Hip Hop, Hegel, and the Art of Emancipation

Jim Vernon

Hip Hop, Hegel, and the Art of Emancipation

Let's Get Free

Jim Vernon
York University
Toronto, ON, Canada

ISBN 978-3-319-91303-2   ISBN 978-3-319-91304-9   (eBook)
https://doi.org/10.1007/978-3-319-91304-9

Library of Congress Control Number: 2018942226

Cover image: labsas / Getty Images
Cover design: Fatima Jamadar

Printed on acid-free paper

This Palgrave Macmillan imprint is published by the registered company Springer International
Publishing AG part of Springer Nature.
The registered company address is: Gewerbestrasse 11, 6330 Cham, Switzerland

ACKNOWLEDGEMENTS

In the early autumn of 2014, just after completing a research project on Huey Newton and the Black Panther Party, I found myself couch-bound for several months with a virus that frequently left me without the focus to read. I don't quite recall how it started, but at some point in my effort to stave off boredom by randomly clicking on everything that came into my YouTube feed, I suddenly realized—much to my embarrassment and just like in that Portlandia skit—that I had "missed Hip Hop". Given my vintage, I grew up a fan of Run-DMC, Public Enemy and the Beastie Boys, but other than that I had little interest in rap music, and like many—I would actually guess most—people, I knew virtually nothing about the Bronx community that created the original culture, the emergence of which was virtually and tellingly simultaneous with the wind-down of the state war to suppress the Panthers. During my recovery, my old friend Adam Tisdelle supplied me with records, books, documentaries, and anecdotes that rapidly made me a passionate fan of Hip Hop's musical and poetic legacy, but more importantly a devoted student of the astonishing history of the broader culture's birth. Right around then, Bruce Gilbert invited me to speak at his excellent conference on Hegel and Romantic Art at Bishop's University. As I alternately re-read Hegel's lectures and absorbed my loaned Hip Hop library, the arguments of this book took shape; so, my thanks first and foremost to Adam and Bruce for setting me down this path.

A book like this is only possible with continual support, advice and critique from others. For conversations large and small, I'm extremely grateful to Duff Waring, Eve Haque, Jay Lampert, Lorraine Code, Karen Houle,

Alice MacLachlan, Gamal Abdel-Shehid, Nicola Short, Nalini Persram, Jennifer Bates, Antonio Calcagno, John Burbidge, George di Giovanni, Rinaldo Walcott, Kamala Kempadoo, various first-year cohorts of York University's Social and Political Thought Program, the Duquesne University chapter of Minorities and Philosophy, Philosophia at York University, and everyone who heard about it and contacted me to discuss the project or just to let me know the name of Prodigy's last album. For two decades, I've been blessed to be part of the quasi-existent Ontario Hegel Organization, which remains the greatest laboratory for speculative work on Hegel around and has provided a welcoming and challenging home for my scholarship. Just as I completed the first full draft, the Hip Hop gods put me in touch with Serouj Aprahamian, who graciously provided me with extensive and revelatory critical comments, as well as some key sources that, as yet, remain largely absent from the scholarly literature; I look forward to watching his ground-breaking scholarship develop. A very special hat tip to Amy Invernizzi at Palgrave Macmillan for believing in this project and to the anonymous referees both for reading my work with sympathy and care and for pushing me to confront my own blind spots.

My parents, Joe and Joan, gave me the strength to do this work; my in-laws, Ashesh and Runjoo, assured me it would come out one day. My strongest ally and frankest critic will always be Prapti, whose influence is all over these pages; and Miko would often stop barking long enough for me to complete a critical section, so she gets a treat.

Finally, I'd like to express my gratitude to Hip Hop's Bronx pioneers, whose work and words forced me to radically rethink much of what I thought I knew about art, freedom, and their essential connection and destiny. The names in this book represent just a handful of the heroes who should appear on stamps for the enormous gift and responsibility they have bestowed upon us. Inadequate of a gesture as it may be, this book is dedicated to them and to all those who work to keep their history, work, and promise alive.

CONTENTS

CHAPTER 1

Introduction

This book takes its subtitle from the debut album by *dead prez*,[1] but in it I aim to show that the phrase succinctly encapsulates the general principle of Hip Hop[2] as a cultural movement, as well as the most fundamental and enduring lessons offered by G.W.F. Hegel's philosophy of art. To be more precise, I argue that Hip Hop's early history charts a course remarkably similar to the one offered for artistic creation in general in Hegel's *Aesthetics*.[3] The parallels, of course, will not be exact; as Hegel notes, "on account of its nature, at once material and individual, the work of art issues essentially from particular conditions of the most varied sort, amongst them especially the time and place of its origin" (34/I, 55), implying that "every work of art belongs to *its own time, its own people*, its own environment" (14/I, 30). Such differences in context must always be attended to in efforts at the philosophical comprehension of artistic movements, and this is particularly true for a movement as unique and contested as Hip Hop. Nevertheless, I hope to show that the resonances between the trajectory Hegel traces for art in general and the early development of Hip Hop in particular are both numerous and substantial enough to make us rethink not only the nature and viability of Hegel's much-maligned,[4] and until recently much-ignored,[5] philosophical aesthetics, but the origin, nature, and enduringly vital lessons of Hip Hop as an aesthetic culture.

While the early history of Hip Hop has been frequently celebrated by academics and journalists,[6] there remain questions concerning precisely why (a) the culture developed in the precise time and place of the South

© The Author(s) 2018
J. Vernon, *Hip Hop, Hegel, and the Art of Emancipation*,
https://doi.org/10.1007/978-3-319-91304-9_1

1

Bronx in the mid-1970s; (b) it developed as a series of artistic, rather than more directly political, forms of expression; (c) these forms cohered into a complete and self-determining *culture*, replete with its own ethical order and one which expressed itself in novel, interrelated forms of painting, dance, beat-centric music, and oral poetry; and (d) this culture undertook the specific historical shifts and developed the specific internal tensions that we have seen and continue to witness as it spread beyond the confines of its geographic origin. In this book, I argue that Hegel's philosophy of art can aid us in understanding the Hip Hop community's transition from total social alienation to some form—even if extremely limited, and eventually systematically repressive—of social inclusion via the specific mediation of an artistic culture grounded in its distinct and novel forms of sensible expression. Moreover, while scholars of the *Aesthetics* have sought to revive its relevance in recent years, few have given any consideration to popular art, let alone populist artistic cultures like Hip Hop, in their work.[7] Unfortunately, "gallery" art still governs most of the discourse in philosophical aesthetics, and it dominates Hegel-inspired scholarship to an even greater degree.[8] In what follows, I aim to show that this arguably elitist tendency is precisely what Hegel objects to in artistic creation, as well as in the philosophical comprehension of it; moreover, I argue that Hip Hop's community base and immediate appeal not only align it with Hegel's aesthetic Ideal, but help clarify the latter's nature to a greater degree than Hegel's own examples and history can. Thus, the fundamental thesis of this book is that Hegel's *Aesthetics* and Hip Hop culture are mutually illuminating.

This is, to say the very least, an unorthodox pairing; in fact, there's good reason to be deeply suspicious of it, and from both sides. Given the intensely marginalized position of its pioneers, there has long been concern within Hip Hop that theoretical inquiry into the culture signifies the "appropriat[ion of] its indigenous knowledges and practices merely in order to annex them to academic modes of knowledge".[9] Because the artistic practices forged by the citizens of the South Bronx were quickly arrogated for the economic and cultural benefit of others, there is justifiable concern that inquiries such as this one do little more than "raid hip-hop for ideas to fuel [...] academic careers, while giving nothing back to the culture".[10] Put more bluntly, when a white scholar suggests that we can grasp a cultural movement now nearly synonymous with Black resistance through the lens of a philosophical edifice as canonically Eurocentric as Hegel's, it frankly *should* raise suspicion among those who quite rightly seek to ensure that the question posed to the culture "is not: 'Of what significance could I (or the ubiquitous academic 'we') declare [Hip Hop] to be?'" but rather "What are [Hip Hop's] own modes of signification, intelligibility and reference".[11] Even in the academic field of Hip Hop studies, where Continental philosophers are often invoked in the process of unpacking the culture's aesthetic and political import, given his infamous and often brutal anti-Black racism,[12] there has been understandably little interest in possible insights from Hegel.[13]

On the side of Hegel studies, there is also good reason "to be skeptical that anything of value can result from trying to project Hegel into the future",[14] and not only because of the failings of his perspective noted above. As everyone with even a cursory knowledge of his *Aesthetics* knows, Hegel infamously declares that art "is and remains a thing of the past [*ein vergangenes*]" (11/I, 25). While much recent work on his lectures has emphasized the possibility of art's enduring importance, it has also largely reflected Hegel's own comments about the varied forms of "fine" artistic creation and appreciation within leading modern states, after the decline of art's classical peak.[15] In focusing on the forms of modern painting or scored music, most scholars typically accept Hegel's diagnosis about the irreducible pastness of collectively lived *aesthetic cultures*; but as I hope to show, it is precisely as a collective and self-determining aesthetic culture that Hip Hop must essentially be grasped.

As suggested above, I wholeheartedly agree that concerns about the appropriation of Hip Hop culture are valid in *every* academic attempt at articulating and explaining it, and are thus certainly and obviously warranted in a case as counterintuitive and contentious as the one proposed in this book. While only the full argument which follows can address this charge, I would simply note from the outset that I agree with Nelson George that there can be "no single organizing theory for understanding hip hop",[16] and merely seek, here, to add what I believe is a potentially quite illuminating voice to the fray. While Hegel has long been my focus academically, my use of his aesthetic framework, here, is primarily dedicated to elucidating the arc and import of Hip Hop's early history. I aim to show not only that Hegel's account of the conditions that compel the emergence of communal, aesthetically focused cultures, as well as of their historically unfolding trajectory is remarkably similar to the context and progressively developing stages of the original Bronx culture, but that his understanding of art's guiding principle and essential purpose strongly resonates with the self-understanding expressed by Hip Hop's pioneers and organic intellectuals. On the Hegel side, my reading of his *Aesthetics* is also unique, but, as with Hip Hop, the complexities and tensions within that text, as well as his broader thought, are deep and serious enough to validate diverse schools of interpretation; in fact, the version of Hegel I present here could arguably only have been revealed by examining his thought in the light of a living aesthetic culture like Hip Hop.

Correspondingly, I do not seek here to "refute" the work of Hip Hop studies scholars, and certainly have nothing whatsoever to teach either the organic intellectuals who emerged from the movement or its pioneering and/or contemporary practitioners; nor do I seek to explicate and defend each aspect of Hegel's theory of art against every possible criticism, or even to fully defend the somewhat heterodox reading I offer against all challenges from within the literature.[17] However, I do hope to both convince Hegelians, Continental philosophers, and philosophers of art that there is much to be learned about the nature and explanatory power—as well as the fundamental limits—of Hegel's account of art's essence and destiny by drawing him into Hip Hop's orbit, and to convince scholars working on Hip Hop that a compelling, unifying, and in some ways revelatory account of the culture can be found in at least the core of Hegel's account of the emergence, achievement, and dissolution of the aesthetic Ideal.[18]

Of course, only the full text below can justify these claims; however, I want to begin by briefly sketching the argument that will be made in their defence by confronting the most glaring problem with this pairing from the side of Hegel's text: the purported "pastness" of art.

The Life, Death and Rebirth of Art's "Highest Vocation"

There is simply no getting around the fact that Hegel declares that "we" no longer produce or relate to art as "we" used to just because the "conditions of our present time are not favourable to art" (10/I, 25).[19] If Hegel insists that art in its "highest vocation" is fundamentally in the past (11/I, 25),[20] then the project outlined above—indeed, any attempt to develop what Robert Pippin calls "a Hegelian understanding of post-Hegelian art"[21]—seems doomed to fail. However, if Hegel thinks art has been superseded, it is not because he believes we have exhausted the forms of sensuous creation, or because we no longer enjoy and appreciate them; rather, it is because he thinks "we", as citizens of modern states, have and through them" (184/I, 242–3), just because mediations like those provided by the state are essentially absent. Art both depends upon and presents the "free configuration of individuality" created by a people themselves as their ideal self-presentation out of external determination; thus, its ultimate result is not any specific art object or form, but a nascent ethical *"community* [as] the spiritual reflection into itself" determined solely through the collective actions of its own members (85/I, 119). By forging a harmony between the *infinitely spiritual* and the *finitely deter-mined*, the aesthetic Ideal at its core and as its vocation founds a community on "the essential content of the moral and the true" which is freedom itself (499/II, 105).[25] In this spiritual community, the artists' "ways of viewing the world constitute *religion"* for themselves and their audience alike, precisely because the experimental, emancipatory, and objective nature of their creative actions—resting on no established ethical order—demands that they be "generally in earnest with this material and its rep-resentation; i.e. this material remains [...] the infinite and true element [of their] consciousness" (603/II, 232, emphasis added). Concretely mani-festing itself as free against the omnipresent constraints of merely received finitude, and moreover taking responsibility for itself through its specific modes of self-determination, the Ideal aesthetic community raises itself towards the development of higher spheres of spirit, justice, and right by living an explicitly created and creative "religion of art".[26] As Hegel puts it regarding his exemplary case of such an Ideal community, the Classical "Greeks knew perfectly well that it was poets who created [their gods]; and if they believed in them, their belief touched upon the spiritual which even so dwells in man's own spirit and is the universal actually effective and moving" in their culture (499/II, 104). The aesthetic Ideal, then, marks the foundational, emancipatory transformation of a people aban-doned to the state of nature into a freely self-determining and unified ethi-cal community through the sheer force of their own power of collective creation; it is the immediately *sensed*, palpably *lived* self-liberation of a spiritual community from a situation of extreme alienation.

Thus, an emancipatory aesthetic culture—or art in its "highest vocation"—really only arises in response to the radical, immediately lived denial of free humanity; conversely, of course, the further removed people are from such alienating externality, the less they stand in need of art to both grasp and claim their right to determine themselves. In most modern states, Hegel insists, externality is now so thoroughly infused with freedom that "our whole spiritual culture is of such a kind that [one] stands within the world of reflection and its relations, and could not by any act of will or decision abstract [oneself] from it" (11/I, 25). Gradually built from the foundation laid by the religion of art, the varied forms of the modern state now surround us, as a kind of "second nature", with "lived" evidence of our freedom. "Being in a state [then] has [...] habit as its form, [and] habit does not correspond with the spiritual *self-conscious* nature of these deeper interests" that manifest themselves in classical art (198/I, 259). If art is the most immediate way in which "spirit liberates itself from the cramping barriers of its existence in externality" (94/I, 131), then art is "of the past" just to the extent that the immediate realm of externality is no longer repressively cramping, and humanity enjoys a mediated world of freedom simply by living, largely by rote, within its institutions.

Of course, even within modern states, cultural products rightly called "art" continue to be both produced and admired; the "pastness" of art only concerns its highest vocation as the "concretely spiritual" expression of a self-emancipating community (78/I, 109). Immersed in institutions of right, Hegel claims, artistic creation is no longer strictly *needed*, because our lived situation enshrines, rather than denies, "spiritual subjectivity with its grasp of its independence and freedom" (519/II, 129); as a result, art ceases to form the spiritual basis of the community.[27] Art, of course, will always remain a creative outlet for free humanity; but, with "no essential 'work' left for it to do",[28] it now becomes the expression of a contingent personal choice—say, for venting frustration or for seeking economic gain—rather than the focus of our essential and necessary collective effort.

Art endures, then, because "in organized states the external existence of the people is secured [and thus] it is only their *subjective disposition and judgment* that they really have on their own account and by their own resources" (184–5/I, 243, emphasis added). What Hegel calls *romantic* art eventually replaces the *classical* Ideal, precisely by forsaking the universal ground of the community to the inclusive institutions of state, and restricting itself to the expression of the merely subjective dispositions of distinct individuals. In romantic modernity, then, art is not created to preach the ethical basis of self-determination that can unite a fragmented and repressed collective into a spiritual and emancipatory community, but to sensibly express the contingent thoughts, desires, or even transitory whims of anyone at all. Such art, therefore, offers not only more varied and refined forms of sensibility, but a broader range of themes as well; thus, we see artists taking the external "up immediately, as it finds it, letting it, as it were, shape itself at will" (531/I, 144), "just as readily [working to] jumble the shapes of the external world and distort them grotesquely" (81/I, 113–4), or even rejecting the achieved universal that the modern state should reflect through an aesthetically expressed "revolt against the whole of civil society itself" (195/I, 195). However, while this ensures that "subjective skill and the art of portrayal are [increasingly] advanced", "the more [...] substantial element is discarded" and thus "the thing which [now] gives satisfaction [...] is the thirst for the present and this reality itself, the delight of the self in what is there, contentment with self, [and] with the finitude of man" (573–4/I, 196). Artists, artworks, and thematic contents thus proliferate, but their creation and reception are "unendingly particular" (194/I, 255), precisely because they primarily reflect arbitrary individuality. Separated from communal life, and with no great task to accomplish beyond expressing divergent and competing subjective interests, even the best romantic art is effectively "consign[ed] to the museum, concert hall, or scholarly library".[29]

The aesthetic Ideal, in short, is a victim of its own emancipatory power. By reshaping the realm of sensation into a reflection of free spirit, art lays the ground for its own supersession by discourses, practices, and institutions that more concretely and stably actualize art's essential truth—human freedom itself. It is in this sense that art is "of the past" for Hegel; for those who live in modern states, it has already done its job, granting us the self-conscious freedom to articulate and concretely produce more stable institutions that preserve the emancipated community as free. And it is precisely our inclusion in this habitual and stable form of actualized freedom that leaves us individually "free" enough to interpret and express our essence arbitrarily and idiosyncratically, rather than essentially and collectively.

Note my qualification: art's highest vocation is in the past *for those who habitually benefit from inclusion in the institutions of the modern state*; however, even as Hegel declares art obsolete, he implicitly leaves open—or, perhaps more accurately, warns of—the possibility for its highest vocation's *return*. On the one hand, characteristically, all too optimistically, and obviously myopically, he claims that in "our contemporary situation, class differences [...] are not tied to birth" (209/I, 273); on the other hand, however, he immediately qualifies the claim as follows:

> But on this account after all we at once link with [this formal legal freedom] the further demand that [every] subject shall, in education, knowledge, skill and disposition make himself equal to the class to which he aspires. But if birth [still] places an unsurmountable obstacle to the claims which a man,

without this restriction, could satisfy by his own spiritual force and activity, then this counts for us not only as a misfortune but essentially as a wrong which he suffers. A merely natural and manifestly [*für sich*] unjust wall of partition, over which his spirit [has] lifted him, separates him from what he was capable of attaining, and the natural, which is only fortified by arbitrary caprice [*Willkür*] into this legal determination, presumes to set insuperable barriers to the inherently justified freedom of the spirit. (A, 210/I, 273-4, trans. modified)

That is, even in contemporary states, the very contingency of individual whim, distortion of harmonious unity, or empty rebellion against modernity as a whole that find voice in romantic art may yet cause contingent differences to enduringly suppress the rightful freedom of some for the benefit of others. Such a conflict between human essence and its external situation, for Hegel, "rests in and for itself on a *wrong* which *true free art has not to respect* [*an and für sich auf einem <u>Unrecht</u> beruht, das wahre freie Kunst nicht zu reskeptieren hat*]" (209/I, 273, trans. modified, emphasis added). Thus, while Hegel does not explicitly thematize this aspect in his lectures—preferring, as always, to defend the progressive march of freedom in the world as though it was in fact enjoyed by or at least significantly benefitted all—he nevertheless is forced to at least indicate that, even if art's highest vocation is in the past for those who are *rightfully included* in modern states, it nevertheless has every right to arise from, and thus has the potential to emancipate, those who *unjustly endure severe forms of exclusion from them*. While most scholars insist (not, of course, without evidence) that Hegel holds that "history is ruled by the principle of non-repetition",[30] and thus that he would be "highly suspicious regarding [the possibility of the renewal of the religion of art] on account of the different conditions that he thinks characterize the modern world",[31] and, moreover, that because "there is only one history and one art evolution, we are unable to say that art *will* develop in the way that it does" in his lectures, rather than that it merely *happened* to so develop in the past,[32] this brief aside suggests that even a Whiggish historian like Hegel must admit that aesthetic history may—under the very kinds of social deprivation that Hegel consistently ignores—*repeat itself*, thus providing a potential avenue for empirically "testing" Hegel's theory of art's progressive development as an emancipatory cultural movement. Art, one might say, *should* be in the past; however, even in the "freest" of modern states, the need for it may yet return.

HIP HOP AS AESTHETIC IDEAL

It is the story of just such a resurgence of art's "essential work" that I aim to tell here. My core thesis is that Hip Hop can be understood as the communal expression of humanity's universal and emancipatory spirit in the realm of sensation, forged by and for a community that was uniquely and radically excluded from participation in the institutions of the modern state. More precisely, I seek to philosophically comprehend Hip Hop as a self-determining, collective *aesthetic culture* that arose to fill the vacuum left by the sudden and catastrophic withdrawal of state institutions from the South Bronx in the early 1970s. Proceeding through a period of tentative, allusive, yet broadly transformative aesthetic experimentation akin to Hegel's account of the *symbolic* mode of art, and building rapidly into a virtual aesthetic religion like the one identified with Hegel's *classical Ideal*, Hip Hop effectively laid the foundation for a cohesive and emancipatory political community; one so vigorous that it effectively forced the state to take—timid, insufficient, and then intensely repressive—steps to variously re-include its members within its forms of habitual organization. The progressive "inclusion" of Hip Hop's community within the wider society, however, drained the culture of its cohesive unity, fragmenting its elements and participants into the pursuit of contingent, often a- or anti-social interests that Hegel associates with *romantic* art. This shift implies a need to move beyond art as the focal point for the collective expression of emancipatory consciousness and, as we shall see, this is precisely the process the enduring Hip Hop community is currently determining. My argument, then, is not only that Hip Hop has undergone "the same growing pains that most of the World's cultures have gone through at their origins",[33] but, moreover, that these growing pains and their aftermath chart a course essentially homologous to the conceptual history laid out in Hegel's *Aesthetics*. Conversely, by examining his lectures in the light of the most potent and world-historical aesthetic culture to emerge in their wake, I aim to diagnose what is living and dead in Hegel's account of art as the sensible expression of human freedom.

Of course, there are obviously important differences between, say, the ancient Egyptians, and then Greeks, who respectively serve as Hegel's core examples of the foundation-layers for, and then consummators of, the aesthetic Ideal and the pioneering artists who arose in the Bronx of the early-to-mid-1970s. Most importantly, while Hegel's exemplary peoples were (in his often quite suspect historical understanding) first unconsciously setting the stage for, then discovering and aesthetically celebrating, the self-determining subjectivity that was eventually enshrined in modern ethical institutions, Hip Hop culture finds its origin in people who—despite the brutal social alienation they endured—already understood themselves to be subjectively free, albeit in and through their contingent, romantic individuality. At the culture's dawn, free individuality was, as it were, both *habitually presumed*, given the community's previous, partial inclusion in the modern state, and *explicitly denied*, by what can only be called their radical *social abandonment*, and this tension affected the specific forms of artistic creation undertaken in the founding of the new "nation". Moreover, while they were returned to a state of external determination by the evacuation of state structures, the nascent Hip Hop community was obviously by no means returned to an *actual* state of nature. Excluded from the state, yet walled within the wealth and cultural products of developed modernity, these artists inherited and utilized an unprecedented panoply of materials and traditions in their immediate situation from which to create the new Ideal.

Accordingly, in what follows, I will argue that Hip Hop names the collectively enacted transformation of the merely received products, as well as the most radically excluded individuals, of modernity, into a unified, emancipatory, aesthetic, and ethical culture. It is my contention that this culture's early history passes through clearly discernible "stages" that reflect what Hegel calls the symbolic, classical, and romantic stages of the evolution of artistic creation. Each of these stages, moreover, undergoes its own internal transformation, beginning with a "severe" period, wherein it remains overly tied to already given materials, and thus still seeks clear and free expression of their form, producing "simple", "jerky", "monotonous" works that reflect the relative "unskillfulness" of their artistic pioneers (616/II, 248); the efforts of these pioneers, however, allow subsequent artists, building on their work, to find the "purely beautiful style" most appropriate to the art form, through which it "mellow[s] into the serenity" of its consummate expression (617–8/II, 249–50); finally, however, the very refinement of technique and beauty of the works becomes, as it were, too great, resulting in art that loses its emancipatory import, becoming merely "pleasing or agreeable" to a general audience (618/II, 251). At this point, the collective practice of artists is fragmented into a series of contingent expressions of "the subjectivity of emotion and feeling in its […] finite particularity" (624/II, 258). As in Hegel's account, each of Hip Hop's developmental stages will be typified by particular art forms, although these will not, as in the *Aesthetics*, begin with architecture, or peak with sculpture. Rather, Hip Hop—perhaps predictably, given the essentially modern situation in which it develops—systematically develops through the art forms Hegel identifies with modern romanticism (and, curiously, in the same developmental order laid out by Hegel): painting, music, and poetry. Thus, I will be using Hegel to justify Afrika Bambaataa's infamous definition of Hip Hop as "a celebration of life [that] gradually develop[ed] each of its elements to form a cultural movement" that is independent and self-determining.[34] Hip Hop's *aesthetic elements* are *Graffiti Writing* (painting), *DJing* (music), and *MCing* (poetry), linked together by *Breaking* (which I will identify, for reasons to be made clear as we proceed, not only with dance, but with a kind of *living sculpture*).

This, we must note, cuts against much contemporary usage of "Hip Hop", which is often used to refer to what I will subsequently call "rap music", or at least some subset of it, rather than the broader, multi-element culture.[35] This is not, however, just a recent phenomenon, as the identification of a Hip Hop culture broader than its now ubiquitous musical poetry has always been a matter of controversy. The odd one out is generally considered to be graffiti, which developed several years before the more intimately connected elements and was also widely practiced beyond Hip Hop's spiritual home in the South Bronx.[36] In what follows, however, I hope to not only build the case for such an identification of Hip Hop with all of its essential elements, but moreover to explain both how and why "rap music" eventually splits from the original culture while continuing to bear its name, and the reasons why so many of its founders, organic theorists, and other defenders have sought to preserve the broader definition in the face of the social acceptance of its most marketable aspect. Hip Hop culture, that is, remains in constant tension with rap music, and I think that Hegel's *Aesthetics*—counter-intuitive as this may seem—can help us understand this fraught and ongoing history.

This emphasis on Hip Hop culture as a *whole*, rather its musical elements in *particular*, proceeds from the primary focus of this book: Hip Hop's first decade, 1969–1979, or the era prior to rap music recordings. While it would be difficult to find any scholars who do not emphasize the vital importance of Hip Hop's origins in understanding its nature and import, most scholarly "examinations of Hip-Hop tend towards a textual over-reliance on rap music",[37] and thus there is a general tendency in Hip Hop studies to focus on the aesthetic, ethical, and political issues that arise concerning, or from, its musical, and especially poetic, aspects.[38] While I agree with most scholars that Hip Hop should be understood as an "artistic response to oppression",[39] because it has been retroactively understood as the seed for the explicitly political discourses present in much rap music, this response has largely been grasped as "a form of aesthetic [...] rebellion against the flames of systematic oppression",[40] which "began as a way for the youth at the time to express their frustrations and to rail against authority figures",[41] by offering "a brutally honest expression of the poverty, oppression, and racism prevalent in inner-city America" and giving explicit voice to "the reality of urban life under the effect of deindustrialization, decay, racism, and marginalization"; accordingly, many hold that Hip Hop "has *always* been a platform for [...] protest".[42]

The problem with such a view, however, is that Hip Hop's poetic element was not only the *last* to evolve within the culture; "conscious" or "political" rap did not develop until its musical poetry had already been *co-opted by forces outside* the Bronx community which created it. Indeed, the dominant academic and popular discourses of Hip Hop, emerging in the period after recorded rap music broke from it, often downplay or even elide the fact that Hip Hop's first decade is marked by the virtual *absence* of explicitly political expression. In what follows, I aim to avoid the anachronism which reads "conscious rap" intent back into the act of adolescents spraying their adopted names on walls or using two turntables to manipulate funk records; rather, my focus will be the expressed self-understanding of the earliest Hip Hop practitioners regarding the emergence and meaning of their art. As a culture largely built from non-linguistic forms of aesthetic expression, Hip Hop began as a culture focused on artistic *form*, rather than the direct expression of any particular political *content*; as Mark Katz notes, while the scholarly "suggestion [...] that hip-hop is a form of protest [...] might be clear in the lyrics of overtly political rap", it is far less clear how the mere process of, for example, "extracting a wordless drum break and pumping it through a sound system at a dance party can be seen as a form of resistance".[43]

Thus, the question I want to pose and hopefully answer concerns *what exactly makes the development of a primarily aesthetic culture concretely political*; that is, this book seeks to explain *how the collective development and appreciation of art can be concretely emancipatory for the community that creates it*. Because so many scholars embrace "the emphasis its artists place on knowing and maintaining its connections to hip hop's origins",[44] and because this connection is broadly—and, in my view, correctly—understood to be informing of the politics of both rap music and Hip Hop culture, it is imperative to demonstrate a non-anachronistic link between its seemingly "apolitical" foundations and its later role as the poetic voice of the oppressed. That is, while I share the common contention that Hip Hop is an essentially political movement, and must be understood as having political import from its very inception, I argue that its emancipatory spirit must reside in *the very development of a collectively determined aesthetic culture*; moreover, I hope to contribute to our understanding of how the early aesthetic culture's original spirit can guide how we think about the possible development of a specifically Hip Hop political movement in the future. In short, this book articulates and defends a theoretical framework for understanding the emergence and ongoing evolution of Hip Hop which justifies the response of pioneering DJ Grandmixer D.ST, who, when asked

> if early hip-hop could be seen as political [...] answered, "There was no agenda. It was sheer unadulterated, 'Let's do something else other than be in a gang.'" But then he paused, adding, "That's politics, actually".[45]

CHAPTER BREAKDOWN

Chapter 2 details the unique socio-economic conditions that the South Bronx endured starting in the late 1960s, just prior to the birth of Hip Hop. I argue that the manifest and sudden roll-back of the political changes won by the Civil Rights and Black Power struggles of the previous decade was not just felt most deeply there, but that the level of state abandonment was so severe that it marked a virtual return to the "state of nature" from which Hegel claims art, as a cultural force, emerges. Suffering the destruction of much of its security through the near-total withdrawal of social services, the Bronx effectively became an independent, stateless territory, radically isolated from the broader social sphere. While the return to gang activity and criminal violence that accompanied the Bronx breakdown are readily understandable, the emergence of an aesthetic, celebratory culture from them is not, and I argue that Hip Hop's emergence cannot be understood as a vocal "cry of rage" against it. Rather, produced almost entirely by adolescents who never knew the protections of a modern civil society, the emergence of Hip Hop art reflects less anger at the state which stifled or neglected them than the compelled, but heroic, re-emergence of the most immediate means through which humanity transforms itself and its world into reflections of its free, creative essence. This need to construct a *self-determined* sense-environment also explains why the Hip Hop community developed *novel* forms of self-idealizing aesthetic expression, rather than simply venting its rage or demands through already available art forms, or other more direct modes of social expression.

In Chap. 3, I examine the first of these aesthetic "elements" to emerge—*graffiti writing*—as exemplary of Hegel's account of the earliest stage of an artistic culture's development. The impulsive "need" for art felt within the state of nature implies that a community's earliest efforts at aesthetic expression are not self-conscious and direct presentations of free humanity, but rather reflect largely *exploratory intimations* of our essence in sensible form. Such *symbolic* art reflects a community's groping search for adequate forms of sensation with which to express themselves as free within a situation that radically suppresses clear consciousness of our essence. We find just such an aesthetic quest in the earliest years of New York graffiti, exemplified by the legendary TAKI 183 in Washington Heights, but reaching its peak in the Bronx in between 1970 and 1973. As "taggers" anonymously spread their adopted, cryptographic names throughout the city, they—in Hegelian terms—enacted a foundational, near-total, and ultimately *architectural* transformation of the cramping barriers of their external sphere into a veritable *temple* for the celebration of humanity's free, spiritual essence. In process, they laid the foundation for an ethical culture grounded in, and defining of, artistic practice and appreciation. So widespread, compelling, and mysterious was this culture that it eventually attracted the interest of the outside world, leading both to a radical alteration in the artistic style and practice of tagging, and to cracks in its lived ethical code. Having constructed a mysterious temple of spirit, it appeared by the end of 1973 that the culture would simply be absorbed into the mainstream, leaving the remaining Bronx community behind.

However, as I argue in Chap. 4, it was precisely at this moment that a young tagger who adopted the name Kool DJ Herc discovered the means to fill the aesthetic temple with an active, lived, and united community. While the symbolic art of graffiti remained limited due to its essentially *indirect* presentation of our spiritual essence, its immediately palpable presentation was created by the *DJs* and their essential aesthetic partners the *breakers*, whose revolutionary acts of self-governing bodily control and self-discovered feats of skill provided sensible proof of the essential freedom that grounds and guides all artistic creation. These artists effectively made spirit flesh through the corporeal display of self-determination in hitherto unimagined feats of skill through "battles" fought within "cyphers" ritually formed around the performers by the devout audience, who judged victors on the grounds of their innovative aesthetic achievements, thus holding them to the community's evolving and self-determined ethical standards. What we see develop in the South Bronx between 1973 and 1977 is nothing less than what Hegel would identify as a collectively lived "religion of art" that united aesthetic objects (in the form of physically present DJs and dancers) and their adjudicating public (in the form of cyphers and informed Hip Hop heads) into a consciously self-determining community.

In Chap. 5, I argue that this "religion of art" was effectively, and necessarily, short-lived, but that its decline nevertheless resulted from the liberating impact of that culture. As Hip Hop's musical elements developed, it moved from the streets of the Bronx to clubs throughout New York where it was inevitably shorn of its community base, its unifying ethics, and thus of the symbiosis between its aesthetic elements, artists, and audience. In Hegelian terms, this move reflects the shift from the classical Ideal to modern *romanticism*, which is characterized by the community's fragmentation, through the rise of contingently individual self-expression as the core of artistic creation. This shift, I argue, was facilitated by the introduction, and subsequent development, of Hip Hop's final aesthetic element, *MCing*, or spoken poetry. Tracing MCing from its emergence as a *rhythmic* accessory to Hip Hop block parties (which reflects "epic" poetry's capturing of the vital details of communal existence in celebratory language), through to its eventual dominance—in particular on record— as the *rhyming* expression of the idiosyncratic imagination of individual poets (what Hegel calls the "lyrical" celebration of infinitely free subjectivity) allows us to chart the arc of early Hip Hop verse from the poetic element of an essentially communal and ritual culture to the focal point of a novel form of global pop music that would come to be known as "rap". Simultaneously, the ensuing popularity of this new form of entertainment allowed for at least some level of social and economic opportunity for the alienated population of the South Bronx. While most of the initial crews disbanded as the unifying ethos of the culture faded, this was in large part because Hip Hop had begun, through the infectious power of its art, to force at least some form of the re-inclusion for its uniquely alienated community into the institutions of the surrounding state.

Which does not, of course, mean that Hip Hop *eliminated* their oppression. The rise of rap music from Hip Hop culture certainly granted *some* Bronx citizens *some* level of inclusion that allowed them to identify, to varying degrees, with the broader public sphere; however, it clearly failed to grant the abandoned community *full* participation—or even stable and beneficial existence—in civil society. Rather, the re-inclusion of the Bronx within the broader state not only introduced to the region a host of state-sanctioned social ills suffered in other, minimally included regions elsewhere, it coincided with the demonstrable *intensification* of their repressive effects in the communities to which rap music, graffiti culture, and other forms of Hip Hop expression were rapidly spreading.

In Chap. 6, I treat two of the dominant reactions within the rapidly expanding and transforming culture of Hip Hop to these new realities. On the one hand, a novel form of rap poetry emerged which gave expression, not to the idealized and/or contingently individual MC, but to the very social conditions that now repressively *contained* (rather than effectively *abandoned*) the marginalized, largely Black and Brown youth who first built the culture in the Bronx, and then more broadly embraced it across the margins of America. In Hegelian terms, this marked the transition from epic and lyric to *dramatic* poetry, written for a broad and fragmented, rather than specific and unified, audience. The mainstream co-option of Hip Hop poetry was largely facilitated by this new "reality rap", which often emphasized the situational stagnation and repression of marginalized communities rather than their demonstrated and universal capacity for self-emancipation. On the other hand, perhaps to counter this trend, organizations grounded in the original South Bronx culture, from Afrika Bambaataa's Zulu Nation to KRS-One's Temple of Hip Hop, began to move *beyond the aesthetic elements* to cultural forms that were *less tied to sensibility*, in order to both more clearly express and carry forward its emancipatory spirit. As Hegel's theory would predict, this involved the introduction of a fifth, non-aesthetic element to Hip Hop—*knowledge*, in forms both religious and philosophical—which more explicitly articulated the universality of humanity that emancipates itself through art, as well as the need to overcome the precise and varied forms of its denial, through racism and other forms of exclusion. While it is arguably the productive unity of Hip Hop's poetic and musical elements, increasingly under the influence of external forces, and its spiritual core as knowledge, identified and preserved by its founders and their followers, that is largely responsible for the existence of so-called "conscious" rap music, the continued dominance of its commercial products at the expense of its spiritual message indicates an enduring tension between rap music and Hip Hop culture, whose future is very much undecided.

This is not, then, a book written by a partisan in any of the lively and vital debates internal to Hip Hop, however broadly or narrowly the term is construed. While I have spent the past few years immersed in the history of the culture, I have never practiced any of its elements and claim no standing in it; in fact, while I've listened to little else during the time it was written, I had very limited knowledge of the history of rap music until I began researching this book. Thus, even though I often cite the critical views of participants and insiders, I have no authority whatsoever to pronounce judgment on any particular claim regarding, say, "where Hip Hop went wrong" or "what Hip Hop should be doing", and do not intend this book to be aesthetically prescriptive. Moreover, while much of the history I recount, here, will be unfamiliar to many readers, the narrative below is not original, nor do I present it as definitive. My training is in philosophy—not history, sociology, musicology, or journalism—and thus the historical details in this book are all derived from either oral histories featuring early participants in the culture or the work of researchers far better suited to the ongoing task of determining the exact chronology of the events at issue. While I believe the framework employed, here, has the benefit of drawing attention to salient historical details that other approaches may overlook or obscure, the history presented here is, of necessity, both partial and epitomizing. My hope is that this book, in some small way, contributes to the development of further historical and theoretical research into the nature and import of the original Bronx culture, and I presume that such work will challenge some of the details, as well as the theoretical analysis, laid out below.

Thus, while I conclude with some thoughts on the import of this book for future scholarship—and while I certainly now have strong opinions of my own on the relative merits of particular artists, events, and trends in the ongoing history of Hip Hop culture and rap music—this is decidedly and simply a book of philosophical aesthetics, albeit one whose theoretical framework and subject matter are essentially political, both in principle and in consequence. By shifting focus away from post-1982 rap music, and back towards the broader culture's pre-recording development on its own terms, my aim is to use Hip Hop to isolate and defend the core and enduring thesis of Hegel's theory of art, precisely in order to use that thesis to articulate, amplify, and philosophically comprehend the voices of Hip Hop's pioneers in their (there really is, in my view, no other phrase for it) *heroic struggle to emancipate themselves and their community through collective forms of aesthetic creation.* Correspondingly, this book sets itself the simultaneous and mutually reinforcing tasks of (a) articulating and defending a particular reading of Hegel's theory of art through an exposition of the historical development of Hip Hop as an emancipatory aesthetic culture and (b) articulating and defending a particular interpretation of Hip Hop culture through an explication of the conceptual development in Hegel's aesthetic theory.

If the MC, theorist and activist KRS-One plays a central role in this book's understanding of Hip Hop culture, it is not simply because he is "affectionately and respectfully called 'the teacher' and 'philosopher' of rap",[46] due to his ability to "bridge[...] the gap between all extremes of the rap audience".[47] Rather, it is because my guiding concern is what he deems "the most important question to Hiphop's identity and preservation: For what purpose does Hiphop exist?"[48]; and I turn to Hegel primarily to articulate and defend his answer: the "force that built our civilizations 10,000 years ago [...] is the same force that has given birth to Hip Hop", whose emergence therefore reflects "the return of the original spark that caused all great civilizations to exist".[49] My goal, then, is to analyse the emergence of Hip Hop at a precise and irreducibly particular historical juncture, precisely in order to reveal its universal and enduring import for our understanding of the essential link between artistic creation and human emancipation.

But it all starts in the place they call the Boogie Down....

NOTES

1. I'm not alone in "biting" the title. Paul Butler, *Let's Get Free: A Hip-Hop Theory of Justice* (New York: The New Press, 2009), does the same, although his book is less a theory of justice, in the philosophical sense, than a (lucid and warmly recommended) critique of the American war on drugs, and the carceral state it feeds.

2. Throughout, I will use this spelling in deference to the arguments of KRS-One, *The Gospel of Hip Hop: First Instrument* (New York: Powerhouse Books, 2009), 63ff. Spellings diverge across texts on the topic (including those of KRS-One, himself), occasionally reflecting a change in meaning. I consistently use this spelling to indicate the broader aesthetic culture, defined below, while many use it to refer more narrowly to certain forms what I will call "rap music" ("conscious rap", "underground rap", or even all rap, etc.). Even in quoted material, I generally refrain from using the term, in any spelling, to indicate the musical poetry alone, and when I do it is usually either noted or clear from context.

3. G.W.F. Hegel, *Aesthetics: Lectures on Fine Art*, Vol. I & II, trans. T.M. Knox (New York: Oxford University Press, 1975)/*Vorlesungen über die Ästhetik*, I, II, II in *Werke* 13, 14, 15 (Frankfurt am Main: Suhrkamp, 1970); pagination in the former is consecutive across the two volumes, but not in the latter, so references in running text will be first to the English version by page number, followed by the volume and page number in the German, in the form (1/I, 13). I limit my analysis, here, to the standard edition compiled by Heinrich Hotho. There has long been debate regarding the validity of Hotho's edition, and much recent scholarship focuses either on the students' transcripts available from the different years Hegel gave the course (e.g. David James, *Art, Myth and Society in Hegel's Aesthetics* (London: Continuum, 2009)) or supplements analysis of the standard edition with consideration of them (e.g. many of the contributions to Stephen Houlgate, ed. *Hegel and The Arts* (Evanston, Illinois: Northwestern University Press, 2007)). As yet, however, there is no single scholarly edition drawn from, or scholarly consensus regarding the relative merits of, the various available sources. Because most work on Hegel's philosophy of art—particularly outside of Hegel studies—is grounded in Hotho's edition, which remains the most complete source available in English, I limit my analysis to the standard German text and translation.

4. As Jack Kaminsky notes, because "[m]odern philosophers [...] have generally repudiated his political as well as his metaphysical doctrines", for many decades, Hegel's "aesthetics [was] treated most shabbily [for u]nlike other parts of his work, it [was] not even [...] subjected to the kind of strict analysis which should precede the act of rejection" (*Hegel on Art: An Interpretation of Hegel's Aesthetics* (SUNY Press, 1962), vii–viii). While there has recently been a resurgence of interest in Hegel's theory of art, many of these texts seek to "disengage his aesthetics [...] from any metaphysical claims concerning the Absolute" (James, 2). As I aim to show in this text, however, the most enduring of these "metaphysical" claims concern *human freedom*, from which no aspect of Hegel's work can be disconnected; his theory of art, perhaps, least of all.

5. Scholars like William Desmond have long wondered why "Hegel's views on art seem to have suffered a certain neglect", despite the fact that his "*Lectures on Aesthetics* have a wide accessibility with an appeal not limited to the professional philosopher" (*Art and The Absolute: A Study of Hegel's Aesthetics* (Albany, SUNY Press, 1986), xi). As Brian K. Etter notes, however, the fact that Hegel's *Aesthetics* "has not received the attention it deserves is largely due to its having so little in common with modern preoccupations" (*Between Transcendence and Historicism: The Ethical Nature of the Arts in Hegelian Aesthetics* (Albany: SUNY Press, 2006), 16). More on this in the conclusion.

6. The gold standard for overall histories of Hip Hop culture and rap music, in my opinion, remains Jeff Chang, *Can't Stop, Won't Stop: A History of the Hip-Hop Generation* (New York: Picador, 2005), but the best single resource on the culture's first decade—the time period which will be my primary focus—is Jim Fricke and Charlie Ahearn, *Yes Yes Y'all: The Experience Music Project Oral History of Hip-Hop's First Decade* (Cambridge: Da Capo, 2002). Other accounts of Hip Hop's general trajectory include Marcus Reeves, *Somebody Scream: Rap Music's Rise to Prominence in the Aftershock of Black Power* (New York: Faber and Faber, 2008), and Nelson George, *hip hop america* (New York: Viking, 1998), but they, like most, tilt their focus to rap music, at the expense of the original Bronx, and then broader, culture. Written during the years of its formation, Steven Hager's *Hip Hop* (self-published, material copyright 1984) is also an essential volume, collecting Hager's pioneering journalism, which (in an early article in the *Village Voice*) offered not only one of the first usages of the term in print, but perhaps the first effort to "make explicit [to a broader audience] that the subcultures of b-boying, rap and graffiti were related" (Chang, *Can't Stop*, 193); it is an expanded edition of the long out of print and extremely difficult to obtain *Hip Hop: The Illustrated History of Break Dancing, Rap Music, and Graffiti* (New York: St. Martin's, 1984). As it is more readily available, citations from Hager will be to the self-published version; because it is un-paginated, and it isn't clear if it will always have the same page numbers by count, I will cite it by chapter number. Joseph C. Ewoodzie, Jr.'s *Break Beats in the Bronx: Rediscovering Hip-Hop's Early Years* (Chapel Hill: University of North Carolina Press, 2017) is perhaps the first sustained academic analysis strictly dedicated to the rise of the culture in the 1970s and raises many of the same questions I do, here; however, Ewoodzie firmly rejects an essentially *aesthetic* answer to them. Rather, the model through which he theorizes the culture's early history primarily concerns how boundaries are drawn around cultural forms, and thus the framework he develops "is not really about hip-hop. It help[s] to explain hip-hop, [but] it can help to explain other new social and cultural entities, like food trucks" (191).

7. There are those, such as James, who quite correctly focus on art's "cultural and historical function within the ethical life of a people" (4), rather than gallery objects. But unlike, for example, those studying rival Continental aestheticians like Gilles Deleuze, there has been little interest among Hegelians to relate his work to more recent, popular forms of aesthetic expression.

8. A case of the exception proving the rule is Alison Stone's *The Value of Popular Music: An Approach From Post-Kantian Aesthetics* (Cham, Switzerland: Palgrave Macmillan, 2016). In "challenging the Western tradition of ranking reason and intellect above all things corporeal" (xv),

Stone seeks to depart from the path of "[m]ost academic philosophers [who] continue to focus on classical music, that is, the broad tradition of Western art music" (xxv), and defends popular music as aesthetically valuable on its own terms; curiously, she does so on both Hegelian and anti-Hegelian grounds. With Hegel, from whom she claims much of the dominant aesthetic tradition's offending "presupposition descends", Stone affirms the intimate "connect[ion of] art with truth" (xxiv); against Hegel, she denies that art "must have serious metaphysical and religious content" which are presumed to have a "rational structure", and argues that popular art reveals that there are "truths to be presented instead [that are] concerned [with] the importance of materiality", and which are thus best presented by works that "entertain, arouse and please the body" (37–8). While she treats some early rap music through this lens in interesting ways, the most revealing difference between our respective takes on both art and Hegel is that "freedom" doesn't merit an index entry in her book; this, perhaps, explains her focus on *popular artworks*, as distinct from my concern with a *populist aesthetic culture*.

9. Russell A. Potter, *Spectacular Vernaculars: Hip-Hop and the Politics of Postmodernism* (Albany: SUNY Press, 1995), 22. In the conclusion, I will consider whether Potter, himself, escapes this charge.

10. Bakari Kitwana, *Why White Kids Love Hip-Hop: Wankstas, Wiggers, Wannabes, and the New Reality of Race in America* (New York: Basic Civitas, 2005), 105.

11. Potter, 22. I replace "rap music" with "Hip Hop" as this reflects the identification of the terms in Potter's text. While agreeing with most scholars that "it is crucial to locate the music (as well as the other elements of hip-hop culture such as graffiti […]) in the specific cultural histories within which it […] emerged" (26), Potter nevertheless argues that "there would be little point in constructing a linear 'history' of hip-hop" (28), perhaps because that would challenge the centrality of rap. In part to contest the centring of rap in Hip Hop scholarship, it is precisely such a linear account that I aim to both detail and justify, here. I return to Potter's concerns regarding the "ubiquitous academic 'we'" in the conclusion.

12. In my view, the finest work on Hegel's writings on African peoples and their harmful legacy has been done by Robert Bernasconi, for example, "Hegel at the Court of Ashanti", in Stuart Barnett, ed. *Hegel After Derrida* (New York: Routledge, 1998), 41–63 and "Hegel's Racism: A Reply to McCarney", *Radical Philosophy*, 119 (May/June 2003), 35–37. For an excellent discussion of the presence of anti-Blackness in Hegel's account of art, see Sander L. Gilman, *On Blackness without Blacks: Essays on the Image of the Black in Germany* (Boston: G.K. Hall and Co., 1982), 93–102.

13. In a rare exception, John P. Pittman, "'Y'all Niggaz Better Recognize': Hip Hop's Dialectical Struggle for Recognition", in *Hip Hop and Philosophy: Rhyme 2 Reason*, ed. Derrick Darby and Tommie Shelby, foreword by Cornel West (Chicago and la Salle: Open Court, 2005), 41–53), uses Hegel's infamous account of the struggle for recognition to explain the role of battles and "beef" in the music; a comparison also briefly suggested by Michael Eric Dyson, *Know What I Mean?: Reflections on Hip Hop* (Philadelphia: Basic Civitas Books, 2007), 24. Like much recent literature, however, these texts conflate Hip Hop with only one of its elements (rap music, and a narrow slice of rap at that), at the expense of the wider culture. They also, in my view, both misconstrue the nature and exaggerate the importance of this legendary passage in Hegel's thought. I challenge the prevalent, "struggle"-based reading of Hegel as a theorist of inter-subjective recognition in "Why We Fight: Hegel's Struggle For Recognition Revisited", *Cosmos and History: The Journal of Natural and Social Philosophy* 9:2 (2013), 178–197, and "Siding with Freedom: Towards a Prescriptive Hegelianism", *Critical Horizons* 12:1 (2011), 49–69.

14. Robert Pippin, *After The Beautiful: Hegel and the Philosophy of Pictorial Modernism* (Chicago: University of Chicago Press, 2014), 35.

15. The most compelling examples, to my mind, are Pippin, Etter, and Benjamin Rutter, *Hegel on the Modern Arts* (Cambridge: Cambridge University Press, 2010).

16. *hip hop America*, ix.

17. Given the diverse audiences for which this book was written, and the counterintuitive nature of the thesis, I have elected to both limit my engagement with the secondary literature on Hegel's theory of art and to reserve it largely for the endnotes. While I engage more deeply with Hip Hop studies scholarship, given the complexity of the texts and history at issue, my consideration of it will be similarly incomplete. I briefly discuss the book's potential import for general trends in both academic discourses more robustly in the conclusion.

18. Thus, I take my work to be an example of what Jane Anna Gordon calls "creolizing theory", cf. *Creolizing Political Theory: Reading Rousseau Through Fanon* (New York: Fordham University Press, 2014).

19. Stephen Bungay, *Beauty and Truth: A Study of Hegel's Aesthetics* (Oxford: Oxford University Press, 1984), 71–5, provides a good survey of some debates surrounding the origin of this claim (i.e. whether it comes from Hegel, Hotho, or the student records of Hegel's lectures that Hotho collected); however, as Rutter notes, in any iteration "no reader of the lectures can remain insensitive to their air of loss or to the skepticism with which Hegel treats the art of his day" (26).

20. Stephen Houlgate, "The 'End' of Art", *Owl of Minerva*, 29 (1997), 1–21, provides a good corrective to some of the more crude readings of this passage, grounded in this qualification.

21. *After The Beautiful*, 53.

22. This connection has often been downplayed in the literature due to an emphasis on the transcendent *divine* in Hegel's thought (see, e.g. Desmond, Etter and Kaminsky). Increasingly, readers of Hegel have come to recognize that what is at stake in his work is the seemingly more immanent "realization of human freedom, [or] the effort to *become* the collective subject we take ourselves [...] to be"; however, they also tend to hold that, philosophically and socially, such "ambition requires a flight at a far, far higher speculative atmosphere than anyone would dare to fly at today [even if] there are elements of Hegel's account that remain valuable" (Pippin, 17).

23. G.W.F. Hegel, *Phenomenology of Spirit*, trans. A.V. Miller (New York: Oxford University Press, 1977), §197–207.

24. While noting that Hegel calls art "a need of Spirit", Bungay nevertheless cautions that we "must not be tempted to [...] equate Spirit with real, thinking human subjects", and should more properly understand it as more general "concept in terms of which anthropological and psychological phenomena can be understood" (27–28). The abstraction of this concept has led some, like Charles Taylor, *Hegel and Modern Society* (New York: Cambridge University Press), 1979, to invoke a kind of transcendent "cosmic reason or spirit" in Hegel, of which humanity is the mere "vehicle" (158ff). In what follows, I defend a more robustly *living, human* form of Spirit, which lies closer to Houlgate's view that "for Hegel, there is no cosmic consciousness or 'world spirit' apart from or outside human existence. It is in human beings alone [...] that being attains consciousness of itself. We are the being-that-has-become-spiritual" ("Introduction: An Overview of Hegel's Aesthetics", in *Hegel and the Arts*, xi–xxviii (xiii)).

25. Cf., Etter, "the Idea found in art pertains to human freedom, so [...] the [aesthetic] Ideal becomes that of human freedom in its focus as well [...] the ideal is not simply an intellectual construct, but rather the artistic representation of the concept of human freedom" (44). As he notes, it may be precisely the idea that "humanity [has] a given nature, out of which emerges certain definite needs [such that] the need for sensuous recognition of our nature is what gives birth to art in the first place" (17), implying that "the traditional value of art [...] lies in its ethical substance and function" (6), that explains the disinterest in and/or condemnation of Hegel's *Aesthetics*; for, in large measure, "the connection between art and ethical content has been rejected by the twentieth century" (39). More on this in the conclusion.

26. On the development of this concept, see Rüdiger Bubner, "The 'Religion of Art'", in *Hegel and the Arts*, ed. Stephen Houlgate, 296–309.

27. This is distinct, I should note, from the claim that art recedes to the past because it has been effectively replaced by the more adequate discourse of philosophy; cf., e.g. Dieter Henrich, "The Contemporary Relevance of Hegel's Aesthetics", in Michael J. Inwood, ed., *Hegel* (Oxford: Oxford University Press, 1985), 199–207. This isn't to say such a reading is inconsistent with Hegel's text; indeed we will discuss the transition to more adequate forms of spirit's expression in Chap. 6. But, the adequacy of this discourse to art's content is less relevant when grasping art's declining role in collective social life than the fact that, as Rutter puts it, "Hegel bears witness in his lectures on aesthetics not to a cessation of artistic activity but to a decline in its significance for human self-understanding" (*Hegel on the Modern Arts*, 6).

28. Martin Donogho, "Art and History: Hegel on the End, the Beginning, and the Future of Art", in *Hegel and the Arts*, ed. Stephen Houlgate, 179–215 (186).

29. Ibid., 181.

30. Bungay, 6.

31. James, 37.

32. Kaminsky, 172.

33. KRS-One, *Gospel*, 192.

34. Quoted in Ivor R. Miller, *Aerosol Kingdom: Subway Painters of New York City* (Jackson: University of Mississippi, 2002), 164.

35. For the views of some pioneers who claim it may be too late to save the original term, see I. Miller, 162–167. While it is increasingly common to treat Hip Hop and (at least certain forms of) rap music interchangeably, there remain those who, even when focusing on Hip Hop's poetic element, draw a distinction between the music and the culture; see, e.g. Cheryl Keyes, *Rap Music and Street Consciousness* (Champaign, IL: University of Illinois Press, 2004), esp. 1–15, the varied essays collected in William Eric Perkins, ed. *Droppin' Science: Critical Essays on Rap Music and Hip Hop Culture* (Philadelphia: Temple University Press, 1996), or any recent public statement regarding the terms by Killer Mike from the brilliant rap duo Run the Jewels.

36. Graffiti's place in Hip Hop culture has been denied both by pioneering painters (e.g. early writers like FARGO: "I don't see the correlation [...] between hip-hop and graffiti [...] one has nothing to do with the other" and BLADE "[Hip Hop] has nothing to do with the original stuff, when [graffiti] writing came along in 1970", both speaking in the film *Just To Get A Rep* (2004; directed by Peter Gerard)) and by, founding musicians like Grandmaster Flash ("You know what bugs me, they put hip-hop

with graffiti. How do they intertwine? Graffiti is one thing that is art, and music is another", Nelson George, "Hip-Hop's Founding Fathers Speak The Truth", in *That's the Joint: The Hip Hop Studies Reader*, 2nd edition (New York: Routledge, 2012), ed. Murray Forman and Mark Anthony Neal, 44–54 (45)). It is worth noting that this attitude is never found among self-identified breakers.

37. Monica R. Miller, *Religion and Hip Hop* (New York: Routledge, 2013), 16.

38. For example, less than a quarter of the 44 essays collected in Murray Forman and Mark Anthony Neal, ed. *That's the Joint* explicitly treat graffiti or breaking, and even DJing is infrequently thematized therein; despite its title, Imani Perry, *Prophets of the Hood: Politics and Poetics in Hip Hop* (Durham, NC: Duke University Press, 2004) concentrates almost exclusively on rap lyrics, barely mentioning breaking and graffiti.

39. Alonzo Westbrook, *Hip Hoptionary: The Dictionary of Hip Hop Terminology* (New York: Harlem Moon, 2002), 64.

40. M.K. Asante, Jr., *It's Bigger Than Hip-Hop: The Rise of the Post-Hip-Hop Generation* (New York: St. Martin's, 2008), 9.

41. Paul Edwards, *The Concise Guide to Hip-Hop Music: A Fresh Look at the Art of Hip-Hop from Old-School Beats to Freestyle Rap* (New York: St. Martin's Griffin, 2015), 47.

42. Julius Bailey, *Philosophy and Hip-Hop: Ruminations on Postmodern Cultural Form* (New York: Palgrave Macmillan, 2014), 6; 9; 34.

43. Mark Katz, *Groove Music: The Art and Culture of the Hip-Hop DJ* (New York: Oxford University Press, 2012), 36.

44. Mickey Hess, *Is Hip Hop Dead?: The Past, Present, and Future of America's Most Wanted Music* (Westport, Conn.: Praeger, 2007), 4.

45. Katz, 40. D.ST is perhaps the most-heard Hip Hop DJ in the world, having provided the scratch element to Herbie Hancock's landmark single, "Rockit". Throughout, I use the chosen names of Hip Hop artists, rather than adding their merely given names; the reasons for this should become clear in Chaps. 3 and 4.

46. Carlton A. Usher, *A Rhyme is a Terrible Thing to Waste: Hip Hop and the Creation of a Political Philosophy* (Trenton: Africa Wold Press, 2006), 67.

47. David Toop, *Rap Attack 2* (New York: Serpent's Tail, 1991), 196.

48. KRS-One, *Ruminations* (New York: Welcome Rain, 2003), 197.

49. KRS-One, *Gospel*, 61.

CHAPTER 2

The South Bronx, or the "State of Nature"

As detailed in the Introduction, a kind of tension haunts the origin of Hip Hop as conceived in this book. On the one hand, the culture arises in America following the decade during which its social institutions had arguably reached their zenith in terms of consciously working to inclusively actualize human essence. Such a situation, in the Hegelian framework, presupposes that art has long since revealed its inherent limitations as an actualization of spirit, precisely because modern and inclusive state institutions now allow individuals to explicitly and habitually grasp themselves as free. On the other hand, I have claimed that Hip Hop fits Hegel's definition of the classical Ideal—that is, that it reflects a communal and emancipatory aesthetic culture—which presupposes that a fundamental need for art is broadly and deeply felt by a people, precisely because they lack the social institutions requisite to habitually free social existence. Hip Hop, then, is conceived here both as an essentially modern phenomenon, built on and from the self-consciously free individual, and as what we might call a timeless one, grounded in and revealing of the essential drive for self-determination that brought us out of the state of nature. It thus reflects the generically universal nature of humanity as a whole and its essential relation to artistic creation, as well as the unique struggle of an irreducibly particular, specifically post-Civil Rights, and primarily African-American community. These tensions find their origin in the specific cultural context from which Hip Hop arose: The South Bronx of the early 1970s.

© The Author(s) 2018
J. Vernon, *Hip Hop, Hegel, and the Art of Emancipation*,
https://doi.org/10.1007/978-3-319-91304-9_2

A PRE-MODERN MODERNITY?

It is virtually impossible to exaggerate the level of social abandonment and alienation that preceded the birth of Hip Hop culture. Founded in and structured by racial hierarchy, by the late 1960s America seemed poised to finally include Black and Brown communities within the higher realms of spirit by extending to them the core institutional protections of a modern state. The years of the Civil Rights, and then the Black and Brown Power struggles had borne considerable fruit (Civil Rights and Voting Rights legislation, Afro-American and Ethnic Studies departments in higher education, poverty programmes, police oversight boards, more diverse and community-based political representation, increased economic opportunity for both entrepreneurs and workers of colour, etc.) at an increasingly accelerated pace. America, in short, seemed to be fulfilling Hegel's predicted role as the "land of the future",[1] providing the leading light of freedom for its time on its march towards Martin Luther King's infamous "table of brotherhood".

However, as King's dream faded into the harsh reality of Nixon's Presidency, the South Bronx (already in the process of being decimated by the construction of the Cross Bronx Expressway) quickly became the extreme edge of a generalized tendency towards renewed racial injustice that would manifestly put the lie to Hegel's unified, Whiggish narrative of historical progress; first through the differential distribution of the effects of a crippling unemployment crisis, and then through the brutal elimination of the Black Panther Party, and similar organizations that corralled the frustration of the disenfranchised youth of the inner city into varied community and political projects.[2] As Jeff Chang succinctly notes, as the 1960s drew to a close, the "optimism of the civil rights movement and the conviction of the Black and Brown Power movements gave way to a defocused rage",[3] whose predictable result was a return to widespread crime, which only intensified institutional discrimination. This regressive shift was typified by the booming Bronx job market in arson, which corrupt landlords used to forcibly evict unwanted tenants and collect insurance on recently privatized social housing.

The state's response to this growing alienation was simply and manifestly to deepen it. Presidential Counselor on Urban Affairs Patrick Moynihan wrote an infamous letter to Nixon in 1970 arguing that "The time may have come when the issue of race could benefit from a period of benign neglect".[4] Nixon vociferously agreed, and varied levels of government ushered in a stream of social service cuts, most tellingly to the fire services that were so badly needed—with seven stations being closed in the continuously burning Bronx—contributing to the eventual loss of over "5,000 apartments buildings with 100,000 units of housing" in the region.[5] The press generally ignored the issue in the early months, in large part because the arson epidemic was "officially ignored" by the fire commissioners, and some "[g]overnment policies actually encouraged arson".[6] Law enforcement in the region had gone from openly and proudly repressive in the pre-Civil Rights years, to at least officially (if rarely in practice) protective after 1964, to effectively *absent* by 1970. Bronx drug dealers like early MC Coke La Rock, for example, initially believed their products were legal, as they never attracted the attention of police even when openly providing their services.[7] As if by cosmic coincidence, heroin and PCP flooded into the inner city, tearing families apart, and adding to the crime spree in the virtually lawless zone.[8] Originally denoting a small section of blocks, over time "the term 'South Bronx' was attached to each new neighborhood stricken by the vicious cycle of poverty, drugs, crime and [...] arson".[9] To local residents, it appeared "as if the laws of the city, or the country, did not apply in the South Bronx",[10] and because the children of the struggling, desperate and addicted were denied even the minimal economic and personal "security that some of their parents and even grandparents knew",[11] they entered the post-1960s world:

> expected to forge and build Black America's future, but with no guidance or grassroots leadership or organizational component to constructively thrust them forward, they lived in an environment that had become comparable to the one in *Lord of the Flies* where children stranded on an island with no adult guidance create a new, brutal social order of their own.[12]

For most, the only protection against junkies and pushers, as well as the only stable structure and seeming economic opportunity, came in the form of street gangs. Gang culture had quite recently been largely either eradicated or co-opted by the Panthers and their cohorts, but suddenly returned in full force to fill various voids left by social collapse, acting both as a kind of surrogate family for members by providing mentorship and protection, and as a makeshift police force for the community by banishing the junkies who terrorized the locals, thereby depriving pushers of customers. Pioneering DJ Grandmaster Flash recalls that in "the early seventies, when they called the South Bronx hell on earth [e]ven the cops were afraid to go there [...] Nearly every kid my age ran with a gang [and so i]f people had a problem, they went to the gangs before they went to the cops".[13] Thus, in a region largely isolated from the benefits and institutions of the modern state, the local gangs "devised their own brand of order for their own small world".[14] However, while they provided some modicum of social structure for the region, they also acted with the traditional impunity of local law enforcement, contributing to the rise in reported assaults "from 998 in 1960 to 4,256 in 1969. Burglaries during the same period had increased from 1,765 to 29,276".[15] Turf was both more tangible and more protective than civil society, and so battles to secure and enhance it ensued, injuring hundreds, sometimes fatally. Students rapidly dropped from schools, which were subsequently "closed and abandoned, after being first starved of music and arts programs, then of basic educational necessities".[16]

In response, when they weren't feebly denying that such problems existed, city and state officials openly claimed to have given up on the region and its inhabitants. George Sternlieb, director of Rutgers' Center for Urban Policy, captured the establishment's attitude of the time by claiming that the "world can operate very well without the South Bronx".[17] By the mid-1970s, several city planners publically advocated "razing the slums of the South Bronx" because it was "beyond rebuilding".[18] In short, crammed into projects gradually burning to the ground from "the fires of abandonment",[19] largely lacking law enforcement protection in an era of rampant and fruitless street violence, and left to fend for themselves in the "neighborhoods hardest hit by post-industrialism" during a staggering recession,[20] the citizens of the "poorest section of the poorest borough of the city",[21] "whose older local support institutions had been all but demolished along with large sections of [their] built environment",[22] effectively lived on an independent, *stateless territory*, one not dissimilar to, but far more extreme than, others dotted throughout the city and country. Thus, the common refrain among Hip Hop founders was that, in the early 1970s, "the Bronx was the world", where they lived by and large as disconnected from the modern state of which they were technically a part.[23] In 1973, a mere matter of months before the "first Hip Hop party", the *New York Times* ran a series of articles on the region, calling it everything from a "jungle" to a "necropolis", reflecting the essential effort of city and state officials to fundamentally *dehumanize* its inhabitants.[24] Enduring a "tragedy [...] perhaps unique in the history of civilization",[25] the South Bronx was, by force of intentional and overwhelming state neglect, effectively returned to something resembling the pre-modern "state of nature". Of course, this state was markedly different than the one with which Hegel begins his *Aesthetics*. While, as KRS-One argues, the "unanimous feeling permeating throughout the inner city [was] the constant feeling of being stifled, held back, hunted, and oppressed",[26] this "externally determined" feeling was lived by those who were, at least technically, citizens of a modern state, and who thus knew the level of social inclusion that should have been their due. That is, "the hip-hop generation was [both] the first to enjoy the freedoms of a post-civil rights world" and "the first to recognize the hollowness of those promises and to bear witness to the effects of the repeal of many of those same freedoms".[27] Those dwelling in inner cities, simply by virtue of being at least formally American, as well as inheriting the self-conception won through the preceding decades of struggle, still conceived of themselves as essentially *free*. However, radically deprived of the institutional safeguards that enshrine and enhance human essence, they also had more reason than virtually anyone else in modernity to interpret their freedom *arbitrarily*, in terms of their own immediately individual isolation from, indifference to or rebellion against the broader ethical order.

Thus, in the South Bronx, modern, "romantic" individuals were left without institutional safeguards, essentially returning to a situation where action operated without reference to a determinate state. As Hegel notes, in an effectively "stateless condition [*staatlosen Zustande*] the security of life and property depends on the personal strength and valor of each individual who also has to provide for his own existence and the preservation of what belongs and is due to him" (185/I, 243, trans. modified). KRS-One, reflecting the addition to this scenario of the romantic conception of freedom, argues that those who became the Hip Hop generation "live[d] in the inner cities where individualism rules" or in a situation where "there [was] no collective quest for equality, righteousness, justice, truth, or reason [...] The general philosophy for such a society is, me and mine!".[28] Survival, let alone any higher self-actualization, depended on individual strength, cunning, ingenuity, and effort; within such a situation, it is understandable that people simply retreat to a form of anti-social and/or radically individual criminality that mirrors those who came to dominate the state's financial and political sectors at the dawn of neo-liberalism.

ART FROM THE FLAMES

What seems inexplicable is the emergence, from this violent struggle for survival and power, of a generalized and widely adopted culture of specifically *aesthetic* innovation and appreciation; in fact, as Joseph Ewoodzie notes, "those who emphasize the importance of social-structural conditions [...] demonstrate that it was *not likely* to have emerged from such destitution".[29] On the Hegelian account of aesthetics, however, it is not the *plenitude* of one's (post)modern surroundings, their infinite possibilities for revision and remix, the proliferation of audiences and niche markets, and so on from which art's highest vocation is called forth; to the contrary, it is precisely "from the *deficiencies* [*Mängeln*] of immediate reality that the *necessity* of the beauty of art is derived" (152/I, 202, emphasis added). For citizens generally included in modern states, of course, these deficiencies are usually gaps or differentials in the application of legal protection or some other form of partial (even if quite serious) deprivation. In such states, (romantic) art forms one among many ways people either push back against the determinations of institutions to make them better reflect, actualize, and include the citizens who live by rote within them, or merely console themselves to their lot therein. In modernity art is not strictly *needed*, but is regularly and predictably produced as, or alongside other forms of, progressive activism, sensuous escapism, implicit acquiescence, or impish rebellion. By contrast, the creative movement that manifests art's "highest vocation" is the outcome of a far more severe situation; one that radically and palpably denies the self-determining freedom of a people by essentially *depriving* them of institutional protection in its entirety. There being no formal institutional order, one must be built from the only "ethical" resources available: the individuals acting as freely as they can within the constraints of their otherwise determined external situation. In such circumstances, "the validity [*das Gelten*] of the ethical order rests on individuals alone" (184/I, 242, trans. modified).

While this point may be relatively uncontroversial (after all, if social institutions do not exist, they could only arise from those who will eventually determine, fill, and enforce them), it alone does not explain why this takes place *aesthetically*. The nascent order produced by gangs in the South Bronx, after all, served the basic function of producing social stability through the activity of "free" individuals; it may have been a profoundly deficient order, but it was certainly an improvement on the situation that begat it. Moreover, it is not difficult to conceive of a situation wherein genuine ethical institutions or organizations proceed directly from the vague order produced by merely selfish or territorial activity, as the Black Panthers and others attempted with a significant degree of success, just prior to the complete collapse of civil society in the region. Even if the violence associated with gangs ensured that such organizations were necessarily short-lived, it would seem more predictable for them to morph directly into community service and development organizations akin to those that gathered the discarded and masses into the Civil Rights and Black Power struggles; in fact, during Hip Hop's early years, the Panthers, the Young Lords, and other organizations still eked out existences locally, and there were also internal efforts to build a "higher order" from gang life that would carry forth the remnants of still raging, and within recent memory highly successful, political struggles.[30] Of course, with sad predictability, the efforts at gang peace brought back some (but actually not much) police presence, accompanied by equally predictable police brutality, and thus one could always argue that the political option was stifled. But then the question remains why the violence seething in the South Bronx failed to simply reach a boiling point—as it had in the immediately preceding years in Detroit, Watts, Newark, and other crumbling cities— and exploded in readily understandable riots.[31] What seems inexplicable is that, coming hot on the heels of both the destructive uprisings and productive inner city politics of the 1960s, the proverbial "cry of inner city rage" manifested itself, not just artistically, but as the creation of *entirely new forms of artistic production*, and which (as we shall see) actually expressed *no* explicit rage against external authority or political rebellion against state repression, but remained operative only within the isolated community itself. The energy one might normally predict would lash out on the surrounding and oppressive order was channelled into novel, *joyous* forms of collective creation in precisely the manner predicted in Hegel's *Lectures*. Why, then, does *novel, creative*, and above all *communal* art arise at such moments?

FROM DESIRE TO SELF-DETERMINATION

According to Hegel, there is something resembling an essentially human *drive* for artistic expression that arises precisely when a people "cannot, in the finitude of existence and its boundedness and external necessity, recover the immediate vision and enjoyment of its *true freedom* [*in der Endlichkeit des Daseins und deren Beshränktheit und äußerlichen*

Notwendigkeit den unmittlebaren Anblick und Genußseiner wahren Freiheit nicht widerzufinden vermag]" (152/I, 202, trans. modified, emphasis added). As essentially free, humanity cannot be satisfied with a life of mere survival, self-preservation, or even arbitrary "free" will, for these necessarily wed us to externally determined, merely contingent, and transient forces and objects. Mere self- and property-preservation, for example, reflects the form of self-consciousness that Hegel calls "desire". Desirous self-consciousness acts on the surrounding world, but only "in accord with [contingently] individual impulses and interests" such that one "maintains himself in them by using and consuming them" and thus "by sacrificing them works his own self-satisfaction" as the contingent individual she is (36/I, 58). Seeking only to actualize the contingently given subject in contingently given circumstances, desire reacts *instinctually* to the external environment, and thus cannot "let the object persist in its freedom, for its impulse drives it just to cancel this independence and freedom of existent things, and to show that they are only there to be destroyed and consumed" (36/I, 58). By extension, the desirous individual cannot legitimately claim to be "free in respect of the external world, for desire remains essentially determined by external things" that it consumes or destroys (36/I, 58). When gangs, for example, essentially took over the South Bronx, untroubled by any aspect of the surrounding civil society, they were consequently left "free" to fight for and enjoy power, money, or kicks; however, their collapse into the aesthetic suggests that this merely negative/negating "freedom" clearly remained unsatisfying, reflecting the fact that an abandoned people "is compelled to satisfy the need for this freedom, therefore, on other and higher ground" (152/I, 202).

Out of the immediate consummation of desire, Hegel claims, this "other and higher ground" emerges initially and inevitably as *art*. Like use and consumption, artistic expression, of course, "is only there in so far as it has taken its passage through spirit and has arisen from spiritual [...] activity" (39/I, 61, trans. modified). The creation of an aesthetic object presupposes, and demonstrates the existence of, a being free enough to create; however, unlike the merely impulsive negativity of desire, *aesthetic* spirit is "productive" (39/I, 61) for it is "distinguished by the fact that it lets its object persist freely and on its own account" rather than "convert[ing] it to [desire's] own use by destroying it" to satisfy merely immediate, subjective interests (38/I, 60). *Desiring* objects to be *consumed*, we remain determined by them, and thus by the interests and habits that derive from our merely given situation; *creating* objects to be *appreciated*, we allow ourselves to sensibly experience evidence of possibilities not simply granted contingently from without, but *self*-determined from within. That which is received from external nature is "only immediate and singular, while *humanity as spirit* [by contrast] duplicates itself" in so far as it "represents itself to itself" by "active[ly] placing itself before itself" for its own contemplation (31/I, 51, trans. modified, emphasis added). In its "highest vocation", artistic expression is the production of *freely created, immediately sensible evidence of our essential freedom from external determination*, or the "altering [of] external things whereon [one] impresses the seal of his inner being and in which he now finds his own [essential] characteristics" (31/I, 51). The novel and broadly communal emergence of such expression results from and demonstrates the "universal need for art" or our "rational need to lift the inner and outer world into [our] spiritual consciousness as an object in which [we] recognize again" ourselves (31/I, 52). Without a state, and seemingly determined by our surroundings, we need art to begin to see ourselves as non-desirously free enough in our world to eventually build the institutions of a free society within it.

Of course, since the desirous subject remains determined by external contingencies, "it is not only with external things that man proceeds in this way, but no less with *himself*, with his own natural figure which he does not leave as he finds it but deliberately *alters*" (31/I, 51, emphasis added). Art reflects the transformation of the world without consumption or destruction, and thereby the recreation of the individual from selfishly desirous to spiritually self-determining. Art, in its highest and most essential vocation, is thus not a matter of personal expression, refined skill, broader cultural perspective, pleasing or challenging distractions, or inspiring gallery visits; rather, it marks *the fundamental, emancipatory transformation,* via *creatively non-desirous and productive action, of the external determination of oneself and one's communally shared world into sensible and lived evidence of our inherent, shared, and essential capacity for the liberating and self-determining transformation of our lived situation*. It lays the foundation for higher, non-artistic transformations of self and world precisely by creating an immersive and participatory environment that sensibly reflects and immediately actualizes our essential capacity for self-determination.

Of course (as I will discuss more fully in the conclusion), the idea that art conveys *any* essential and universal content has largely been abandoned in contemporary aesthetic theory and practice, in no small measure because of its link with the Hegelian narrative of progress from more primitive to more refined states that places both art, and history more broadly, in a decidedly and offensively Eurocentric frame. The various errors, omissions, and outright falsifications in his historical narratives amply demonstrate the power of such a critique, and as a result there is much in Hegel's *Aesthetics* that rightly stands condemned; in fact, it is places like the South Bronx that show this most viscerally and undeniably. However, the demand that we recognize art's vital link to both a universal essence and human emancipation is not exclusive to Hegel; it also finds voice in Hip Hop culture's main philosophical spokesperson—KRS-One.

If "it is the politically unsatisfied that feel oppression most [a]nd most inner-city people are politically unsatisfied", then KRS-One's childhood home of the early 1970s Bronx represents the most extreme form of this dissatisfaction.[32] Absent political inclusion, he argues, true human freedom is impossible, for we remain trapped by the circumstances and contingencies of our given environment and finitude, wherein the "individual is returned to *natural law* where human beings must *fend for themselves*".[33] It is precisely in such circumstances, however, that we learn that we are essentially defined by the "*super* human" in us, or that which can rise above its circumstances, "not the animal human", or that within us which desirously remains determined by its imposed situation.[34] This "super human" is not some mystical quality that escapes human knowledge or exists in a realm of transcendence; it simply names the fundamental capacity for self-determination which is implicitly present in all human beings, but is manifestly denied by severe forms of social exclusion, and which we come to grasp most basically and vitally through art. Like Hegel, KRS-One prefers to summarize the concepts of liberation from desire, true self-consciousness as free, and the intrinsically human capacity for productive creation through which the latter produces the former into the shorthand "Spirit", which is "understood as *the vital principle or animating force within living beings*" or "a causative, activating, or essential principle" that manifests itself in acts of individual and collective self-determination.[35] As in Hegel's account of art, for KRS-One, if it was precisely the collective realization that "all worldly avenues of success [had] been closed" or "the lack of money and other resources that caused Hip Hop to exist",[36] this aesthetic response demonstrates the presence of an essentially human drive for self-emancipation from radical social determination; that is, "Hip Hop seems to be a genetic response to oppression".[37]

Spirit is thus the animating force of all human activity which, when trapped in determining finitude, can manifest itself only in desirous consumption or destruction. An oppressed people is free, but cannot actualize, or even fully *know* itself as such, so long as it remains determined by the constraints that stifle its spiritual essence, or restrict it to the level of arbitrary desire. Thus, one's circumstances, as well as oneself, cannot simply be accepted, exploited, or destructively rejected if we are to grasp and actualize our essence; rather, for KRS-One it is "the ability to add, change, and create or re-create your Self [that] is the first step out of oppression and into self-creation".[38] If true "freedom is self-creation",[39] then the actualization of freedom truly begins when an oppressed people build for themselves a form of personal and collective expression that reflects back to them their essential freedom despite their restrictive circumstances. Before being rigorously thought and formally institutionalized by a repressed people, freedom must be *seen, heard, and performed*, and thus demands a freely *created, creative, and sensible* actualization as its foundational, lived ground.

From Emancipation to the Elements

Which, finally, brings us to the problem of why Hip Hop developed such *novel* forms of artistic expression. One of the dominant myths surrounding the culture is that its precise forms of expression—such as the use of turntables, rather than instruments; or spray paint, rather than oils—were *externally determined* by the impoverished circumstances of their creators. The cuts to arts programmes in local schools certainly support such a thesis, and it is likely that spray paint was found strewn in the various abandoned construction projects in the Bronx during the period of decimation, facilitating the development of aerosol-based visual art. Recent scholarship, however, has drawn attention to the fact that the sound systems used by early DJs were actually far more difficult to acquire than second-hand instruments,[40] and were "often expensive enough that DJs would enlist a gang to protect the system".[41] And while graffiti might have begun with found materials, the early artists generally *stole* their paint and markers from stores, and they could have just as easily stolen fine art supplies as hardware-based ones. Many early music pioneers actually could play instruments,[42] studied graphic design in trade school, or belonged to gymnastics teams at the few remaining boys and girls clubs. It seems, contrary to the myth, that what drove the material construction of Hip Hop was less the relative *ease* with which these forms could be achieved, given circumstances, than the more fundamental drive to create forms of artistic expression that radically and explicitly *broke from* previous forms of painting, music, dance, and poetry. The question, then, is why novelty was prized by a people whose options for expression were so limited?

If the above analysis is correct, then socio-economic circumstances of the residents of the South Bronx can be understood as a kind of modern return to the "state of nature". This realm of external determination, then, would include the presence of romantic art forms that find place in the surrounding state, and which existed as forms of cultural expression within the now-abandoned community from which Hip Hop emerged (e.g. free jazz, spoken word recitation, pop art, or even the "slogan" graffiti of the late 1960s, etc.). As Hegel argues, imitations of surrounding nature fail to express the freedom inherent in humanity precisely because, like desire, they remain essentially determined by the merely given. While those who can, for example, perfectly imitate the song of the nightingale certainly demonstrate an interesting and rarefied set of skills, it strikes (or, Hegel would argue, at least should strike) us as being less than art; however impressive, such imitation remains "nothing but a trick" (43/I, 67), precisely because "from the free productive power of man we expect something quite different from" mere replication (43/I, 67).[43] And just as birdsong imitation, no matter how skilled and accurate, fails to reach the level of true art, for KRS-One, for the "graffiti artist to draw a tree identically to how the tree actually appeared in nature is to kill the tree in her art [for] this is not art in a creative sense, this is photography in a duplicating sense".[44] The emancipatory essence of art reveals that "it befits man better to take delight in what he produces *out of himself*" (43/I, 67, emphasis added), through the creative, rather than imitative, use of our capacities on the external world; and this demands forms of artistic production that, even if falling under the romantic art forms, nevertheless radically alters them in ways hitherto unseen. Hip Hop culture—just so that its community could reclaim its freedom to determine itself out of uniquely repressive circumstances by creating an aesthetic setting in which it can appreciate, admire, and grasp the free nature of its accomplishments—had to create forms of expression beyond the merely given, accounting for the far more difficult to achieve, but thereby more creative and liberating, aesthetic outlets invented in the unjustly abandoned South Bronx community.

CONCLUSION: TOWARDS THE SYMBOLIC FOUNDATION

Art, both in essence and in its highest vocation, has its origin in the immediately felt need for novel and specifically aesthetic self-expression uniquely felt by a community radically excluded from the protections of the social order; it names the sensible process of *individual and collective, experimental self-discovery,* through which a people comes, against the cramping restrictions of situational finitude, *to grasp themselves as freely self-determining in and through a world transformed by their own creative freedom.* Lived, aesthetic cultures emerge as the expressive discourse and existence of the socially abandoned, as they begin to overcome the purely arbitrary and negative freedom of desire and its merely given forms of external expression, in order to actualize themselves as free through acts of self-determining creativity. It is just such a creative discourse—one that can initially "express the collective consciousness" of the oppressed as they aesthetically strive for self-determination[45]—that for KRS-One defines the first of Hip Hop's elements to appear: graffiti writing, through which we will explicate Hegel's account of the foundational form of artistic expression: the *symbolic.*

NOTES

1. In his *Philosophy of History*, Hegel argues that states, like art, move through stages of origin, peak and decline, in terms of their actualization of human essence. No state perfectly actualizes it, but every dominant state contributes to the overall progress of the species. Infamously, he predicts that America is the nineteenth century's "land of the future", and thus the one which will primarily advance human freedom in the twentieth. More on this in the conclusion.

2. Several excellent histories of this remarkably disturbing chapter in American history have been produced, among them Huey P. Newton, *War Against the Panthers: A Study of Repression in America* (New York and London: Harlem River Press, 1996), Joshua Bloom and Wald E. Martin, Jr., *Black Against Empire: The History and Politics of the Black Panther Party* (Berkeley: University of California Press, 2013), Ward Churchill and Jim Vander Wall, *Agents of Repression: The FBI's Secret Wars Against the Black Panther Party and the American Indian Movement* (Cambridge, MA: South End Press, 2002) and David Cunningham, *There's Something Happening Here: The New Left, the Klan and FBI Counterintelligence* (Berkeley: University of California Press, 2004). I explore the links between Panther politics and Hegel's account of free will in "I Am We: Dialectics of Political Will in Huey P. Newton and the Black Panther Party", *Theory and Event* 17:4 (December 2014).

3. *Can't Stop*, 12.

4. Cited in Ibid, 14. For a nuanced and trenchant critique of Moynihan's role in shaping policy regarding race, see Ta-Nehisi Coates, *We Were Eight Years in Power* (New York: One World, 2017), 223–281.

5. Jill Jonnes, *South Bronx Rising: The Rise, Fall, and Resurrection of an American City* (New York: Fordham University Press, 2002), 8. While acting as something of an apologia for key political figures of the era like Moynihan (who wrote its forward) and anti-graffiti warrior Ed Koch (who provided one of its blurbs), this nevertheless gives a good sense of the unique devastation that affected the area, and of the demographic and economic shifts that accompanied it. It is quite telling, however, that there is only one mention of Hip Hop in the book, and then only to the break-dancing trend that swept the nation in the mid-1980s. A quick primer on this history can also be found in Ewoodzie, 20–31.

6. Jonnes, 232; 259. Arson-encouraging policies included the awarding of state resources to rehab totally vacant, as opposed to dilapidated but partially occupied buildings; underfunding, and then eventually abandoning the Bronx Arson Task Force; and giving relocation priority to those who lost their home by fire, leading many to burn their own apartments down just to escape the flames around them.

7. Cf., Hager, Ch. 2. For the record, he sold marijuana, not cocaine; his name was derived from a childhood love of hot cocoa. The cocaine craze in MC names arose in the 1980s.

8. Cf. George, "Heroin couldn't have run wild in the streets without widespread police and political corruption" (*hip hop america*, 37).

9. Jonnes, 8. Given the gang divisions in the region, it should be no surprise that this generalization is contested by many early Hip Hop participants. I thus use the even more general "Bronx" in much of the book, as debates do rage within the community as to which precise local region actually birthed the culture.

10. Ewoodzie, 50.

11. Katrina Hazzard-Donald, "Dance in Hip Hop Culture", in Perkins, ed. *Droppin' Science*, 220–235 (225).

12. Reeves, 14.

13. Grandmaster Flash, with David Rita, *The Adventures of Grandmaster Flash: My Life, My Beats* (New York: Broadway Books, 2008), 24.

14. Jonnes, 236.

15. Hager, Chapter 1.

16. Chang, *Can't Stop*, 18.

17. Ibid, 17–18.

18. Jonnes, 298. The second phrase is a quote from Robert Moses, who is considered by many to be largely responsible for both the initial destruction, and the difficulties in rebuilding.

19. Chang, *Can't Stop*, 15.

20. Usher, 41.

21. Jeffrey O.G. Ogbar, *Hip-Hop Revolution: The Culture and Politics of Rap* (Lawrence: University of Kansas Press, 2007), 3.

22. Tricia Rose, *Black Noise: Rap Music and Black Culture in Contemporary America* (Middletown, CT: Wesleyan University Press, 1994), 34.

23. Cold Crush Brothers DJ Tony Tone, quoted in Fricke and Ahearn, 67. Compare to the voices presented in the 1960s Bronx gang documentary *Rubble Kings* (2016; dir. Shan Nicholson).

24. Cited in Katz, 17.

25. Jonnes, 7.

26. *Ruminations*, 41; 40.

27. Jeff Chang, "Introduction: Hip-Hop Arts: Our Expanding Universe", in *Total Chaos: The Art and Aesthetics of Hip-Hop*, ed. Jeff Chang (New York: Perseus, 2006), ix–xv (xi).

28. *Ruminations*, 38, 103.

29. *Break Beats in the Bronx*, 7, emphasis added.

30. For example, in 1971 the Ghetto Brothers, after the sudden and shocking murder of one of their members, took inspiration from the Young Lords and Black Panthers and called for a cessation of violence, brokered a peace treaty among local gangs and sought to marshal these forces into community service organizations. The victory celebrations that arose in the wake of this treaty were key antecedents of the block party culture that would come to define Hip Hop. This legendary episode is best seen, rather than read, and luckily has been the subject of two documentaries, *Rubble Kings* and *Flyin' Cut Sleeves* (1993; directed by Henry Chalfant), as well as a moving graphic novel, Julian Voloj and Claudia Ahlering, *Ghetto Brother: Warrior to Peacemaker* (New York: NBM Publishing, 2015). It is worth noting that the Ghetto Brothers also had a house band, whose live instrumentation, Latin-tinged sound and overt political messages leave it far removed (as we shall see) from the music of early Hip Hop.

31. There was widespread looting, of course, during the infamous blackout of 1977, which is often invoked as central to Hip Hop's political development. By then, however, Hip Hop culture had arguably reached its communal peak and was already starting its cross-over into social acceptance outside the Bronx.

32. *Ruminations*, 41.

33. Ibid., 43, emphasis added.

34. Ibid., 52.

35. Ibid., 77.

36. *Gospel*, 35.

37. Ibid., 795.

38. *Ruminations*, 63.

39. Ibid., 154.

40. Pioneering DJ Grandmaster Flash, for example, couldn't afford even a decent home stereo growing up, let alone a block-rocking system, and so he learned electronics in order to take the available "stuff that was half-disabled and put it back the best way" he could (quoted in Toop, 63).

41. Edwards, 43. On the active *choice* to use DJ equipment over instruments, see Joseph Schloss, *Making Beats: The Art of Sample-Based Hip-Hop* (Middletown, CT: Wesleyan University Press, 2004).

42. Cold Crush Brothers founder Charlie Chase, for example, switched from playing bass to DJing after watching pioneers like Kool Herc and Grandmaster Flash, cf. Juan Flores, "Puerto Rocks: New York Ricans Stake Their Claims", in Perkins, ed. *Droppin' Science*, 85–105, and Ewoodzie, 153–8.

43. As Houlgate argues, if "beauty is truly to be the expression of human freedom [...] it must itself be freely created by human beings rather than simply found in nature" ("Introduction: An Overview", xv).

44. KRS-One, *Gospel*, 444.

45. *Ruminations*, 175.

CHAPTER 3

Graffiti Writing, or the Symbolic Stage Art

*Ra was all-powerful, and he could take many forms. His power and the
secret of it lay in his hidden name; but if he spoke other names, that
which he named came into being.*
Egyptian Creation Narrative

Prologue

While graffiti certainly existed in the city as far back as could be remem-
bered, nothing in its practice was noteworthy enough to warrant much
popular attention until 1970, when the enigmatic "cryptogram" "TAKI
183" began to appear throughout the New York City transit system.[1]
Within a few short months, the cypher was so widespread (appearing in
multiple Boroughs, in thousands of iterations) and mysterious (bearing no
further appended messages or graphics, as well as no clear referent) that the
New York Times investigated. They determined, to a fair amount of surprise, that it was simply the encoded name—a variant on the Greek diminu-
tive of Demetrius, along with the street number on which he lived—of "an
unemployed seventeen year-old with nothing better to do than pass the
summer days spraying his name wherever he happened to be".[2] Such boredom would, of course, be rampant among teenagers in a mid-recession
metropolis; it was precisely the circumstances that produced it which fed
the epidemics of drugs, gangs, and crime in New York at the dawn of the
1970s. What was noteworthy, however, was that TAKI alleviated his boredom through an act that appeared to serve no conceivable purpose, and

© The Author(s) 2018
J. Vernon, *Hip Hop, Hegel, and the Art of Emancipation*,
https://doi.org/10.1007/978-3-319-91304-9_3

yet was incessantly repeated in a manner that indicated deep significance, yet without explicitly revealing its nature. While neither TAKI, nor those who built this new wave of graffiti along with him,[3] could have known it at the time, it was this simple, impulsive, and enigmatic process that laid the ground for the aesthetic culture that would come to be called Hip Hop.

Building a Temple of Spirit: Symbolic Art

In the Hegelian framework, artistic expression arises from a community that has been sensibly surrounded with determining constraints sufficient to manifestly deny their essentially free humanity. In this "state of nature", aesthetic creation is more a *compulsion* than a decision, emerging from an *urge* simply *to* express themselves, without clear knowledge as to precisely *what* to express or *how* best to do so. Without a determinate content to represent, or a particular form in which to express it, art proceeds from and makes manifest the fundamental human need to determine oneself and one's environment, beginning at the level of sensation, by *unconsciously* transforming the given to the created, or the repressive to the expressive. Still more determined than free, but starting through creation to grasp their freedom in the limited ways available, an emergent aesthetic culture reflects the *impulse for transcendence* within and from the alienating given, and thus must make use of the options for such creative transformation already present within it.

Thus, the first, largely unconscious, "aim of art is precisely to strip off the matter of everyday life and its mode of appearance" that deny free spirit (289/I, 373), and to re-shape them such that they now reflect it as the cause of their existence in new form. An artist emerging from the state of nature, as it were, is compelled to "take possession of things [found] in nature, [and] arrange them, form them, strip off every hindrance by his own self-won skilfulness, and in such a way that the external world is changed into a means whereby he can realize himself" as free (257/I, 332). Art arises then, as

> humanity, torn from its most immediate, first connection with nature and from its subsequent, merely practical, relation of desire [*nächsten, bloßprak-tischen Beziehung der Begierde*], spiritually steps back [*geistig zurücktritt*] from nature and its own singularity and now seeks and sees in things a universal, implicit, and permanent element. (A, 315/I, 408, trans. modified)

Hegel calls this emergent art *symbolic* because it remains intimately tied to the externally given—both in terms of the expressive forms available and the creative subjects who take them up—and thus it can only *indicate*, rather than clearly express, its essential ground. Because the earliest artists struggle within and against finitude, they continually find themselves "confronted by what is external to [themselves as free, i.e.] external things in nature and human affairs" (300/I, 390). We do not shift from strictly desirous and determined self-consciousness to consummated self-determination, or even to a clear aesthetic representation of our free essence; rather, suspending desire and confronting objects non-practically, we still find ourselves surrounded by a world which is "an 'other', which nevertheless should be for [us] and in which [we] strive[…] to find [ourselves] again" [*sind ein Anderes, das doch für ihm sein soll and worin er sich selbt* […] *wiederzufinden strebt*] (A, 315/I, 408, trans, modified).

While Hegel notes that humanity's earliest efforts at symbolic expression simply seek to find the universal essence in things as given (as, e.g. in certain forms of animism), the determining power of the given in such efforts remains too strong to count as *artistic* creation. The cramping barriers of the external cannot simply be *imaginatively infused* with spiritual meaning by individuals; they must, to some extent at least, be *sensibly overcome*. Symbolic art *physically transforms our lived environment*—and by extension *our merely desirous subjectivity*—out of the most basic, immediate inkling of freedom available to us within it, and thus in a manner that "seem[s] to point to a mysterious, concealed truth which needs to be deciphered".[4] Symbolic artists are, in a sense, searching for the appropriate aesthetic expression of spirit, or engaged in the "*mere search* for portrayal [rather] than [demonstrating] a capacity for true presentation" of human essence (76/I, 106). Symbolic art, then, is a kind of *impulsive search for an adequate expression of our implicit spirit in and on a situation that radically denies it*; thus, "the whole of symbolic art may be understood as a continuing struggle for [the] compatibility of meaning [human essence] and shape [formed material], and the different levels of this struggle are not so much different kinds of symbolic art as […] modes of one and the same contradiction" (317–8/I, 411–2). Art's symbolic stage is marked by a kind of infinitely variable alteration of "actual natural objects and human activities" (323/I, 419) found within the "state of nature", that experimentally "corrupts and falsifies the shapes that [the artist] finds confronting" her (300/I, 391), in a kind of quest to aesthetically puzzle out the very meaning of our capacity for creation itself. It is the experimental renovation of the immediately lived environment and existence of the alienated into one that begins to reflect free creation.[5] This is precisely why the art form that Hegel primarily associates with the symbolic emergence of the aesthetic is *architecture*, typified by the great, public constructions of ancient Egypt.

While Hegel followed developments in Egyptology quite closely, he was also given to speculations both fanciful and disturbing about it, displaying his relative ignorance as well as reinforcing his Whiggish tendencies; his assertions regarding the ancient civilization's specific nature are therefore often of little historical value.[6] While we will, of necessity, make use of his discussion of Egyptian architecture in what follows, our focus will be on the aspects common to symbolic art in general, or those which proceed from its concept, in order to distance Hegel's core account of freedom's first form of aesthetic expression from his Eurocentric and simplistic account of the linear progress of civilizations. While this undermines his invocation of the unified human "we" that increasingly actualizes itself through its temporal development (and, of course, passes from East to West at just the right moment), it is worth noting that Hegel also details the varied modes of symbolic art developed throughout history (from Zoroastrianism to the stories of his contemporary Ludwig Tieck, by way of Aesop's fables, Islamic devotional poetry, and more), thus revealing that symbolism is not the exclusive property of any artist, time, or people. On his reading, symbolism exists whenever human spirit is only *intimated* in art, rather than clearly expressed, in a manner typified by the sweeping architectural renovation he locates in the singular genius of Egypt.

Architecture best captures the nature of symbolic art, for Hegel, because it works on the most immediate materials in our environment, and in a way that thus lays closest to mere desire, while nevertheless remaining manifestly aesthetic. Architecture does not work on refined materials perfectly amenable to expressive intent; rather, its "material is matter itself in its immediate externality [...] and its forms remain the forms of inorganic nature" already given to us (e.g. symmetry, balance, etc.) (84/I, 116–7). While Hegel grounds the fundamental role of architecture in the affinity between the unconscious, indefinite grasp of human essence with the "equally abstract" material of "matter as such, [or] what has mass and weight" (635/II, 276), what is more vital in architecture is that it visibly "raises an enclosure" (84/I, 117) against the constraints of merely given externality, and in a manner which is clearly not geared towards survival or consumption, but seems designed "to reveal a universal idea to others" (635/II, 273, trans. modified), even as the precise nature of that idea remains unclear. Shelter is a practical need, while architecture concerns "manipulating external inorganic nature such that it is transformed into an artistic, external world of spirit" (83–4/I, 116). While shelter primarily exists to be lived in, architecture demands to be *seen and understood*; it co-opts the materials, forms, and capacities present within the state of nature in order to construct "an independent symbol of an absolutely essential and universally valid thought, [or] a *language*, present for its own sake, *even if silent*, for spiritual beings" (636/I, 273, trans. modified; emphasis added). If shelters mutely keep out the elements, architecture "build[s] into what has no inner meaning of its own a meaning and form which remain external to it because this meaning and form are not immanent to the objective world itself" (631/II, 267).[7]

Symbolic architecture is thus something like an *immersive cryptogram* that surrounds a community in implied hope that they will collectively come to decipher its implicit message. It is drawn from merely given finitude (the necessity of constructing and inhabiting shelter, the given existence of material with mass for such construction, the natural capacity we have to transform given objects to satisfy needs, the physical forms of symmetrical and stable arrangement found in nature, etc.) but also freely, aesthetically raised above mere desire (sensibly distinct from natural or merely serviceable dwellings, expressively "readable" as constructed to be somehow understood, open to the community as a whole for interpretation and appreciation, etc.). Its creation reflects subjects as they merely exist within nature, with their contingently individual, "vague and general ideas, elemental, variously confused and sundered abstractions of the life of nature", as well as in their impulsive quest to express the "thoughts of the actual life of spirit" (637/II, 274); both to themselves and to an as yet non-existent, but implicitly presumed, spiritual community.

In sum: symbolic art, typified by architecture, reflects a form of sensible creation still inextricably tied to the merely given forms of subjectivity and materiality within the "state of nature", but which nevertheless expressively struggles to "work [itself and its situation] free from the jungle of finitude and the monstrosity of chance" (84/I, 117). Architecture names the non-practical or -desirous construction of enveloping edifices "which stand there independently [...] and which carry their meaning in themselves and not in some external aim or need" (632/II, 269). By constructing an immersive cryptogram to be "read" by others, a foundation is laid for the creation of other forms of artistic (and, ultimately, religious and political) actualization, precisely by revealing "in an artistic way, even if in an external one, the will to assemble" within a space created by and for human spirit (84/I, 117, trans. modified).[8] It is precisely this capacity to aesthetically express the possibility for the gathering of a spiritual community that leads Hegel to associate architecture primarily with varied forms of the *temple* (cf., 84/I, 117). Art begins by constructing a non-natural, creatively transformed environment for free, spiritual beings in a world that denies their essence, and thereby announces—albeit in an imperfect, merely indicative way—their common capacity for free, spiritual self-determination. Symbolic art thus marks the creation of a visual and immersive aesthetic enclosure within and through which individuals can gradually come to explicitly grasp themselves as self-determining creators.

Of course, inner city residents in post-1960s America could hardly be expected to "re-run" a history identical to that portrayed in Hegel's account of symbolic art. Already conscious of themselves as (albeit individually, arbitrarily, and thus not truly) free, one would not expect to find the worship of the divinity of light, the obsession with the cycle of birth and death, or the postulation of the soul's immortality that occupy so much of his discussion of the symbolic; if the primary tension of symbolic art is to be found here, it will thus not proceed through the same variants, stages, or themes. Moreover, in post-industrial economies, architecture is manifestly unavailable as a mode of emancipatory expression for small communities, let alone for the most socially abandoned. Given their absolute neglect by state institutions, there could be no hope for the citizens of the Bronx to independently rebuild their crumbling dwellings to the state of merely functional shelter, let alone to conceive of, and construct, fresh and novel temples of spirit like the pyramids. Architecture, then, was both too outdated (in an era dominated by the romantic arts) and out of reach (in a situation characterized by extreme class and race divisions, scarce land, and expensive materials) to ground a new aesthetic community. However, while Hip Hop is of necessity rooted in the time and place of its origin, KRS-One nevertheless argues that there is a sense in which it simultaneously marks "the return of an ancient people, with ancient skills rooted in the earliest experiences of human consciousness".[9] Its founding artists creatively employed and worked over the detritus of their finitude in order to express a spirit higher than mere survival and desire, and in so doing effectively constructed the temple within which the broader culture of Hip Hop could be built. And the "architects" of this temple were the New York graffiti writers whose work reached its aesthetic peak in the South Bronx between 1970 and 1973.

GETTING YOUR NAME OUT

As Jack Stewart notes, in a broader sense, graffiti is one of the oldest as well as the most static forms of artistic expression[10]; the scrawling of phrases on public walls dates back at least as far as the first century BCE, and its illegal application in major cities reached significant proportions in decade preceding the birth of Hip Hop (with, e.g. the scrawls of the activists of Mai '68 in Paris or "Free Huey" and related political slogans across the United States, the rise and spread what Norman Mailer called "smut writing" on bathroom walls, etc.). However, if "the form and content of graffiti remained remarkably unchanged until the mid-1960s", something different seemed to happen "when much larger-scale graffiti began appearing" in some of the most economically depressed areas of New York City.[11]

This shift in style began with the street gangs that, as we saw in the previous chapter, re-emerged to fill the void left in the wake of the state's abandonment of inner city communities. As we have seen, the young people who joined gangs were primarily concerned with preserving the integrity of the only world they were allowed to know—their local territory. As the 1960s entered their ebb and the gangs resurfaced, graffiti was often used to mark "the boundaries of their turf". For this task, small letters, representational images, or clean and precise stencils simply would not do, nor would "safe", out of the way locations to paint; turf control required not only a simplification of message (primarily just the nicknames of members used within the local set, sometimes accompanied by the set name), but an increase in both the scale of the letters (i.e. "the size of the names grew to match the magnitude of the warnings") and the frequency of writing as well (for spaces needed to be re-secured in the wake of elemental damage, city or business clean-up, rival gang cross-outs, etc.).[12]

More importantly, the emergence of this new style of graffiti, with its focus on recognizable name, broadly legible size, stable duration, and steady frequency of "tags", was quickly and almost inexplicably eclipsed by that of another breed of writers, initially referred to as "loners". Either unaffiliated with gangs or simply seeking a form of expression outside of them, these writers "helped to usher in one of the few major changes in the history of graffiti" by co-opting the new scale of lettering and simplicity of message in the service of one and "only one intention: to get their names out" by "writing" them virtually everywhere.[13] This change led to what is now the most recognizable form of graffiti: the "tagging" of some piece of public space with the *invented name* of the writer, solely in order to make said name visible to as broad a public as possible. And while "loner" graffiti may have also emerged in other cities, it was in "New York [that] the idea would achieve its full promise", in particular in the wake of TAKI.[14]

Unlike the largely political graffiti that dominated public space in the previous decade, and even the gang and moniker forms of graffiti that immediately preceded him, TAKI's tags had no specific message to convey; even though he was "getting his name out", because he had made it cryptographic, he could not be clearly identified as its author.[15] His scrawls appeared totally impractical, for—as he himself admitted—his hobby could achieve nothing external to the act of tagging itself.[16] Moreover, there was no traditional aesthetic charm to his earliest "scribbles", so one could not even claim that they were beautiful, or in many cases even all that visually interesting. Rather, the sole justification he provided for adorning any and all possible surfaces with the basic scrawl of his cryptic name was: "I was bored, and I didn't want to get involved with drugs, so I started writing my name around".[17] This could, of course, simply have been the idiosyncratic manner in which a contingent individual dealt with the stifling situation of the times. However, the spread of his "tag" "seemed to have a profound effect on the city's youth".[18] Himself following JULIO 204,[19] TAKI's all-city coverage inspired countless followers whose "tags" spread like contagion throughout the city, and emerged especially from the deeply alienated enclaves within Brooklyn, Harlem, and above all the Bronx. The question, then, is why this boredom and alienation was alleviated in a manner that was simultaneously so novel, so time consuming, so widespread, so cryptic, and so seemingly pointless? What, in other words, is in a name?

For Hegel, art begins with "unconscious symbolism", in which "the sensuous representation [of our essence] is not, as art demands, formed, shaped, and invented by the spirit, but rather is immediately found and enunciated in the external existent" (331/I, 428, trans. modified). Unconscious creation consists of our taking up something merely given in our situation, or from "the individual objects of nature [or] individual human attitudes, situations, deeds, actions", and the like, in a manner which nevertheless presents them as "shaped by *imagination* and *art*" (323/I, 418). By crudely, but creatively, altering the merely received, unconscious symbolism sensuously demonstrates that the "universal [essence] and that individual [object] are represented and expressed as immediately one" (331/I, 428, trans. modified). And it is precisely this "*urge* which seeks to […] present to our contemplation and imagination the inner meaning [i.e., the essential] through the outward shape [i.e., the given] and the significance of the outward shape through the inner meaning" that we find in the tags of TAKI and his confederates (351/I, 453, emphasis added).

Emerging from the collapse of modern social institutions, of course, the early graffiti writers habitually inherited the Romantic grasp of *individuality* as the locus of human essence. The essential freedom that grounds this individuality, however, was denied and suppressed in the most excluded areas of the city, reducing it to the level of merely arbitrary desire. Having grasped free individuality as essential, but finding it externally determined and alienated, TAKI impulsively transformed the merely received aspects of his individuality—his contingently given childhood nickname and street address, each a "*merely* natural and sensuous object [that] presents itself" as given (352/I, 454, trans. modified)—into an *aesthetic marker*, presenting for public display an enigmatic, yet evocative "symbol" whose very lack of clear message "alludes immediately outside itself at something else which yet must have an inwardly grounded affinity with the shapes presented and have an essential relationship with them" (352/I, 454, trans. modified). It is precisely this unconscious, yet obsessive creation—the posing of a sensible "riddle" whose ultimate meaning and import is unclear, even to those who create it—that defines, for Hegel, the symbolic stage of art, and which laid the foundational gathering space within which the broader aesthetic culture that came to be known as Hip Hop developed.

In TAKI's wake,[20] graffiti spread in both a form and a quantity that had never been seen before. This "spontaneous group activity" that seemed to be emerging from the most impoverished areas of the city was possible precisely because graffiti is a form of sensible expression that one "could attempt without education, talent, or money".[21] However, in virtually every case, when asked, the early Bronx writers offered either no justification for what they did, or reasons as weak as their predecessor.[22] TOPCAT 126, for example, simply claimed "I was never a real graffiti artist. I just used to do it when I didn't have anything else to do. I just had time on my hands",[23] just as TAKI claimed "it is something he just has to do".[24] In fact, early practitioners rarely thought of themselves as artists (which in the modern, romantic era generally connotes both the conscious deliberation of individual creators and/or the desire to please or provoke a specific intended public) and even rejected even the term "graffiti" (which would lump their work in with that of bathroom smut poetry, the unaesthetic defacing of surfaces with slogans, etc.), emphatically preferring simply to be called "writers". As Bronx writer BAMA I puts it, "it wasn't even, 'Let's make some art, let's do something pretty.' Because that's a little too straightforward".[25] The very impracticality and seemingly unjustifiable nature of early graffiti—the uncontrollable "need to scribble on everything you see" a precise cryptogram meaningful to few, if any, others that made it appear as merely reckless and pointless vandalism continuous with, rather than disruptive of, the gang violence that preceded it[26]—was precisely, and arguably *only*, what identified it as a distinct form of artistic creation. Begun impulsively, by a handful of actors, for most who tried it, "[h]itting their tags became an addiction",[27] which nevertheless internally developed, with little to no outside influence, into a "legitimate folk art".[28]

The evolution of wall writing, while certainly not identical to, and obviously far more compressed and localized than, Hegel's account of the symbolic regime of art, nevertheless bears striking similarities to its three central features. First, as noted, symbolic art's "figures are drawn from the presently given [*Vorhandenen*]" rather than consciously invented by the imagination (337/I, 436, trans. modified). For graffiti, in line with its post-Romantic development, the primary figure is the *name*, which was typically either drawn from one's contingently given individuality (as with the condensation of the "name and home street" tags of early writers like BARBARA 204, TRACY 168, JUNIOR 161, and EVA 62), but more often reflected stylized versions of them (EL MARKO 174), or idealized self-descriptions (as with WICKED GARY, SOULFUL SONNY, and RAY A.O., which stood for "All Over", indicating his planned coverage of the city), while some used these traditions to make even more mysterious riddles (Z73, e.g. chose her name because she was born on the 26th of the month and started to write in 1973, hiding behind the standard "name and street" format). Other tags were drawn from a mix of the contingently personal and the given cultural environment (COLA 188, HULK 62, IZ THE WIZ), or the habits and/or desires of the writers (STAY HIGH 149, SUPER COOL), and some names were chosen simply for their visual impact (SNAKE 131), even without sufficient understanding of what made them so noticeable (as with the infamous tag, HITLER II).[29]

In every case, however, these names were (and this is the second feature of symbolic art) unconsciously "applied to universal meanings" (337/I, 436). TAKI's notoriety offered an intriguing prospect to the early generations of writers. His tag was mysterious (even after his identity was determined, there were still few people who knew exactly who he was, and virtually none could pick him out of a line-up), and yet he was nevertheless more famous than many of the city's most powerful citizens (no-one in New York could be unaware of him because his name was legible everywhere they went, and among writers he reached almost mythic status). TAKI's tag represented no-one in particular, but rather was the specific manifestation of the creative impulse present in every (potential) graffiti writer in general, and his cryptographic name was more important and acknowledged than his person. In his wake, it was generally understood within the nascent graffiti culture that "[w]riters were *supposed to be mysterious* figures who never revealed their identity to outsiders",[30] rather than authors of "advertisements for oneself" in search of personal recognition.[31] Tags not only "protected [writers] from discovery, [but] gave their work *an air of mystery*",[32] and as tagging developed "secrecy was part of the form" of aesthetic creation.[33]

Which leads to the third feature of symbolic art. While something drawn from the world is applied to a universal meaning, its specifically *symbolic* character results from the fact that it nevertheless remains "the fact that the particular existents should not actually *be* the absolute meaning for intuition, but rather should only *indicate* it" (337/I, 436, trans. modified).[34] TAKI's tag "meant" nothing more than the drive to compulsively write the name, for reasons and with import not even he fully comprehended. Those who immediately followed in his wake may have been at least in part looking for recognition (e.g. from the *Times* or other media outlets), but as it spread through the city, such fame clearly would not be won by specific individuals, at least in any direct way. It was, in a certain sense, *graffiti writing itself* that demanded social recognition; however, since it was simply a sprayed collection of the arbitrarily chosen names of a small subculture of socially abandoned teenagers, it was unclear what, if anything, it precisely indicated or demanded. Graffiti clearly meant *something*, both to the individuals making it and to the community who were immersed in it; the tags themselves, though, gave no clear indication as to how the movement or its participants were to be understood, even among the writers themselves. As Hegel puts it, in symbolic art the "spirit" that produces it "is not yet clear to itself" (352/I, 454, trans. modified), and thus it does no more than pose a "riddle" to its community through aesthetic means. Symbolic artists set themselves and their audience, as it were, the "spiritual task of the self-deciphering of the spirit" which is driven to produce art, yet "without actually attaining to the decipherment" of it (354/I, 457).

GOING ALL CITY

This is why Hegel claims that the Egyptians "are the original people of *art* [*das eigentliche Volk der Kunst*]", despite the fact that "their works remain mysterious and dumb, mute and motionless" (354/I, 457, trans. modified). While the specific form of this claim certainly relates to Hegel's infamous and indefensible misunderstanding of the nature of hieroglyphic languages and the people who used them,[35] it nevertheless clarifies the very nature of art's foundational role in his account of human self-understanding, as typified by clearly meaningful, but (largely still) puzzling constructions like the pyramids. For Hegel, when a people is, due to repressively alienating circumstances, *compelled* to create—as we find in the "rapid and concentrated alteration of [the] visual environment" that occurred in the early 1970s in New York[36]—this is indicative of our inherently human drive to discern our essence, or "interiority" at a time when situational restrictions render us unable to discern and "speak the clear and distinct language" that adequately expresses it (354/I, 457, trans. modified). Mass, symbolic art movements indicate a kind of collective struggle for self-discovery, or "Spirit's unsatisfied urge [...] to make conscious its own interiority, as interiority in general" (354/I, 457). Our very effort to transform the given aesthetically, rather than practically (e.g. to build temples, rather than shelters; to saturate the city with cryptic names, rather than slogans, demands, or warnings), intimates our essential transcendence from the constraints of the given; yet our earliest efforts at expressing that essence remain beset with the very finitude that we struggle to transcend. Symbolic art cannot yet clearly express our essence, but indicates a people's struggling with and against its own finitude, in search of (the meaning of) its free infinitude, by giving release to the impulsive "pressure to bring this wrestling with itself before itself by means of art" (354/I, 457). Symbolic art "means" nothing in particular (the pyramids don't "mean" human freedom or spirit any more than they "mean" the immortality of the soul); rather, its import lies in just this individual and collective *faith* in the transformative power of the human aesthetic impulse to gain knowledge of what, as yet, it can merely intimate.

And this is precisely what struck Norman Mailer when researching one of the first major essays on New York graffiti. Perplexed by the "passion[...] to write the name" found in all taggers, he writes (speaking of himself as interviewer in the third person):

Tentatively he offers a few questions about the prominence of the name, of why people use that word. He hesitates how to pose the question—he fears confidence will be lost if he is too abstract, or to the contrary too direct, he does not wish to ask straight-out, "What is the meaning of the name?" but, indeed, he does not have to—[early writer] Cay [161] speaks up on what it means to watch the name go by. "The name," says Cay, in a full voice, Delphic in its unexpected resonance—as if the idol of a temple has just chosen to break into sound—"The name," says Cay, "is the *faith* of graffiti." It is quite a remark. He wonders if Cay knows what he has said.—"The name," repeats Cay, "is the *faith*".[37]

While Hegel invokes different temples in his account, in titling his essay after the claim, Mailer pinpointed what is essential to symbolism. The faith of graffiti lies not in *one's own* faith in *one's own* name (or, for that matter, in any *particular* artist or art object), but rather in the *graffiti community's* faith in *the* name, or in the collective, impulsive process of artistic creation as such, as it emerges from determining finitude. And this faith is the meaning of the name precisely because something transformative *was* obviously occurring—both in the artists themselves and in their community—through the broad, sweeping, and aesthetic alteration of their lived environment achieved through tagging, even if the precise nature of this transformation remained as yet unclear. In literally coating the city's infrastructure with cryptographic expressions of individuality, graffiti writing, much like the still-mysterious pyramids, constructed a temple of the human spirit inside a realm of determining and alienating externality.

The analogy between omnipresent aerosol tags and the Egyptian genius for mammoth, cryptographic construction, of course, will no doubt appear somewhat strained. However, this comparison was occasionally voiced by early writers, most forcefully by Bronx legend PHASE 2:

Letters are structures that you can build off of. Do you look at a building and say, 'What does this building mean?' Or do you say, 'That's a beautiful building'? Do you have to able to read hieroglyphs to appreciate them? I can relate to hieroglyphs as a form, and *the form relates back to me* [...] It's not about writing letters, it's about righting letters. I call it "hieroglyphics".[38]

For his part, Hegel extends his account of the symbolic genius of Egypt beyond its curiously inscribed tombs, reminding us that the:

people of this wonderful country were not only agriculturalists, they were builders; they dug the ground *everywhere*, excavated canals and lakes; in this *instinct for art* they not only produced the most prodigious edifices above the ground but also with equal vigour constructed equally immense buildings, of the most enormous dimensions, in the bowels of the earth. The erection of such monuments [...] was a *principle occupation* of the people. (354/I, 457, emphasis added)

Thus, it is not the specific nature of Egyptian architecture, or even architecture itself, which defines the symbolic foundation for art's development; rather, it is the *communally enacted and all-encompassing transformation* of a repressively determining external realm into one that begins to reflect human creation. We see this in the fact that, by 1971, "Manhattan, the Bronx, and Brooklyn were *covered*, if not *saturated*, with graffiti" whose origin and import seemed as mysterious to most New Yorkers as that of its Egyptian precursor.[39] In TAKI's wake, hundreds of alienated youth were driven to scribble cryptographic names on every surface, from the largest to the smallest, above ground and below; in process New York was "transformed into a grand public performance" within which every citizen was necessarily immersed, such that tagging and the city itself eventually became synonymous.[40]

WILD STYLE AND HITTING TRAINS

Symbolic art's need for broad coverage is reflected, moreover, in graffiti's essential concentration on the *subway system*. Most early writers tagged the insides of subway cars, station signs, and walls not only because they promised a far larger audience than any individual building or billboard on one's home turf, but also because they were constructed in forms that readily lent themselves to graffiti. In process, certain "stations became clubhouses" also known as "writers corners" where artists would meet to share materials, information, or techniques.[41] Starting in around 1971, however, writers "hit the outside of subway cars with large masterpieces and grand designs" that greatly expanded both the audience and transformative nature of graffiti.[42] On the one hand, subway cars had extensive reach, with the most coveted lines travelling throughout the entire city, and while the insides of the cars forced riders into confronting the tagging culture, the outside panels were imposed upon riders and non-riders alike, as they moved across the varied above-ground lines, thus representing, in the confining metropolis, the "ultimate surface for maximum exposure".[43] On the other hand, however, this wider and more distant viewership for tags demanded new developments in "the verve of their lines and their relative proportions [so that they] caught the eye more than others" as the trains passed.[44] Thus, with the move to train cars, a new spirit of creation caught hold of the writers, which leads us to four further links with Hegel's account of art's symbolic origins, and reflects the peak of the development of graffiti writing as a communal art form.

First, symbolic art, as we have seen, neither proceeds from, nor attains, clear and adequate expression of its spiritual content. It reflects the communally enacted transformation of the lived environment from one of external determination into one that begins the process of individual and collective spiritual reflection, and for this task there is necessarily no set programme available to be followed, or shape to be forged. Therefore, Hegel argues, the symbolic artist "has no recourse but to *distortions*, since", in order to transform them into aesthetic symbols, she of necessity "drives particular [externally given] shapes beyond their firmly limited particular character, [and therefore] *stretches* them, alters them into *indefiniteness*, and *intensifies* them beyond all bounds" (334/I, 432, emphasis added). Symbolic artists, working without knowledge of the aesthetic form most adequate to expressing human essence and with merely found materials and forms, are compelled to experiment with a seemingly infinite variety of forms in their quest for the meaning of creation itself.[45] Thus, for Hegel the early development of an artistic culture implies a kind of *continual experimentation* with style and image.

Which goes some way towards explaining why it is precisely such distortions that rapidly formed the focus of subway graffiti. While the earliest tags were "simple, unadorned, unpretentious and practiced in a clandestine manner", as the competition between writers, as well as the potential surface area and audience for tags increased, tags could only stand out in the increasing clutter of scribble if writers invented "better, larger, and different graffiti".[46] Thus, the move to subway cars was accompanied by an era of "eccentric tampering" with letterform, such as the "ornately bizarre" distortions in ALL JIVE 161's stylized "J", or the "awkward[ly] elongated" letters of SNAKE 161.[47] Some writers began choosing names simply for the possibilities for distortion contained in their letters, and within a few months, the very legibility of the names themselves became a matter of difficulty even to insiders thanks to the "colorful, wild, and fanciful curlicues and geometric shapes" incorporated into letters by some writers.[48] Quite quickly, the cutting edge of this "wild calligraphy" became, for virtually all concerned, "indecipherable, like cuneiforms from another culture", even for those who not only knew that it was a name, but even which name it was.[49] As these "new visual languages" developed, writers like PHASE 2 "continued deconstructing the letter into hard lines, third eyes, horns, drills, spikes, arches, *Egyptian pharaohs and dogs*, pure geometrics" and the like, while others, like FUTURA 2000, incorporated an "almost *architecturally* precise line and an understanding of industrial design" into their tags.[50] Subway graffiti did not simply increase the potential audience for tags; its bewildering variety of distortions and experiments expressed the "haphazard collisions of ideas and style"[51] or what Hegel calls the "continuing struggle for compatibility of meaning and shape" (317/I, 412) that defines symbolic art. This marked a shift from clearly legible, but cryptographic name, to tags which were known to be such names, but remained riddles to discern due to a "style that featured highly fractured forms which seemed to bounce of each other at oblique angles", which was soon christened "Wild Style",[52] coincidentally echoing Hegel's claim that symbolism represents the "first, still *wildest* [*wildesten*], attempts" at aesthetic creation (334/I, 432, emphasis added). The development of graffiti, then, created a virtually architectural, immersive space of aesthetic creation by covering its external realm with an infinitely varied riddle whose limitless distortions necessarily suggested more than they revealed.

Secondly, what makes the earliest efforts at artistic production reflect human spirit, as distinct from individual desire, is precisely their radical *impracticality*. Art arises when merely given desire is forsaken for that within us which transcends it, even though this inner realm of spirit is as yet indeterminate. Hegel claims that this aesthetic "liberation [from the given] can only take place in so far as the sensuous and natural is apprehended and viewed in itself as *negative*", because the merely given situation and subject are precisely that from which we experimentally seek emancipation (A, 347/I, 448, emphasis added). Through symbolic art, spirit is implicitly grasped as the negation of finitude in all of its forms, up to and including our own natural body, or "specific being". As Hegel reminds us, the negation of specific being is well-known before the dawn of art, for the "immediate and therefore natural negation in its most comprehensive mode is *death*" (A, 348/I, 450), against whose negation, of course, we *practically* seek protection (as with pre-architectural shelter). In *aesthetically* negating the given, however, we must forsake the merely given drive for self-preservation, in much the same way that we replace merely protective shelter with aesthetically (and often dangerously) constructed architecture. Freedom, like death, negates our specific being and thus, in our earliest grasp of it, spirit "is interpreted as having to enter this negation as a determination accruing to its own essence and [thus] to tread the path of extinction and death" (348/I, 450). Implicitly grasping themselves as free from, and thus negating of, finitude, but as yet unconscious of the forms that determinately actualize that freedom, symbolic artists initially associate the presence of spirit with the primary mode of negation available in external determination: individual death. It is precisely this spiritual preoccupation with death that Hegel (again, problematically) locates in Egypt's giant tombs and corpse embalming, through which the "honour paid to the dead [...] is not burial, but perennial preservation as corpses" (355/I, 458).

We do not, of course, find a death-cult in graffiti; what we do find, however—in a manner that accords with the infamous dawn of self-consciousness in the *Phenomenology of Spirit*—is an obsession with the *risk* of death. Because the outside of cars could not be adequately painted in the new styles within the short time that a train was parked in the station, writers began to brave the yards in which they sat overnight, especially in the Bronx which housed the main holding areas. This greatly increased not only the chance of arrest (fewer places to hide, more security than the stations, higher penalties for trespassing, etc.), but the risk of serious bodily harm. Many apprehended writers were instantly "subjected to corporal punishment by the officers" that arrested them and there were "serious concerns [of] being injured during a chase" in effort to escape, including "the possibility of [...] even losing their lives by falling, being electrocuted by the third rail, or being hit by a passing train".[53] These very real (and often realized) possibilities were not coincidental to the practice; rather, the "risk of injury or death [...] were important ingredients upon which the subway graffiti phenomenon fed" and taking such risks was as important to both the writers and the recognition they could gain as stylistic developments or broad coverage.[54] As Hugo Martinez—an academic who was among the first to try to "legitimize" graffiti by moving it from the trains to galleries—recognized, the "element of danger, rebellion [in graffiti made it] like a *ritual*".[55] The visionary writers who founded Hip Hop culture "knew that the fear and excitement that stimulated them on the tracks injected an important quality into their graffiti" that, if unspecifiable, was nevertheless essential,[56] and later generation writers like the legendary LEE were inspired not just by the visual impression of tags, but by "the death-defying wizards of style" who produced them.[57] Moreover, as Grandmaster Flash recalls, the risks of tagging made a significant impact on those in the broader community that formed its audience: "the respect those cats got—oh man! Because of the trains, they were known and respected all over the city. They had to be, dangerous like it was. You couldn't help but bow down for what it took to be out there".[58] Thus, in the early tagging culture, "[d]efying physical danger and the authorities [was] as important as style innovation".[59]

Third, for Hegel, symbolic modes of aesthetic presentation, only hinting at our essence, are effectively *static*, exhibiting in themselves none of the *motion* that (as we will see) he associates with the explicit presentation of freedom. In Egypt, for example, he claims that the "colossal statues of Memnon" are notably "motionless [...] stiff, and lifeless" (358/I, 462); nevertheless, these immobile icons symbolically indicated the living presence of free spirit, for each did not "signify[..] itself but hint[ed] at another thing with which it has affinity and therefore relationship" (357–8/I, 461). These statues, Hegel claims, were tellingly constructed "facing the sun in order to await its ray to touch them and give them sound and soul" (358/I, 462). Unable, like the living "human voice [which] resounds out of one's own feeling and one's own spirit without external impulse", these representations could not directly signify our free essence in themselves (358/I, 462). "Taken as *symbols*" however,

> the meaning to be ascribed to these colossi is that they do not have the spiritual soul freely in themselves and therefore, instead of being able to draw *animation* [*Belebung*] from within [...] they require for it light *from without* which alone liberates the note of the soul from them. (358/I, 462, emphasis added)[60]

Symbolic expressions of spirit, as architecturally external, are themselves static, but can implicitly refer to our free essence, in part, by incorporating the relation to a motion external to themselves in their very construction.

And for early writers like PHASE 2, it was clear that "letters tell a story, they are always moving forward. They almost represent motion, and almost represent individuals", and the distortions of wild style certainly gave static pieces a vibrant appearance.[61] The move to train exteriors, however, allowed them to *actually move*,[62] and many writers began to take on the influence of the movement of the subways in their tags, thus reinforcing the fact that the "illusion that the stylized letters are in motion is part of the energy expressed through graffiti".[63] As they sped across an elevated bridge, for example, where many onlookers saw "the sides of cars, the designs became almost cinematic as they moved in and out of view",[64] and writers quickly began to devise tags meant exclusively for viewing in motion. In yet another coincidence, contemporary slang for tags made "distinctive so they would stand out" as they quickly passed by, was to make the name "sing".[65]

Fourth—and most importantly for Hip Hop's future development—as the legal framework of the state came tumbling down around them and the gang influence faded away, the tagging community took on the task of constructing a fragmentary and shifting, but nevertheless real and lived, *ethical code* that underpinned the practice. As wall-space became increasingly scarce, police pressure became increasingly intense, risk became increasingly serious, and artistic skill became increasingly refined, writers were forced to develop "an honor system that guided [the] subculture of spraying".[66] These informal rules were in part related to the surrounding, state-based community (e.g. never hit a private home, church, or local-owned small business, etc.), but were primarily *internal* to the relations between writers in the nascent graffiti community itself. Ethical standing could be won by achieving broad coverage of the city with one's name, as well as by developing a unique style for, and internal variety to, one's tags, or through the extreme difficulty or risk involved in a particular "hit" (those requiring more time, offering less "cover" from security, involving necessary near-misses with the third rail or moving trains, etc.). As the graffiti community expanded, a collectively enforced ethical code ensured that those who had achieved such standing had rights over novice, "toy" writers, who could not, for example, adopt an already established name, at least without indicating—and more importantly *earning*—lineage. As the early tags gave way to the larger bubble letters known as "throw-ups", and eventually to the half-, whole- or multi-subway car paintings known as "masterpieces" (or simply "pieces"), rules developed for the use of already occupied space (e.g. never cross out an existent tag with your own unless the same tagger had already crossed out yours; a throw up can cross out a tag, but can in turn be crossed out by a piece, provided they "burn", or aesthetically best the buried work, etc.). Given the risk of injury and death that accompanied the art, it is perhaps unsurprising that perceived violations of this code, if they could not be addressed aesthetically (e.g. by crossing out or burning all of the tags of an offending writer), were settled by a fight (called a "fair one", at least when between two writers, although forms of mob justice for serious offenders were not unknown).[67] The aesthetic revolution of graffiti, then, laid the ground for an essentially *ethical* transformation of the abandoned communities of modern society; one which importantly was not directed at assimilation into the surrounding state, but which immanently emerged from the participants and core practices of the artistic community itself. As the preceding indicates, the rules were not meant to preserve the tagging community as it existed, or to include or accept the individuals who formed it as they were; rather, they necessarily had the effect of *forcing participants beyond their previously given limits*, making them more skilled in their chosen field, more knowledgeable about the history and pioneers of their evolving community, more respectful as well as more critical of the contributions of their fellow "citizens", and above all driven to raise themselves to the level where they could contribute to the community's development themselves. Tagging was thus not an impish act of narcissists who just wanted to be noticed or to act out; rather, the "trains that were painted were incredible artistic feats" that were there to be both respected and bested, and this demanded a set of communally determined and enforced rules[68]—rules taken so seriously that early writers like COCO 144 "compare it to a samurai code".[69] Writing, thus, demonstrated that collective and individual creation, under particular conditions, had a "higher vocation" than mere individual expression; because the "heart of this whole culture [was] style *and* respect",[70] tagging could actually serve as the foundation for the possibility of a *progressively evolving, increasingly self-determining ethical collective*.

Thus, much as in the foundation of Hegel's emancipatory aesthetics, the most radically excluded members of a crumbling civil society used graffiti—which seemingly reflects "an art for the joy of making it, to prove that [one] could"[71]—to transform the inner city from a grey and oppressive "battle zone" into a kind of immersive temple, in which the free creative agency of the individuals who created and appreciated it was sensibly, if only symbolically and thus imprecisely, reflected back to them.[72] Through this process, new bodily capacities were discovered, new forms of expression were created, and a new aesthetic and ethical culture was eventually built, known initially only to the taggers themselves, but eventually producing a sympathetic and almost equally committed audience. While wealthier Manhattanites, who still retained a strong interest in the surrounding institutions of right, often condemned subway trains covered with paint and marker scrawls as a kind of alien and fearsome blight—eventually reflected in the (then-Mayor) "'Lindsay theory' that graffiti writing 'is related to mental health problems'"—as one of the earliest published statements in support of tagging put it, the effect of the images within the communities that primarily produced them was actually the "cheering up [of] the depressing environment in the poorer areas of the city".[73] The radical alterity of this culture to the habitual or repressive structures of modernity, as well as to its dominant art forms, is reflected in the widely cited words of Claes Oldenburg, "You're standing here in the station and everything is grey and gloomy and all of a sudden one of those graffiti trains slides in and brightens the place like a big bouquet from Latin America".[74] Growing out of the collapsed ruins of the promise of the 1960s, graffiti writing converted post-war America's most alienated community into a nascent and entirely novel ethical community via the transformative faith of and in its mysterious, stylized, and enveloping aesthetic names.

THE DECLINE OF THE SYMBOLIC

For many early observers and participants, however, subway graffiti in New York reached its peak of development in roughly 1973.[75] Within a handful of years, successive "generations" of writers had moved from what was essentially a larger version of the printing in previous graffiti to a recognizably self-contained and radically novel artistic culture with multiple styles, attendant rituals, internal criteria for aesthetic evaluation and ethical codes regulating the behaviour and contributions of its participants, despite the fact that its "practitioners [...] had no illusions that what they were doing might be called art", at least as the term was generally understood in romantic modernity.[76] However, in a preview of what would happen to the broader Hip Hop culture—virtually simultaneous with the point of graffiti's aesthetic peak—outside observers involved in the institutions of the surrounding civil society (universities, art galleries, social welfare organizations) began to appreciate the graffiti being created as well as its apparently liberating effect on the repressed youth of the city. Among the first was the aforementioned Hugo Martinez who, in the Fall of 1972, transformed his admiration into an "intention [...] to get the best writers off the subways and channel their energies and talents into graffiti as a fine art—to redirect their work to so-called legitimate surfaces".[77] Martinez's intentions were certainly noble (he helped found the United Graffiti

Artists which provided something resembling a union for writers making the move from trains to galleries or murals, set early pay rates for artists unaccustomed to negotiating them, etc.), and efforts such as his were often welcome (many young people facing potentially desperate futures were often understandably eager to cash in on their hard-won pastime, and to have expert guidance in doing so); however, it is also clear that the civil society helpers and the newly organized "writers didn't fully realize that when they moved from the mass transit system to their own canvases in a studio environment, they ceased to make graffiti and began to make *paintings of* graffiti", introducing a split between the technical practice of painting and the ethical culture of tagging.[78]

As we have seen, graffiti was not simply defined by its use of markers or spray paint to stylistically present names, but involved a collective aesthetic practice deeply tied to *all* the elements listed above: compulsive writing, mysterious cryptograms, genuine risk, external motion, getting one's name out, wild and original distortions, broad imposition on an immersed public, and ethical rules and corrective punishments exacted on transgressors. Less about the resulting paintings than about spiritual and communal explorations of the act of free creation, graffiti writing was inextricably tied to forms of subjectivity and collectivity that were built around, but ultimately transcended, the tags themselves. As it moved to galleries, however, a new "emphasis on aesthetic quality"—focused on "design factors" and critical acceptance "very different from the emphasis writers had placed on quantity of hits and pieces", risk, experimentation, and adherence to ethical rules—began to take hold.[79] For three years, graffiti's "development had been insular", and focused on the wild experimentation with and broad distribution of the name itself, but by 1974 "graffiti writers began to reflect an awareness of broader influences in their work", incorporating figural elements (faces, caricatures, logos), as well as political themes and "more distant sources" such as gallery art itself.[80] The new design elements, and often accompanying studio work, required a "calm deliberateness"[81] foreign to both the panic of a trip to the train yard and to the raw and untutored bravado of the early writers who undertook such missions "out of innocence" and thus "were creating it [even though they] didn't even know what [they] were creating".[82] Quasi-formal apprentice systems developed for training writers, who were recruited to help bring "studio graffiti" onto the train yards, where painters produced what genuinely looked like museum pieces, some of which city officials even eventually allowed to run, as graffiti became a tourist draw for the city.[83]

Thus, as graffiti made the move from the trains to the galleries, extra-cultural criteria from the surrounding art world seeped into both aesthetic practice and appreciation in the field, altering the nature of not only the practice of writing, but the subjects creating it and the ethos of their cultural community. Originally seeking in the tagged name an unspecifiable form of recognition for an as yet undetermined but implicitly projected community of spirit, many writers after 1973 "seemed to have come to the tracks with aspirations of becoming artists" in the gallery system, which was becoming a clear and precise path to individual inclusion in the surrounding state.[84] Having originally been abandoned by mainstream society, the newly minted "artists" (an appellation that, by 1975, stuck more or less permanently) now found themselves competing for acceptance within it.

Competition had, of course, always been a part of tagging, as reflected in its ethics and the shifts in its aesthetic forms, but the emergence of "fine art" graffiti radically altered its meaning; artists now competed less for risk, coverage, innovation in style, or the ethical standing in the community that could be won through them, than for personal visibility and economic achievement within the surrounding state. Only by dominating space with high quality pieces could one hope to be recruited to the gallery scene, with its promise of more direct self-expression and financial rewards. This quickly attracted wealthier, less alienated artists to the increasingly trendy scene, putting substantial *pressure* on the public space available for writing, thus changing the nature and intensity of competition. As LSD Om recalls, a "writer of the times [back then] was a person that wrote his name with some sort of style and respect, not to go over other people. It seemed in the beginning there was a lot more respect—people didn't go over each other. There was plenty of room, it wasn't cluttered up with names".[85] But as the flood of new writers descended upon the walls, predictably, by "early 1973, crossing out was becoming hostile [as the ethical] code against writing over another's work broke down".[86] Cross-out wars and "fair ones" spread, as did more "painterly" techniques, which could both erase any trace of old wars and place one in better stead with the gallery system, where one could gain real social recognition and gain for oneself, not just for "the name".[87] Press coverage began to reflect this shift, as articles moved from covering the graffiti phenomenon as a whole (the mystery of TAKI's tag, the explosion of tagging in his wake, what its presence meant, how society should respond) to "[p]resenting the writers as artists [who] had invented something very special, *a personal expression* that went *far beyond old-fashioned graffiti*".[88] The communal expression of human spirit that sought a way out of desirous individuality through an aesthetically grounded ethics in some ways simply led back to the place from which it began, as absorption into the dominant culture transformed graffiti into a mirror of—rather than an enclosed and emancipatory ritual space carved out within—romantic and fragmented modernity.

Many writers, in process, lost faith in the name and gained faith in their individual selves and the art world in which could find personal fame and favour; others, of course, stayed underground, or otherwise tried to retain what of the culture they could as tagging entered into a series of complex relations with external forces that claimed it, exploited it, and altered it, while simultaneously opening up avenues of social and economic inclusion for many, through the gallery and mural scenes that began to build around them.[89] But for many of the pioneers, writing would never be the same, and the tensions between its subterranean, spiritual origins and its co-opted, marketable face would soon spread across the globe.

CONCLUSION: FROM THE SYMBOLIC TO THE CLASSICAL

In terms of our Hegelian framework, we might say that the first half decade of graffiti writing charts a typically symbolic expression from its "severe" stage of growing pains through to its communally unified, ethical, and self-determining "classical" height up to its period of "romantic" decline. Emerging from the ruins of the Bronx to transform the city into something resembling a mysterious, aesthetic temple built from uniquely individual contributions to a self-determining and evolving community, graffiti (at least in part) dissolved into just one of many art forms, presented in a variety of personal ways, and taken up for a variety of contingent reasons, offered up to the few modern citizens who cared to search out the latest trends in the galleries, murals, and even just walls that decorate the fringes of a habitually free society.

However, if graffiti was forever altered by its acceptance by the dominant social order, there is also a sense in which it had already fulfilled its purpose. By taking "revolutionary control of public space",[90] in the precise manner that it did, it had already achieved the highest vocation of the symbolic form of art: "the construction of a temple to be an enclosure for a person who himself belongs to fine art" (662/II, 304).[91] By 1973 taggers had laid the necessary foundation for a broader and more consummate artistic culture that not only built on the gains of graffiti, but both incorporated and brought to full fruition its essential ethical and artistic practices. For Hegel, the foundational work of symbolic art serves primarily to create an aesthetic enclosure that cryptically indicates to its participants and audience that there is a free spirit within them, which they can come to know precisely by sensuously presenting themselves as free. It creates an expansive and immersive "sanctuary" whose "primary purpose [...] is only the erection of a work which is a unifying site [*Vereinigung*] for a nation [...] a place where they assemble" (637/II, 275, trans. modified).[92]

In Hegel's account, of course, this site facilitates the transition from Egypt to Greece, which rests on his assertion that an aesthetic community can only make one contribution to art's (and thus humanity's) progress; an unjustified leap that conveniently facilitates the placement of the "unconscious" and "conscious" stages of art at the peak of the East and the foundation of the West. By way of internal critique of Hegel's Eurocentric fantasy, in the next chapter, I hope to show Hip Hop's true birth reveals how the *same* specific and local community can expand its own self-understanding and capacity for self-determination, precisely by *internally* developing the more appropriate aesthetic means for collective self-expression that his account of cultural progress demands. That is, I aim to show that it is no coincidence that, in the autumn of 1973, at almost the exact moment that graffiti began to be absorbed by the surrounding order, deep within the ritually painted walls of the Bronx, a young writer who tagged "CLYDE AS KOOL" solved the riddle of the name by discovering how to fill the temple with a more aesthetically clear presentation of spirit.

NOTES

1. Jack Stewart, *Graffiti Kings: New York Mass Transit Art of the 1970s* (New York: Melcher Media, 2009), 20. TAKI likely began in 1969, but went "all city" the next year, as graffiti entered the subway system. More on this below.

2. Craig Castleman, *Getting Up: Subway Graffiti in New York* (Cambridge: MIT, 1997), 135. While cited far more widely than Stewart, this book primarily treats the graffiti of the late 1970s and early 1980s, and thus the period after its pioneering "Golden Age"; the same is true of the classic text by Henry Chalfant and Martha Cooper, *Subway Art* (New York: Thames and Hudson, 1984).

3. While Stewart, like virtually all scholars of the art, cites Philadelphia as the geographical origin of "tagging", recent research by Serouj Aprahamian, "Debunking the Historical Hype: A Look Into The True Origins of Wall Writing", available at https://www.bombingscience.com/debunking-the-historical-hype-a-look-into-the-true-origins-of-wall-writing/ (accessed October 2017), has uncovered not only photographic evidence of similar markings in New York perhaps as early as 1967, but even scholarly treatment of it beginning in 1969 (Herbert Kohl, with photos by James Hinton, "Names, Graffiti, and Culture", *Urban Review* 3 (April 1969), 24–37), raising significant questions about the scholarly and popular consensus regarding the Philadelphia story. The kind of wall writing from which TAKI derived his style may go back to 1964, and some even claim the practice goes back as far as 1960. While we cannot rehearse the details, here, the specifically *cryptographic* forms of graffiti that form my focus, here, do seem to have begun with in the later 1960s, when writers like JULIO 204 compressed the previous style (which clearly indicated the "name and street" of the writer, as in "Papo of 87th Street") into a new form; and Taki's employment of this enigmatic form and broad coverage went far beyond the mid-1960s writing that Kohl claims was written by those who "knew who [their] audience would be [...] It would be [their] friends and enemies, the kids on the block" (28), and which centred on names that were largely derived by gang and clique affiliation (what he calls a "peername" (32)), manifesting a far more clear and direct message. South Bronx writer CRASH, for example, firmly claims that real "tagging" was born in 1968 (cf. I. Miller, 163); however, as with much in early Hip Hop, there are conflicting claims about when and with whom particular developments originated, and thus some of the details, here, may need to be amended in light of ongoing research like Aprahamian's, in whose debt I stand for calling my attention to many of these vital and underexplored issues.

4. Stephen Houlgate, *An Introduction to Hegel: Freedom, Truth and History* (Oxford: Blackwell, 2005), 232.

5. Compare Etter, "the unique impulse to create art resides in the particular need for the sensuous recognition of what we are and what the world is [...] In other words, the need for art originates in the need to surround ourselves with reminders of who we are and what kind of world we truly live in. [...] [A]rt is [not] a purely intellectual mode of perception: the need for art arises precisely because we have a sensuous nature, and art is directed to that side as well as to our intellectual or spiritual side by its union of the sensuous and the spiritual" (16–7).

6. Two of the best correctives to Hegel's account are Jay Lampert, "Hegel and Ancient Egypt: History and Becoming", *International Philosophical*

Quarterly, XXXV (1995), 43–58 and Charles C. Verharen, "'The New World and the Dreams to Which It May Give Rise': An African and American Response to Hegel's Challenge", *Journal of Black Studies* 27:4 (March 1997), 456–493.

7. As David Kolb argues, for Hegel, "architecture [...] provides a first (external) overcoming of externality. It is the art of the external because it posits and proclaims its own externality as a [...] way of transcending that externality" ("The Spirit of Gravity: Architecture and Externality", in William Maker, ed. *Hegel and Aesthetics* (Albany, State University of New York Press, 2000), 83–95 (84)).

8. As Etter writes, to "ornament public space appropriately—that is, with *decorum*—is to affirm its dignity [as well as] our worth as human beings" (169).

9. *Gospel*, 77.

10. Cf., Stewart, 13.

11. Ibid.

12. All citations in the paragraph are from Stewart, 13. While he is referring to the questionable foundations of graffiti in Philadelphia, Kohl also cites gang membership and the marking of enclosed turf as vital in graffiti's foundations in New York.

13. Ibid.

14. Ibid., 16. For those who insist that tagging first developed in Philadelphia, the pioneering "loners" in that city are generally identified as "Corn Bread" and "Cool Earl"; but, again, see Aprahamian on the evidence for claims of the timeline of their work. Perhaps more pertinently, however, Cornbread began writing to impress a particular love interest (originally writing "Cornbread Loves Cynthia" throughout his neighbourhood), which distinguishes his purpose from that which dominated New York writing, especially after TAKI.

15. While the "name and street" structure of his tag certainly proceeded from earlier forms, as Hinton's photos reproduced in Kohl's essay reveal, these earlier tags generally lacked Taki's *mysterious* nature. It may seem a small leap from tags like "Foxie of 100 St." and "Al the Killer of 115" to TAKI 183, but the level of interest and scrutiny faced by Taki's tag as well as the rapid spread of both the cryptographic tag-form and the accompanying mystery regarding authorship indicate a qualitative change both unique to New York and specific to the manner in which graffiti laid the foundations for Hip Hop's development. As I. Miller notes, pioneering "[a]rtists like PHASE 2 argue that [New York graffiti writing] has no direct precedents" (13).

16. Cf. TAKI quoted in Castleman, "You don't do it for girls; they don't seem to care. You do it for yourself. You don't go after it to be elected president" (135).

17. Ibid. As he puts it elsewhere, "it was what you do when you're sixteen, you know. Other guys go drinking, break into cars. We'd go out writing at night" (Ewoodzie, 33).

18. Castleman, 135–6.

19. JULIO 204 (who may have begun tagging in 1967) is generally acknowledged as TAKI's mentor, although an early arrest seems to have led to a short career, explaining his relative obscurity (cf., Hager, Ch. 2). He is certainly a key figure in the shift out of the more local, clique-based graffiti, but it may be that, using his real name did not have the aesthetic impact of the more mysterious tag of his protégé. TAKI did use a given nickname, but it was likely obscure enough to create the air of mystery that, as we shall see, is essential to graffiti writing.

20. Although many claim that it was the fame afforded him by his coverage in the *Times* that was primarily inspirational, Hager insists that taggers in "the Bronx had been writing similar graffiti long before the article on Taki appeared" (Ch. 2), although this may refer to the mid-1960s gang and clique tags, rather than the more mysterious style of TAKI and JULIO.

21. Stewart, 19; 42.

22. In an otherwise excellent primer on graffiti, and the subsequent—and vastly different—culture of "street art", Anna Waclawek treats both as species of a "mode of protest" that reflects "a desire to belong to a city's visual cultural" and "reclaims space for a more diverse public" (*Graffiti and Street Art* (London: Thames & Hudson, 2011), 43–44). Admittedly, many of the early writers do claim their work was an act of rebellion against their confining conditions (it was, after all, illegal, and was certainly condemned by their parents and local authority figures, and reflected a manner of gaining recognition within a local and subversive subculture); however, given the age and the radical alienation of those who invented it, we would hardly expect *clearly political* intentions to be present in its pioneers, and such accounts downplay the essentially impulsive and unconscious nature which is tied to the "addictive" nature of the art form that she otherwise conveys so convincingly. While it was common among early writers to talk about "doing damage to the system" through their work (I. Miller, 21), when writers like COCO 144 retroactively recognized its political import, their phrasing exposes its cryptic and symbolic nature: "*Unconsciously* it was a way of screaming out and saying, 'This is me, and I'm not your household doormat'" (I. Miller, 47, emphasis added). Of course, the unconscious nature of its emancipatory import is by no means a critique of graffiti; it simply helps make sense of the relationship between tagging's essential content and its unique aesthetic form.

23. Stewart, 42.

24. Hager, Ch. 2.

25. Stewart, 42.

26. PAUL 107, *All City: The Book About Taking Space* (Toronto: ECW Press, 2003), 7. While this author obviously encourages no-one, those interested in taking up the art might like to consult this near-perfect how-to manual.

27. Stewart, 30.

28. Hager, Ch. 2.

29. See I. Miller, 57–65, for a fascinating history of the varied rationales behind early name choices.

30. Hager, Ch. 2, emphasis added.

31. Cf. the legendary writer PHASE 2: "For quite a while nobody knew I was PHASE 2. I told my friends not to tell anyone. That was the fun of it. You could sit around and people would say, 'Damn, you know who I want to meet? PHASE 2.' And I'd be sitting right next to them" (quoted in Stewart, 71). While recent sociological work tends to focus on fame as the primary motive for the artists (e.g. Nancy Macdonald, *The Graffiti Subculture: Youth, Masculinity and Identity in New York and London* (New York: Palgrave, 2001), or the documentary film *Infamy* (2005; directed by Doug Pray)), any achieved recognition would have been extremely ambiguous in the earliest years.

32. George, *hip hop america*, 11.

33. I. Miller, 16.

34. As Kaminsky notes, while the subsequent art of the classical ideal "can give us direct insight into living beings themselves [symbolic a]rchitecture can at most *suggest* life and power" (62, emphasis added).

35. For discussion, see my *Hegel's Philosophy of Language* (London: Continuum, 2007), Ch. 2.

36. Stewart, 55.

37. *The Faith of Graffiti*, documented by Mervyn Kurlansky and Jon Naar, with text by Norman Mailer (New York: Praeger, 1974), 5. This is the catalogue from the first Museum Of Modern Art show on graffiti photography, and it has since been supplemented by Jon Naar, *the birth of graffiti* (New York: Prestel, 2007). See I. Miller for reactions early writers had to Mailer's general portrayal of their culture.

38. I. Miller, 41; 70, emphasis added.

39. Stewart, 28, emphasis added.

40. Ibid., 43.

41. Ibid., 28.

42. Ibid., 41.

43. Ibid., 43.

44. Ibid., 47.

45. As PHASE 2 argues, "Some people say they've perfected wild-style. That's impossible. You can't perfect something that has no limit" (quoted in I. Miller, 87).
46. Stewart, 35.
47. Ibid., 64–5.
48. Ibid., 35–38.
49. Ibid., 170.
50. Chang, *Can't Stop*, 15, emphasis added.
51. Stewart, 66.
52. Ibid., 116. Compare with Waclawek, for whom wild style names the "virtually unreadable" pieces whose "letterforms […] are illegible, sometimes even to other writers" (19); or I. Miller, who claims that "[w]ild-style burners, unreadable to the uninitiated, gave writers a feeling of secrecy in the midst of their public expressions" (86); or Grandmaster Flash, who vividly describes being overwhelmed by train cars that "won't be quiet. Keeps shouting at me to pay attention. […] Giant machines covered in art. Covered in style. Styles so wild, so you can hardly keep up. Letters and numbers so worked up, it takes a minute to figure out where one stops and the next one begins. Like some kind of alien alphabet" (*The Adventures of Grandmaster Flash*, 29–30).
53. Stewart, 53.
54. Ibid., 54. In the words of Tracy 168, subways were targeted for two main reasons: "The train would shoot over to Brooklyn and somebody over there would see your style. But there was also more adventure on the trains. Daredevil stunts like jumping from trains to platforms would really get the adrenaline going" (Hager, Ch. 2).
55. Quoted in Stewart, 84. Compare I. Miller, for whom "writers painted in *ritual contexts* adapted to their twentieth-century urban life: deep down in dark tunnels, among homeboys (initiates), and with an air of mystery" (127, emphasis added).
56. Stewart, 84.
57. I. Miller, 98.
58. *The Adventures of Grandmaster Flash*, 31.
59. I. Miller, 125.
60. While Hegel notes that "higher criticism has cast doubt on this" claim, he nevertheless suggests that, "just as minerals rustle in water, the voice of these stone monuments [could be assumed to proceed] from the dew and the cool of the morning and then the falling of the sun's rays on them" (358/I, 462). The accuracy of the story is less important than Hegel's insistence that static statues symbolically receive motion from something outside, which nevertheless essentially becomes a part of them thereby.
61. I. Miller, 41.

62. In fact, writers incorporated motion into their work from the very beginning. Before the move to subway exteriors, many tagged the sides of city buses, which could be hit while they were moving, by taggers who jogged alongside them (this was called "motion writing" (Ibid., 112)).

63. Waclawek, 19.

64. Stewart, 43.

65. Ibid., 46. For discussion of the import of moving trains to early artists, see I. Miller, 89–92.

66. Sacha Jenkins, "The Writing on the Wall: Graffiti Culture Crumbles into the Violence it Once Escaped", in Raquel Cepeda, ed. *And It Don't Stop: The Best American Hip-Hop Journalism of the Last 25 Years* (New York: Faber and Faber, 2004), 288–299 (288). Its most enduring and widespread elements are summarized well here, as well as in Waclawek, 27–8, William "Upski" Wimsatt, *Bomb The Suburbs*, Revised 2nd Edition (Chicago: The Subway and Elevated Press Company, 1994), 41–2, and Stephen Powers, *The Art of Getting Over: Graffiti at the Millennium* (New York: St. Martin's Press, 1999), 154–5.

67. For examples of this code operating in practice, see the documentary *Style Wars* (1983; directed by Tony Silver) or Powers, 106–7.

68. SHARP speaking in I. Miller, 126.

69. Ibid., 130.

70. VULCAN, quoted in Ibid. (emphasis added).

71. Stewart, 203.

72. Ibid., 33. As I. Miller puts it, "[t]hrough their paintings, writers indicated that […] 'If mass transit is for the masses […] we want it to look like us'" (45).

73. Castleman, 137; 140.

74. Ibid., 142. This is also cited, e.g. by Mailer.

75. This is the judgment, for example, of Stewart, as well as most of the taggers interviewed in Hager, and Hager himself. TRACY 168, in his preface to *Graffiti Kings*, claims that graffiti's Golden Age "died in April of 1974" (Stewart, 5).

76. Stewart, 83.

77. Ibid., 84.

78. Ibid. I. Miller agrees that in the "translation from train to canvas [graffiti] art ceased to be an act and instead became an object" (158).

79. Stewart, 84.

80. Ibid., 140–1. As we will see below, the tension between grassroots creation and institutional assimilation is, in many ways, the general problem posed by Hip Hop's entire history, as well as by Hegel's *Aesthetics*. For discussion of the second boom in "graffiti art", which accompanied Hip Hop culture's global spread, see Chang, *Can't Stop*, 167–211, or Castleman.

81. Stewart, 146.
82. Hip Hop activist Jacqueline Hines, quoted in KRS-One, *Gospel*, 516. She applies the point more broadly to Hip Hop itself, although in the next chapter, I argue that the full culture was much more conscious of its creative action and purpose than the early writers were, as well as more wary of the possibility of assimilation to the broader society.
83. The most famous case was the "Warhol Soup Cans" mural, painted by Lee and Fab 5 Freddy in the late 1970s, which ran for "at least three or four years" before being taken down (Fricke and Ahearn, 283).
84. Stewart, 175.
85. I. Miller, 130.
86. Stewart, 95.
87. Although, of course, these were not immune to ethical violation. This war on "painterly" subway cars is the primary theme of *Style Wars*, as well as Hollywood's first Hip Hop film, *Beat Street* (1984; directed by Stan Lathan). The original, superior screenplay by Hager is reprinted in *Hip Hop*.
88. Stewart, 84, emphasis added.
89. For an oral history of how some pioneers resisted the co-option of tagging by the art world, see I. Miller 152–62.
90. KRS-One, *Gospel*, 118.
91. As Etter puts it, "the vocation of [symbolic] architecture in general [lies in] fashioning external nature into an enclosure for the human spirit" (164).
92. As Richard Dien Winfield notes, the liberating effects of architecture can be felt, among other ways, in "buildings that unify a nation, both in the task of construction and, upon completion, by providing a focal point of gathering" ("The Challenge of Architecture to Hegel's Aesthetics", in William Maker, ed. *Hegel and Aesthetics*, 97–111 (102).

CHAPTER 4

DJing and Breaking, or the Classical Stage of Art

Prologue

In the only real attempt to capture Hip Hop culture in cinema—Charlie Ahearn's *Wild Style*[1]—infamous graffiti artist Zoro (played by late 1970s writer LEE) keeps his identity secret from everyone, including his on-again, off-again girlfriend Rose (LADY PINK). Only an old writing confederate, Phade (Fab 5 Freddy), who has since retired to move into party promotion, knows Zoro's secret. While most of the film concerns the adventures of Phade and Zoro as they begin to discover the money and fame possible through connecting graffiti with the broader art world, its guiding thread concerns the preparations for a massive street party Phade has been asked to curate at a destitute park. He agrees to provide DJs and MCs who can draw the hottest dancers to the event, and enlists Zoro to spray-paint a mural on the park's bandshell to provide a kind of immersive environment within which the jam can take place. In the most crucial moment of the film, the camera continually cuts between Zoro's process of painting, pioneering DJ Grandmaster Flash rehearsing turntable tricks in his kitchen, and the elite street dancers of the Rock Steady Crew practising their moves in anticipation of the event, visibly demonstrating the inextricable unity of graffiti with the emergent arts of what came to be called rap music and "breaking". Having guessed his secret, Rose visits the park where she finds Zoro unable to make progress on the outline of a shrouded and mysterious figure flanked by giant, menacing hands. She pushes him to explain what he is trying to convey, and he replies:

J. Vernon, *Hip Hop, Hegel, and the Art of Emancipation*,
https://doi.org/10.1007/978-3-319-91304-9_4

> I'm trying to paint this figure in the middle [...] I already got the hands, like on the side, like the hands of doom and they're like representing the city and the environment around this artist, right? And what I'm trying to draw is the artist in the middle, and he's like....like...painting all by himself in his own world.

Rose, having guessed that the figure is the mysterious Zoro himself, chastises him for placing *himself* at the centre of his work:

> I don't like your mural, I don't like the idea [...] I'm just telling you the truth, alright? Zoro this, Zoro that, we don't wanna hear about it! You're only worried about Zoro. Concentrate on what the whole thing is about: it's a jam! Rappers are gonna be comin' down, they're gonna be the stars of this thing, not you.

With this Zoro has an immediate and ecstatic change of heart, and radically shifts his conception for the painting. The camera cuts to the now-finished work and, while the giant hands remain on the sides of the mural, the mysterious figure has been transformed into an immense *star*, painted at the heart of the stage. The hands no longer threaten the central icon, but both *shelter* it from the outside world and *empower* it with lightning bolts that feed its broad glow. In a brief and totally anomalous animated sequence, the lightning shoots out from the star, spreading its energy over the entire park. The animation ends, revealing the amphitheatre filled to capacity with partiers, and the mural is now the enveloping home for a community gathering combining rap music and dance.

While the focus on rappers as stars belies the vintage of the film,[2] there is perhaps no better portrayal available of the transition from the decline of graffiti through its Romantic appropriation by the gallery and mural scene, to the emergence of a complete and celebratory Hip Hop culture grounded in its four aesthetic elements through the street parties of the Bronx. And it was on August 11, 1973, at 1520 Sedgwick Avenue that Kool DJ Herc discovered the key to bring it all together.

FROM THE TEMPLE TO THE RELIGION OF ART

As we have seen, while implicitly revelatory of free humanity as its source, audience and goal, symbolic art remains too cryptographic to explicitly reveal the essence to which it points; it poses a riddle, but cannot clearly present its solution. Thus, Hegel claims, symbolic art implicitly demands its own transition to a truly "adequate mode of configuration [which] achieves what true art is according to its concept" (427/II, 13, trans. modified), wherein "the thing, through and in its external appearance, declares its spiritual content [*die Erklärung ihres geistigen Inhalts gibt*]" (426/I, 546, trans. modified). Arising from the symbolic, however, the adequate presentation of spirit cannot simply be presented "in its infinite form [...] i.e. it is not the *thinking* of itself", as we see, say in a people whose stable circumstances allow for the philosophical comprehension and political actualization of essence (431/II, 18); those who emerge into the realm of self-knowledge from the riddle of the symbolic continue to focus on *art* to express their essence, precisely because they remain bound by unjustly imposed circumstances to determination by their "immediate natural and sensuous existence" (431/II, 19). However, even if these new artists continue to "revert to the natural" in seeking to express their essence, the efforts of the preceding symbolic artists have granted a kind of clearance within which new creators can come to more explicitly grasp, and more adequately present in sensuous form, humanity "as dominant over the external" (431/II, 19). Thus, symbolic art serves to create a "sanctuary [*Heiligtum*]" (A, 639/II, 278) for a still-aesthetic "spiritual assembly [*Sammlung des geistes*]" (A, 648/II, 289) to more adequately express itself as free. The question, then, is what "natural shape and externality" can be creatively presented such that it "lifts the spiritual to the higher totality where it maintains itself in its opposite, posits the natural as ideal, and expresses itself in and on the natural" (432/II, 19)?

To be more precise: art must work within and on finitude, but after symbolic art lays its ground, classical art can and must discern the most adequate material for sensibly expressing the free humanity which symbolic art strove to present, as well as the most adequate forms of that material's transformation. Post-symbolic artists, then, are tasked with finding forms of finitude which can clearly *embody*, rather than merely *indicate*, the infinitude of self-determining freedom. As Hegel argues,

> since the objective and external [realm], in which spirit comes to intuition, is, in accordance with its concept, thoroughly *determinate* and *particularized* at the same time, it follows that free spirit, which art causes to appear in a reality *appropriate* [*gemäß*] to it, can in its shape in nature only be *spiritual individuality* [emphasis added]. (432/II, 19, trans. modified)

In other words, the riddle posed by the symbolic is solved precisely by focusing artistic presentation on the living, free subject implicitly presupposed and revealed by all artistic production. This implies several key transformations away from, as well as continuities with, art's symbolic foundation.

Art cannot simply present free humanity in general (i.e. the philosophical concept of human essence), because it essentially retains the sensuous and therefore particular nature of symbolic art, which must now simply be shorn of its mystery. If "humanity [in general] constitutes the centre and content of true beauty and art", it nevertheless remains true that as the "content of art [...] humanity must appear under the essential determination of *concrete individuality*" (432/II, 20, trans. modified, emphasis added). The merely implicative tag of graffiti then, must give way to the visible presence of the subject that lies behind it and to whom it called.

This does not mean, of course, that art's mission is satisfied if the contingent individuals who create graffiti are simply identified for public display; the recognition offered particular individuals within the surrounding worlds of museum art, after all, is what led to the demise of the ethical order of the early graffiti culture. Rather, what must be aesthetically presented is the free humanity (that can be) responsible for such art, or the universal capacity within every subject to overcome their determining circumstances through creative and dedicated work. Thus, the truly aesthetic "form is essentially the *human*, because the externality of the human alone is capable of revealing the spiritual in a sensuous way" (433/II, 21, trans. modified). Art demands less that we peek behind symbolism's curtain to see the individual behind the name, than that we come to aesthetically present the corporeal, particular finitude through which we all appear to be determined as essentially in harmonious unity with the self-determining freedom commonly shared by all human beings. Thus, "in so far as art's task is to bring the spiritual before our eyes in a sensuous manner, it must get involved in [...] anthropomorphism, since *spirit appears in a satisfactory [genügener] way only in its body*" (A, 78/I, 110, trans. modified, emphasis added).[3]

Of course, our corporeal finitude is not *naturally* expressive of spirit. Human beings are not merely free but, like all entities in the natural world, also determined, and we have seen that this implies that they are most immediately affected by desire, practical need, and other forces; that is, "in the human form there are dead and ugly things, i.e. [things] determined by other influences and by dependence on them" (434/II, 22). Classical

art, then, cannot simply bring focus away from our determining surroundings to the body so determined; rather, "it is precisely the business of art
to expunge the difference between the spiritual and the merely natural,
and to make external corporeality into a beautiful, through and through
cultivated, animated and spiritually living figure [*gebildeten, beseelten und
geistig-lebendig Gestalt*]" in its sensuous presentation (434/II, 22, trans.
modified). Because the body "counts in classical art no longer merely as a
sensuous determinate being, but only as the determinate being and natural shape of spirit [it] must therefore be exempt from all the deficiency of
the merely sensuous" as given (78/I, 110, trans. modified).[4] If the immersive environment of the symbolic ensures that "the inorganic external
world has been purified [...] and made akin to spirit [such that] the god's
temple, the house of his community, stands there ready" for a more adequate presentation of spirit (84/I, 118), then the problem of the classical—
in a curious resonance with the climax of *Wild Style*—is precisely how to
aesthetically present "the *lightning-flash of individuality* [*Blitz der
Individualität*] striking and permeating the inert mass, [or how] the infinite [...] form of spirit itself concentrates and gives shape to something
corporeal" (84/I, 118, emphasis added)?[5] Hegel's answer, here, is dual.

On the one hand, the need for an idealized presentation of the human
form primarily links the classical Ideal with *sculpture* (cf., e.g. 84–5/I,
117–8). The human body, as it stands, is not only beset with the contingencies of desire and need, but by the physical forces of gravity, openness
to injury, and disequilibrium which continually remind us of its external
determination. Sculptural presentation of the human form, however,
allows it not only to be shown in three dimensions and thus *as a body*, but
in a material that allows it to appear as *free from our natural limitations;*
that is, as "no longer processed either according to its mechanical quality
alone, as a heavy mass" or "splintered into the play of accidents and pas-
sions" (85/I, 118, trans. modified). "Sculpture is [thus] more ideal" than
nature (490/II, 92), because its "consummate plasticity [*vollendete
Plastik*]" (719/II, 374, trans. modified) allows for a corporeal, yet far
more variable and free, presentation of "spatial forms of the human body"
(706/II, 358). Sculpture most adequately presents the "free vivacity [*freie
Lebendigkeit*]" (724/II, 379) of the "perfectly animated [*vollkommene
belebt*]" (726/II, 381) human body as it would be were it to be "purified
from the defect of finitude" (432/II, 14). Hegel calls this essential "unity
of the spiritual and the natural" "divine" (453/II, 46), because he finds it
best exemplified by classical Greek sculpture which manages to convey the

divinity of the gods while nevertheless "individualiz[ing] the character of the gods into an entirely specific human form [that] perfects the anthropomorphism of the classical Ideal" (490/II, 92). The focus on anthropomorphism is key, for on Hegel's reading the Greeks did not seek or earnestly posit a divine realm *apart* from this world; rather, they "shaped human activities into actions of the gods" (480/II, 79) in a form of sculptural presentation that "lays hold of the human form as the *actual* existence of the spirit" (705/II, 357). Thus, in the classical stage of art, the aforementioned "person who belongs to fine art" is to be "set up by sculpture as a statue of the god" (662/II, 305) in spirit's immersive temple.[6]

On the other hand, however, even the most "spiritual" sculpture remains an inert object that merely exists within a world of externality, and thus is not immutable, invulnerable to the elements, or even mobile. Sculpture, then, is not sufficient on its own for the aesthetic presentation of spirit, for it retains the mark of mere finitude and stasis, and thus cannot always "convey [...] spiritual movement, distinction from the external world or differentiation within" it (797/III, 17). What sculpture essentially reveals, then, is that the "determining principle" of art itself lies not simply in the creation of palpably "divine" individuals, but in their "spiritual reflection" by an audience or community that grasps itself as freely self-determining therein (85/I, 119). This is why Hegel claims that, while the "sculptures of antiquity leave [we moderns] somewhat cold" due to our habitual grasp of freedom through state institutions (797/III, 17), for the Greeks who "worshipped" them, they sensuously revealed how "spiritual individuality emerges into and completely masters the body in which it has real existence" (797/16). Thus, "when [symbolic] architecture has built its temple and the hand of sculpture has set up within it the statues of the god, this sensuously present god is confronted [...] by the *community* [*Gemeinde*]" whose reception of its spiritual content fulfils its mission (A, 85/I, 119). While the sculpted form of an idealized human body presents the classical Ideal, it is the community's participatory understanding of its import for themselves that truly solves the riddle of the symbolic. Thus, the harmonious "unity [of finitude and infinitude] which the god has in sculpture" is only consummated when—like lightning—it "disperses [*zerschlägt*] into the plurality of the inner lives of individuals whose unity [as a community] is not sensuous but purely ideal" (85–6/I, 118). When an aesthetic community that can grasp the spiritual content presented by sculptural bodies as the sensible expression of the freedom within their own "divine" corporeality is assembled in the temple, then art has essentially fulfilled its "highest vocation", or reached its Ideal peak in what can justly be called a "religion of art".

As with the symbolic form of art, of course, we cannot expect Hip Hop culture to utilize the means of the ancients to accomplish this spiritual goal. Much like architecture, sculpture of the kind Hegel identifies with the classical Ideal remains both too unfeasible (requiring expensive and durable materials, highly refined training through apprenticeship, protective and stable enclosures, etc.) and too static (more immobile than the already aesthetic subways, let alone radio, television, and other saturating moderns mediums) to serve as a viable means of spiritual expression. Moreover, unlike Hegel's Eurocentric vision of Greece accomplishing what the Egyptians never could, Hip Hop was forged precisely by those who produced, admired, and had their surroundings transformed by the symbolic art of graffiti, giving the lie to Hegel's ungrounded belief that "peoples" only have one aesthetic truth to offer the world. But if Hegel is right about the link between artistic development and the communal emancipation of a suppressed people, and there is merit to my contention that Hip Hop reflects the trajectory of Hegel's Ideal, then graffiti—precisely by constructing an immersive and implicitly spiritual environment—would be seen to clearly give way to a "classical" focus on sensuous presentation of the *idealized human form* that, moreover, would have the power to *draw together a community* whose very gathering in a space dedicated to such presented forms explicitly elicits a collectively self-determining self-conception in its members. Given the circumstances in the South Bronx, this obviously requires a presentation of the human that is both more readily attainable by the most radically abandoned victims of late capitalism, and more aesthetically appealing to a romantically modern, largely African-American, and post-Civil rights community to express their essential freedom. This, I argue, is the essential contribution to Hip Hop culture made by the *breakers* and the *DJs*, both of whom find their foundation in the revolutionary insight of Hip Hop's Founding Father.

Filling the Temple: The Classical Elements

Kool DJ Herc's career began contingently enough. The young Clive Campbell spent much of his childhood enthralled with his father's pastime of collecting records. A Jamaican immigrant, Herc was exposed in his early, pre-Bronx life to "soundclashes", or large community parties wherein DJs battled for supremacy in terms of record selection, sound system, and unique mix.[7] While largely unknown to the residents of the Bronx, the soundclash tradition nevertheless resonated to a certain degree with the newly developed New York disco scene, which was gradually replacing the concert ballrooms of the 1960s with a record-based dance party that took over not only the local clubs, but also many of the local parks as professional DJs began to take their mobile units outside in the summers, and which thus may have had the more decisive influence on his eventual calling.[8] Herc (whose nickname was drawn from his "Herculean" height and athletic prowess) also tagged and carried some of the tinkering skills that he developed by altering "writing" materials over to modifying his father's powerful sound system, which the elder Campbell inherited after managing a failed band; once he determined how to maximize the output of the system, Herc earned his father's permission to begin DJing at some local events. Thus, the varied contingencies of time, place, family history, cultural background, and unique individuality all conspired to grant Herc the use of extremely powerful speakers, a PA system and a pile of records drawn from outside the mainstream of popular culture. These contingencies were first put to aesthetic use in August of 1973 when, again by chance, his sister asked him to DJ a party to raise funds for new back-to-school clothes, which began Herc's career of hosting regular parties in the recreation room at the housing project in which he lived on Sedgwick Ave.[9]

While, "[l]ike any proud DJ, he wanted to stamp his personality onto his playlist",[10] Herc also knew that the DJ's job was "giving the people on the floor what they were supposed to be hearing",[11] and he knew that his father's reggae records wouldn't resonate with the Bronx attendees. Drawing and pleasing a local crowd, however, also meant eschewing the contemporary disco and rock that dominated the club scene and FM radio. In order to resonate with the South Bronx graffiti community, Herc experimented with different records and eventually gravitated to the music of Baby Huey, the Isley Brothers, and "James Brown which represented the Black Power movement" of the previous decade in musical form, and which seemed to have an immediate and unique impact on the local crowd.[12] Drawing together the intense audio system of the soundclash and the disco scenes with the harsh-but-funky sound that emerged from the previous decade's Black Liberation struggles, it instantly became clear that in Herc's early parties "something was different. The funk that he threw on the turntables, and the soul that came across with [their] African beats, was something" that resonated with his community in a way other music simply could not.[13]

The popular dances of the disco era would have fit uncomfortably with these harsher rhythms but—curiously coincidental to Herc's emergence as a new brand of DJ—some of the regional dances began to blend with more recent influences (e.g. "the shuffling, sliding steps of James Brown; the dynamic platformed dancers on Don Cornelius's syndicated Soul Train television show; […] the athletic leg whips and spins of kung fu movies"[14]) in a manner that "developed gradually" into new forms of dance, that passed by various names, such as "burning", "rocking", or "up-rocking",[15] and coincidentally "the kind of music that Herc was playing was really conducive to this [new] style of dancing".[16] Many of the hard-edged funk and soul records of the late 1960s/early 1970s typically contained a section—variously known as the "break", the "breakbeat", the "get down" and the "sure shot"—where the melody and harmony parts would fall away, leaving only the thumping percussion and/or bass. During these brief fragments—"when the band would drop out and the rhythm section would get elemental"[17]—he noticed that the "rocking" became especially intense. While standard dancing certainly occurred throughout his events, it was when "the break c[a]me on [that] the [rockers] hit the floor, [and] start[ed] doing their different dances", whose moves seemed as fresh and far removed from the surrounding culture as his records were.[18] Herc "carefully studied the dancers" and concluded that "people was waiting for certain parts of the record" in order to move.[19]

Thus, precisely because his parties were for dancers, and because Bronx dancers preferred to perform their newly discovered moves on the "breaks", Herc began to consciously build his set around them. At first this meant "searching for songs by the sound of their break, songs that he would make into his signature tunes".[20] Even the longest of these breaks were quite short, however, so it quickly became clear that he needed to "make the beat last for a long time to keep [them] dancin', 'cause once the words come on [the rocker] stops dancin'".[21] Using the two-turntable set-up that allowed disco DJs to smoothly flow from track to track, he learned to locate the song's "break" by vision,[22] and, switching between the two turntables, he strung the breaks from all the favoured records one after the other in a kind of cycle, in what he called the "Merry-Go-Round". This allowed Herc to "extend a five-second breakdown" in the middle of a song into a self-standing "five-minute loop of fury" that moved from break to break, and would drive "the dancers from climax to climax on waves of churning drums".[23] Eventually, full songs were reduced to being a preface to, or respite from the real action, as the new breed of Bronx dancers primarily "wanted to hear breaks after breaks after breaks after breaks".[24]

While the Bronx dancers—who, in part due to their obsession with dancing on the "break", Herc came to dub "b- (as in break) -boys and -girls"[25]—were "what drove the music forward",[26] it is equally true that Herc's revolutionary Merry-Go-Round method pushed the dancers to new, as yet unseen heights,[27] thus reflecting the other meaning of "break", which was local street slang for "doing shit above normal".[28] The basic rocking being done in 1973 was gradually supplemented with footwork performed on all fours on the ground, and then with spontaneous gymnastic routines or "power moves" and seemingly gravity-defying "air moves"; in all styles, dancers consciously sought to achieve what was previously almost unimaginable for human bodies to perform. A regular crew of breakers led the festivities at Herc's parties, drawing more attention to the events which, precisely because Herc for long stretches was "playing nothing but breaks", now centred on "a new dance form that was nothing but devastating moves".[29] As the beats grew more intense and propulsive, and dancers more athletic and graceful, the parties quickly increased in size, to the point where they had to be moved *outside*, into the concrete blocks that had already been saturated with symbolic graffiti. Because the "[a]uthorities had long abandoned large parts of the Bronx[,] renegade party-starters never had to worry about permits and police" for outdoor events, making it even more convenient than partying indoors, where community rooms needed to be rented and some landlords enforced fire codes.[30] Herc's Merry-Go-Round thus began to saturate the region, extending across the distinct groups formerly divided by gang and racial tension, as his booming speakers echoed throughout the surrounding area at parties that would eventually stretch into the eight-to-ten-hour range, and draw crowds that would soon number in the hundreds, producing something resembling a *secular mass*.[31] As legendary b-boy Trac 2 puts it, "Kool Herc, when he started bringing his jams out into the streets, where everybody could enjoy the music, and everybody could enjoy that type of atmosphere [at that point] it became more of a community coming together than a community being divided. We didn't have a place where we could all come together, and I think that's what Hip Hop is".[32]

What is unclear, however, is precisely *why*. Why were dancers, during the ascent of the extravagant spectacles of disco, prog, new wave, and glitter rock, drawn to isolated and comparatively monotonous breaks, rather than the more emotionally enveloping melodies and harmonies of the era's popular music? Why weren't breaks accompanied by a dance that not only was not similarly repetitious and standardized (as in, e.g. the "pogo" that accompanied the almost-equally minimal and nearly-contemporary new "punk" rock), or similarly harsh and aggressive (as in, e.g. the "mosh-ing" that would soon develop in the crumbling urban centres that anchored the hardcore punk movement of the late 1970s), but which was built on the seemingly opposed values of continuous novelty, kinetic ath-leticism, and technical precision? Nothing within the situational contin-gencies of the Bronx, Kool Herc's upbringing, or the cultural influences on the early breakers alone can answer these questions. In what follows, I'd like to show that a speculative reading of Hegel's classical Ideal, at least to some degree, can.

Before doing so, however, we should note that the "imperfect" art of dance is virtually absent from Hegel's lectures (627/II, 262); moreover, for Hegel, classical sculpture achieves such an adequate presentation of spirit that it forms a world unto itself, and thus stands in no need for essen-tial relations to other art forms, like music. As in much of his account, the reasons for these claims remain unclear, and it is precisely such assertions that lead to the common and compelling charge that Hegel omits details and tensions inimical to some a priori vision of logical development. It is thus imperative that we focus our attention on both the most essential criteria for the classical Ideal, rather than the details of Hegel's typically questionable account of Greek paganism, and the self-described aesthetic practices of the breakers and DJs, rather than imposing an abstract struc-ture upon them. Following Herc, then, let's start with the break.

FROM BREAKS TO BREAKERS

As we have seen, classical art rests on symbolic foundations, which in turn make aesthetic use of externally given materials. While post-symbolic art-ists must build from the foundations laid by previous creators, in order to produce "the ideal work of art", they must "rise above the merely sym-metrical" (247/I, 320) or natural forms of organic presentation. However, just as it is not the organic nature of the human body, but its *merely given* form, that is superseded, externality as such is not completely rejected— that is, "regularity is [not] wholly superseded"—for this would require leaving the realm of the sensible entirely (247/I, 320). Rather, classical art begins when regularity is taken up into a work that is more spiritually expressive, or when it is "reduced to a mere foundation" for higher productions (247/I, 320, trans. modified). In unpacking this tension between the givenness of natural forms like symmetry and the aesthetic presentation of spiritual individuality within the external, Hegel draws an analogy to the regularity of *beat* in music.

Visible objects, like wall tags, that exist "together in space can comfortably be seen at a glance", while musical notes, by contrast, have a temporal existence, wherein "one moment has gone already when the next is there" (249//I, 322). On their own, nothing within the notes themselves determines that they should be apprehended as one phrase or piece; no individual note sets up any expectations for what will come, or recollections of what preceded. Such apprehension, Hegel argues, is only possible insofar as the notes are related to a solid *foundation* from which determinateness can be derived, that is, "the regularity of the musical *beat* [*Regelmäßigkeit des Takts*] which produces a determinateness and a *continuously recurring pattern*" (249/I, 322, emphasis added). The unifying symmetry of the beat is "not something belonging objectively to the notes and their duration" (249/I, 322–3); a horn stab, for example, tells you nothing about whether it is in standard or cut time, just as the wordless vocal exclamations of James Brown can be interchangeable across tracks with vastly different grooves. However, it is only insofar as a regular beat provides a steady foundation that the evanescent, sonorous particulars can be held together in an "abstract unity" (249/I, 323). This suggests that beat is not heard from the outside, but *felt* on the inside, as the solid foundation upon which the spiritual apprehension of music rests,[33] and thus "it is not the note that moves us in our inmost being; it is this abstract unity [of regular beat] *introduced into time by the subject*" that makes music aesthetic and therefore spiritual (249/I, 323, emphasis added). Hearing and appreciating music, then, presupposes a *subjective contribution*, and it is the regularity of beat that shows us how it is that we help "construct" the very existence of music as a sensuous object, thereby revealing the existence of our inner freedom from merely received particulars. The beat lays a spiritual foundation for art just because it is strictly *in us* in a way the timbre of a string, or the pitch of a note are not. As Hegel puts it:

> To the note as such [i.e. as purely external particularity], and to time, to be divided and repeated in this regular way is a matter of indifference. The beat therefore appears as something purely created by the subject, so that now in listening we acquire the immediate certainty of having in this regularization of time something purely subjective and indeed the basis of the pure self-identity of the subject. (249/I, 323, trans. modified)

This is why "the beat resounds in the depths of our soul" (249/I, 323) and reveals "a magical power to which we are so susceptible that often, in hearing music, we beat time to it without being aware of the fact" (249/I, 322). The beat *makes us move*, just because it proceeds from our essential and free spirit. What, then, occurs when we confront music that is "all beat"?

As Joseph Schloss argues, while the "break is a rupture in form created by suppressing particular instruments (and, by extension, their melodic and rhythmic contributions to the groove)", nevertheless this "suppression serves to accentuate musical absences, [thus] creating a sense that *a contribution is required from listeners* to restore the music to its proper state".[34] In a way, reducing music to the beat sensibly presents what our contribution to it had been (the beat was there all along, although what we "heard" was the melody, harmony, lyrics, timbre, etc.), and this presentation thus draws out of us a kind of spiritual awareness of our contribution to the music (which we had previously, e.g. simply tapped along with our feet, nodded with our head, or counted "inside"). By virtue of its reduction to beat alone, then, "the break is reaching out to the listener", revealing to them that it is in fact they who make the music whole.[35] The break is the beat that we had felt, now brought to the fore such that this spiritual effect can become consciously clear; isolating it *within* the track brings to light our contribution, and makes us anticipate the return of, or need for, other elements, granting us new appreciation of our own internal, unifying activity.

Isolating the break *from* the track, however, *leaves that anticipation hanging*, for we forestall returning to the non-rhythmic sonorous elements; our contribution to the music, in other words, is being *made for us*, precisely through the musical aspect that best makes us aware of it. Thus, if the break calls us to our spiritual task of supplementing what is heard, it simultaneously demands of us a contribution beyond that of counting time. Since the beat that we internally "tap out" is brought into focus, and in a manner that nevertheless also presents an absence to be filled, it is perhaps inevitable that our "contribution takes the form of dance", which physically externalizes the inward activity reflected in the beat.[36] Isolated rhythm presents to us an incomplete musical object, but in such a way that it leaves us only able to "fill the silence with motion".[37] If breaks "impel b-boys to dance",[38] this is precisely because, as pioneering DJ and "Master of Records" Afrika Bambaataa would later put it, the "break-beat is that part […] in the record that lets your god-self just get wild".[39] One can still, however, raise the question as to why the break compels us to dance, rather than, for example, to supply the melody or harmony that has dropped out, or to otherwise accompany the isolated beat, either through instruments or vocalization. More pertinently, we still need to explain why this dance was specifically built around the performance of radically novel feats of skill.

On Hegel's account, if sensibly presenting the spiritual foundation of music draws our attention to our own inner essence, it is nevertheless equally the case that, "since concrete *spirituality* and its individuality serves as the starting-point and essential content of the Ideal, the harmony with external existence has also to be displayed as originating from *human* activity and as *produced* thereby" (253/I, 328). Art's highest vocation is achieved when, through it, humanity sees itself as freely self-determin*ing*, rather than externally determin*ed,* and thus if art must revert to the natural in order to display human spirit, it simultaneously needs to present the body "as dominant over the external which, as one side of the totality of the inner self, exists no longer as purely natural objectivity but, without independence of its own, is only the expression of spirit" (431–2/II, 19). This requires an aesthetic reconfiguration of the human body, such as the "releas[ing of] the arms and legs from the body" which allows them to be freely "moved in various ways" (201/I, 263). Free human spirit must rise to an embodied self-presentation that clearly marks its distinction from the externally determined "animal" body (434/II, 22). Thus, we must work to find "sculptural" "modifications which [only] the spirit, immanent in a living body, [can] introduce[…] into this corporeal sphere" (715/II, 368), through which to sensibly make clear to ourselves the spirit which wills them. These modifications present a subject "raised above their body so that they feel their shape, their limbs, as if they were a superfluous appendage" (484/II, 84), displaying a mastery of our corporeality through a "flawless externality, from which every trait of weakness […] has been extinguished [and which] corresponds to the spiritual inwardness which is to immerse itself in it and therein attain an embodiment" (483/II, 83). Classical sculpture, then, is necessarily and "properly involved an inquiring into the nature of the human figure" that can palpably present the spiritual.[40]

Similarly, and echoing Afrika Bambaataa's quote about our "god self" above, we might say that the early breakers brought sculpture's divine capacity to transcend our natural limits to the dance floor, precisely because they appeared to "do *impossible moves* that no-one else could do".[41] Breakers prided themselves on doing "shit with [their] feet that people didn't understand",[42] given not only its foreignness to popular or traditional dance culture, but the manner in which it "pushed [...] the limits of human anatomy".[43] Pioneers like the legendary Spy could repeatedly prop their bodies "up on one hand to generate flurries of legs and feet", building on the work of others like Robbie Rob, who could stun crowds by balancing his "body upside down on a single elbow and toe point".[44] It is important to recall that these feats were "designed not only *for* teenagers, but *by* teenagers"[45]—sometimes even by pre-teens—adding to their seemingly inhuman achievement. Breaking provided those assembled at Herc's parties with the improbable sight of radically un-tutored and infamously awkward adolescent bodies reaching heights of corporeal grace and prowess hitherto unimaginable even by professional dancers,[46] and seemingly (since there was no forum besides block parties in which to display such skills, and certainly no hope of monetizing them) only for the purpose of communally presenting their actualized capacity for reaching such heights. Add to this the fact that it was often performed on hard concrete, softened, if at all, only by discarded cardboard or linoleum—and thus continuously courted injury for its participants, who often visibly rose above pain to achieve or hold a move—and it seems reasonable to conclude that breaking had a vastly different cultural meaning than virtually all contemporary, and arguably most previous, forms of dance. Herc's discovery of the break pushed "the dancer to enter a heightened world where ideas about space and time and spirituality [...] could be addressed through raw physicality",[47] just as for Hegel "the artist's task is to make raw objects express our deepest concerns, to make something like marble into something like freedom".[48] Bronx breakers *palpably manifested* in their own persons the "*spiritual* animation [*geistige Beseelung*]" that Hegel demands of classical sculpture (786/II, 456), and thus Herc's discovery of the unique musical element of Hip Hop can be said to have drawn the free essence concealed within the body into explicit sensible expression through its unique form of dance.

Of course, if beat-driven dance, in general, allows artistic expression to be manifestly displayed as originating in human activity, Hegel's association of this "classical" expression with the calm repose of sculpture nevertheless seems to place it at a distance from the kinetic moves of the early breakers, to say nothing of "their essential relationship to the DJ" who accompanied them.[49] Thus, we must not only look more closely at the characteristic features of the classical Ideal in Hegel, but more importantly at the aesthetic developments that accompanied the early Bronx party scene.

SKILLS

As argued above, if art emerges from our determining entanglement with "external nature [within which we] stand[...] precisely in a relation of *dependence*", then its classical peak must palpably reveal that humanity has risen beyond it into a self-determining relation with finitude (256/I, 332). This demands the sensible demonstration that we have indeed "cast off this dependence" on the given, and can now "play freely and cheerfully with the means put at [our] disposal" (256–7/I, 332–3). As Hegel reminds us, "the fact that I must keep myself alive, eat and drink, have a house and clothing [etc.] is of course a necessity for the externals of life" (257/I, 333), so art cannot liberate us from nature as a whole; however, the sculptural Ideal must sensibly present our essential capacity for self-determination within externality, and thus must provide palpable evidence of our capacity to alter our environment, and ourselves, by our own spontaneous, creative, and consciously willed activity. What is at stake in art's classical stage, then, is less the specifically sculptural production of human figures (which proceeds, not from the concepts at play, but from Hegel's linear, unitary, unjustified model of art's development across historical cultures) than the embodied depiction of our shared capacity for self-determining transformation of our merely received finitude. Post-symbolic art, to fulfil its highest vocation, must clearly and sensibly reveal its ground and goal in a free humanity that can "take possession of things in nature, groom [*zurechtmachen*] them, form them, [or] strip them of every hindrance by [its] own *self-won skillfulness*" (257/I, 332, trans. modified, emphasis added).

And it is precisely this freely, skilfully creative transformation that we find in the work not only in the early dancers, but perhaps even more clearly in the DJs who gathered them into assembly. By drawing upon the merely given and habitually employed materials in his environment (turntable-based dance parties, pre-recorded music, concert PA systems, etc.), and inventively tinkering with them in a manner hitherto unseen (isolating breaks, discovering the Merry-Go-Round technique, increasing power for sound systems beyond their understood limits to create earth-shaking sound, etc.), Kool Herc creatively appropriated and re-arranged them into a form that rendered their previous nature almost unrecognizable; and, perhaps most importantly, their new presentation was uniquely and sensibly attributable to the creativity of the *visibly present* DJ. On the one hand, Herc's legendarily loud system could overpower the constant noise from the expressway and housing destruction; thus, Hip Hop's musical element effectively "sealed partygoers from the din of the city, almost physically separating them from the outside world",[50] solidifying the temple within which the embodiment of human spirit could appear. On the other hand, "the idea of repeating breaks for dancers [...] represented a crucial reconception of [...] the function of the record and the turntable", transforming it from a mere "playback device [into] a means for manipulating sound" with infinitely free creativity.[51] By creating an aesthetic enclosure of sound for ceremonial gathering among the painted walls, within which the artist would appear as the presiding, self-determining figurehead, Herc was palpably "denying the typical power-lessness of adolescence [...] and resisting the poverty, despair, and decay that pervaded the Bronx".[52]

As Herc attracted imitators, each DJ (carrying forward the emphasis on competition from the graffiti culture from which most emerged) sought to stand out by their unique capacity to re-configure merely given materials into novel form. While Herc's repertoire of breaks was limited, and his manipulation of them often haphazard (or, in Hegel's terms, "severe"),[53] the succeeding pioneers built on his inventions to advance the art of breakbeat DJing into a self-contained and self-determined art form. Afrika Bambaataa was called the "Master of Records" because of his knack for discovering danceable breaks in the most unlikely of sources (everything from 50s doo-wop singles, to German electronica, to children's television show theme songs), gathering thousands of records from every conceivable genre and "remixing" even the most habitually familiar sources into a continually shocking and shifting collage of beats. Grandmaster Flash (who briefly tagged under FLASH 163, and gave breaking a try until he was voted out of his first crew for losing his first battle), recognizing the potential in Herc's discovery of the break loop, "turned it from an explosive but haphazard party trick into a precise and astonishing DJ technique" that would be adopted by all subsequent Hip Hop DJs.[54] His revolution was to "work out a way of playing just the funkiest few bars from a record, then repeat that little chunk, and repeat it, and repeat it, all the time keeping a beat" thus providing "the perfect soundbed for breakdancers to go wild to".[55] Seeking to "take it further than Herc [by] answer[ing] questions he wasn't thinking to ask",[56] the teenage Flash, "without having any idea if it was [even] possible, [...] locked himself away like a scientist experimenting with potential solutions",[57] even going so far as to build the electronics necessary to master "cutting" the same break from two copies of the same record on time,[58] with perfect precision so that a 5-second section could be looped indefinitely into a rock-steady tempo for breaking. This became known as the "quick mix" theory, which involved treating the vinyl label as the face of a clock, adding a sticker or crayon line for a "hand", and discerning the break's placement from the hand's clock-position.[59] He also pioneered methods such as "back cutting", or audibly reversing the record before replaying the same selection, revealing the physical sound of the needle being scraped backwards on the record as a form of musical performance in itself. This was furthered by his protégé Grand Wizzard Theodore, who may have invented,[60] but at a minimum refined for precise aesthetic use, the technique now known as "scratching", which involved manipulating one copy of the record, as well as the fader between the two, while the other spun, switching between them to create a virtual melodic line with the electronic noise from one over the steady beat of the other. He also pioneered the "needle drop", wherein a break loop was made with only one copy of the record, by manually lifting, then replacing, the needle without losing time.

I draw attention to these well-worn stories of invention in early Hip Hop DJing precisely because they reflect the emancipatory "hard-won skillfulness" that Hegel demands of the classical Ideal. As noted above, there is little truth to the popular myth that early "practitioners had to use samples because they couldn't afford instruments".[61] If, indeed, it was increasingly difficult to procure instruments and/or lessons within the crumbling region, it was no more, and arguably far less, challenging than both acquiring and assembling professional-sounding equipment along with hundreds of obscure records tracked down for often quite brief clips, to say nothing of discovering—without guidance of any kind—their viable modes of aesthetic manipulation.[62] Unlike, say, the pioneering extensions of harmony, rhythm, and timbre made by 60s icons like James Brown, Archie Shepp, and Sly Stone, Hip Hop DJs did not pursue modifications (however radical) *within* existing forms of composition. Rather, they made an explicit and conscious effort to take the far more difficult road of *moving completely away from received forms of musical expression* (melodic theme, harmonic development, verse/chorus/bridge structure, virtuosic solos, etc.), towards ones that emphasized the *skilful remixing of the merely and manifestly given to reflect self-determining free creation*. In a sense, what "makes Flash's achievement even more astonishing" is that it was *not* produced by necessity, discovered haphazardly or even, as in early graffiti writing, pursued unconsciously; rather, it "was no accident. He knew what he wanted to achieve" and why, and struggled hard to both create and master the requisite techniques and build a sound system and record collection adequate to conveying it.[63] This is no doubt one reason that KRS-One claims "[f]rom the very beginning [...] Hiphop has struggled for self-determination".[64] Moreover, the emphasis on *physical presence* in DJ culture (in distinction from the hidden work of mysterious taggers) suggests that the early culture was defined as much by its *palpable presentation of the self-determining creative capacity to alter the merely received*, as it was by its technology- and break-specific sound. This passion for refined, self-developed, palpably demonstrated skill carried over into its even more physical *dance* element, as one frequently hears early breakers recite variants of the claim that "you can't just do it two hours a day and say 'OK, I'll do it when we go to the jam'. I used to eat, piss, shit, drink, think b-boyin'".[65]

Furthermore, one must always recall that these discoveries were made against a backdrop of radical social abandonment. Basic urban necessities like electricity were often either absent or unreliable in housing complexes owned by corrupt landlords more interested in driving their tenants away than in servicing their needs, making it even *less* convenient to focus on musical forms that required a reliable energy source. Thus, the 1970s jams were only made possible by quite literally *taking power* from the surrounding state, as a "party in the park would entail wiring the sound system to a lamp post",[66] a process aided by the self-directed research DJs were making into the hardware of their sound systems and turntables. Methods of safely running extension cords dozens of feet from viable and hazardous sources to preferred party areas were developed, and electrical skills became as vital as aesthetic ones, increasing the heroism of DJs and their confederates to the level of graffiti artists, who continued to decorate the blocks that now hosted celebratory gatherings of these varied aesthetic and technical inventions.

Thus, in early Hip Hop culture, virtually everything—from the sonic envelopment of the jam, to the break-centric records selected, to the novel forms of their presentation, to the very power through which they were played—required, and palpably demonstrated, conscious and freely self-determining control of both the surrounding environment and their own bodies by the adolescents who pioneered the culture.[67] Whichever aspect of a block party one considers, in Hegel's words, "everywhere there peeps out a new joy in fresh discoveries, the exuberance of possession, the capture of delight; [...] in everything man has present before his eyes the power of his arm, the skill of his hand, the cleverness of his own spirit, or a result of his courage and bravery" (261/I, 338) precisely because its artists "in the execution of [their] work [are not] hindered by any technical incapacity" (438/II, 27). This is perhaps why KRS-One claims that in essence "Hip Hop in and of itself is a human skill produced by the human Spirit".[68]

GATHERING THE COMMUNITY

Of course, these technical yet aesthetic wonders were not the work of isolated and mysterious "loners", as in the pioneering transformations of graffiti. Rather, DJs played *parties*, gatherings of breakers and appreciative spectators. While their unique modes of aesthetic production differentiated them from the surrounding culture, their work was primarily made "for a *public* which sees and enjoys the work of art" (263–4/I, 341, emphasis added). Hip Hop arose as a *people's culture* and,[69] as such, inevitably infused its aesthetic creation with the local community's "customs, outlooks, and ideas" (264/I, 342). This goes some way to explaining why Hip Hop, contrary to widespread myth, did *not* originally manifest itself as a "cry of rage" against local conditions, but as an explicit effort to draw ever-larger collectives into the temples of spirit through the essentially and overwhelmingly *cheerful* sounds and moves of DJs and the animated feats of breakers.

However, because it needed both to appeal to the individuals who would form its ethical community and to manifest the novelty of free creation demanded of true art, Hip Hop's aesthetic and ethical ideas necessarily arose through the modified adoption of the art of previous generations, just as for Hegel the "Greek artists obtained their material from the national religion in which what was taken over from the East by the Greeks had already begun to be reshaped" (439/II, 28). We see this, for example, in the aforementioned fact that Herc and the early DJs generally eschewed contemporary disco and rock for the sounds that accompanied or emerged from the preceding Black Power era. On the one hand, "older soul and funk music was familiar [to his crowd] because it was what their parents played at home", and thus the general palate of their playlists reflected the music with which their audience was raised[70]; on the other hand, much of the era's funk and soul explicitly spoke of the essential need for self-determining collective action among an oppressed people, which undoubtedly resonated with the post-Civil Rights generation who became the Hip Hop one. Thus, Hip Hop as a collective culture was founded on material both *habitually familiar to the community* and *manifestly expressive of human spirit as free.*

However, merely *replicating* these sounds would leave the DJs, and therefore their audiences, unfree in their creation and enjoyment of the culture, amounting to nothing more than the embrace of given habits. If classical art must present works that speak to a people, it must nevertheless do so in a manner that reveals the freedom all essentially possess to transform themselves and their situations. As Hegel puts it, if "purely historical exactitude in external matters [such as those of] locality [...] constitute the subordinate part of the work of art, [they nevertheless] must give way to the interest of a genuine content that even the culture of the present day regards as imperishable" (270/I, 350); this, perhaps, explains why the musical material was "remixed" by Hip Hop's pioneering DJs into a form both radically novel and implicitly familiar. This process reached its peak with Afrika Bambaataa, who would routinely add spoken word recording of Malcolm X, Huey Newton, Martin Luther King, Jr., and other Black liberation leaders of the preceding decades into his mixes.[71] As Hegel suggests, in order to populate the sculpture-filled temple with an emancipatory community, the Ideal artist takes cultural "content, existing in and for itself [*ein anundfürsichseiender Inhalt*]", and "adopts it and freely reproduces it out of [her] own resources" in forms that sensibly reveal their origin in her skilful manipulation (439/II, 28), thereby demonstrating that "tradition and original creation can be wholly united" (478/II, 77). Herc's isolation of the break "made partygoers hear their parents' records as music of their generation",[72] confirming KRS-One's claim that "Hiphop has communicated with itself by developing a language that relies upon the transformation of already existing languages".[73]

Through all of these techniques and practices, the "[e]arly Hiphoppas gave themselves authority through the mastery of certain skills unique to their environment and lifestyle",[74] through which they constructed, as it were, Hip Hop's collective "We" out of the self-determining "I" of each Hip Hop artist, while simultaneously holding each "I" to the evolving standards of Hip Hop's "We". To fully grasp the manner in which this formed an aesthetic community, however, we must deepen our grasp of the intimate link between the individual performers who presented their *idealized shapes* for consideration by their public, and the assembled crowd who made their work a celebratory and ritual *party*. And this is seen most clearly in the most "sculptural" figures of early Hip Hop—the breakers.

CHARACTERS, CYPHERS AND STYLE

As we have seen, just because art is the sensible presentation of finitude infused and dominated by spirit, the "truly free individual[…], as the [aesthetic] Ideal requires it, has to evince itself, not only as universality, but no less as concrete particularity" (236/I, 306). *Divine* figures, Hegel argues, accomplish this best, not because they inhabit or invoke a realm beyond human affairs and limits, but rather because "the gods seem to bring about what is alien to man and yet actually accomplish only what constitutes the substance of his inner heart", thus reflecting the creative "powers dwelling in him" as free (228/I, 296). Wedding the finite and the infinite, the classical Ideal is best presented in and through a "*particular* divinity which, like everything particular, has a sphere of particulars around it, or confronting it as its opposite, out of which it emerges and which can retain its own validity and value" (468/II, 65, trans. modified). Thus, as the ineradicably particular presentation of free spirit through the vivacious animation of the human form, there is no *single* adequate expression of the Ideal; rather, there are of necessity a "*plurality* of shapes" of this body through which spirit is expressed (486/II, 88). If we are to learn from ideal bodily presentation that we are *all* free, then there must be a plurality of exemplars of our spiritual "divinity"; this what Hegel means when he claims that "[p]olytheism is absolutely essential to the principle of classical art" (486/II, 88).

Of course, since Hegelian "divinity" merely names the manifest link between spirit and corporeality, the "polytheism" essential to classical art need not take the same theistic and sculptural form as it did in classical Greece. Shorn of the mythological trappings of both the Greek pantheon and Hegel's occasionally fanciful vision of antiquity, what remains is an "ideal which has existence, [and thus] has *character* [for w]ithout character, no [spiritual] individuality comes on the scene" (482/II, 82). Classical art need not present sculptural gods, but it must display "a plurality of individuals [...] endowed with the specific character of a particular person" (487/II, 88); aesthetic character, however, cannot be that of a *merely given* person, as it must be clearly linked with "the universal which is the source of the particular" (487/II, 89). Thus, it is not the contingent particularity of individuals that forms character, but the *idealized particularity that is revelatory of universal essence within.* Classical art, through character and action, sensibly presents human individuality as both particular and universal, or finite and infinite, thereby fulfilling art's "highest vocation" to aesthetically "make the human form express something *spiritual*" (727/II, 383). And it is precisely this "divinity" that we find in the breakers that demanded breaks, as well as in the DJs who supplied them.[75]

As Schloss notes, even today, it "is unusual for b-boys and b-girls to dance under their given names"; rather, as with DJs and (as we will see) MCs, the common practice is for breakers to adopt *alter-egos*, explicitly identified as characters in aesthetic performance. While these names sometimes drew upon contingent aspects of the given personality of the individual, unlike the cryptic tags of the early graffiti artists, these characters generally "had deep meanings" for their bearers, precisely because they were not symbolically *hiding behind* their names, but visibly and continuously *performing under* them at block parties[76]; such names, then, indicated a breaker's aesthetic *self-image*, through which the bearer manifested his- or herself in public. While the name was often (although not exclusively) self-selected, maintaining it, or being recognized through it presupposed that the character's "self-image has been verified by the community"; one's Hip Hop identity, then, "ties [them] not only to [their] community, but to a whole history of social interactions and artistic choices" that reinforce the individuality of the breaker's character within it.[77] The universality of the community, in other words, is constituted by the individualized characters who populate the block party, but that very individuality is grounded in, and serves to reinforce, the universal Hip Hop community that grants social and ethical validity to it. Thus, the self-image posited by name and character in early Hip Hop moved beyond both the cryptic pseudonym of early graffiti as well as the merely received characteristics of subjective particularity by tying the legitimacy of one's "divine" presentation to the nascent, self-determining ethical order arising through the aesthetic culture. Breakers adopted characters just in order to posit their individuality as equally specific to themselves in unique aesthetic presentation and universal to the Hip Hop community itself in essence and import. There are consequently at least six central features common to both early Hip Hop practitioners and the polytheism of Hegel's classical Ideal.

First, while the symbolic concerned itself with transforming the appearance of surrounding externality, the classical must present an idealized form of human individuality itself; this is why one of its principle distinguishing features is its preoccupation with *adornment* (cf. 258/I, 334). By adornment, Hegel simply means the unnecessary and elaborate decoration of oneself with materials that could otherwise be used practically. The wearing of, say, gold takes a costly and difficult to attain metal with an obvious number of pragmatic uses, and transforms it into a decorative sign of one's lack of determination by needful circumstances. An individual, in "so bedecking himself [...] shows that [even] the costliest things supplied by nature [...] these rarest and most resplendent things should not count as merely natural, but have to show themselves on *him*" as their bearer, determiner, and reference (258/I, 334). As Hegel notes, this may seem irresponsibly selfish to outsiders, but it marks an expected and liberating moment in the development of a radically alienated people. Rising to consciousness of themselves as creatively free, he argues, it is imperative that a people forsake concerns about the merely given "distress and poverty" that surround them, for it is these "which art precisely demands shall be set aside, so that it can redound to the fame and supreme honour of every people to devote its treasures to a sphere which, within reality itself, rises luxuriously above all the distress of reality" (258–9/I, 335).[78] Costly, attention-grabbing adornment palpably reveals one's indifference to the needs of merely received individuality in favour of the self-determined and beautiful presentation of aesthetic character.

This helps explain why the emergence of Hip Hop culture, proper, was accompanied by a revolutionary transformation in *fashion*. To the extent that it had a custom of clothing, tagging's style was largely determined by practical concerns (e.g. the "hooded jackets or sweatshirts, worn by graffiti writers to hide their identity and protect their heads from the wire fences at subway yards",[79] large coats and backpacks to help them steal or carry supplies, etc.); by contrast, block parties, built around the characters of the breakers and DJs, evolved co-extensively with a fashion movement that emphasized "pure bright colours", and in a manner radically distinct from the surrounding disco and rock fashions (258/I, 334).[80] Hip Hop cultivated a novel, DIY style that not only emphasized "flash and uniqueness", but within which "creativity [was] valued more than cost",[81] as evinced by the fact that "[c]ustomization became [a key] point of distinction".[82] Hip Hop fashion pitted attention-grabbing, colourful, and unique constructions against the anonymous, weathered, and merely functional dress that was broadly perceived to typify poverty and alienation.[83]

While adornment is one, immediate way in which an artistic culture sensibly presents the human form as blissfully indifferent to natural needs, Hegel reminds us that (secondly) "what especially belongs here is the beauty of the human form as it is developed in [...] *skill in contests at the games*" (760–1/II, 425, emphasis added). Public contests of ability push particular individuals beyond the pre-competition limits of their finitude, while consciously channelling their bodies into modes of self-surpassing directed at nothing more than the presentation of an idealized human figure for appreciation by others as manifestly self-determining. Contest presents the human form pushing past its given limits through acts of consciously willed self-cultivation designed to excel within collectively determined standards. Thus, in competition we "find human activity put into the background so far as it is restricted to merely natural needs and their satisfaction" (467/II, 64), and specifically *aesthetic* contest demands that, even if the "human form as an expression of spirit is [merely] *given* to the artist", nevertheless the "model for mirroring the spiritual inner life is presupposed in the shape, specific traits, posture, and demeanour of the body" (715/II, 369). This helps explain the central focus within Hip Hop culture on *battling*.

A battle is quite simply a contest between Hip Hop artists for supremacy in their chosen aesthetic element. This, of course, extends from the competitive spirit of graffiti, which itself in part descends from the combative nature of gang culture, and thus, on the surface, battling seems to reflect the contingency of teenage individuality and circumstantial limitations. Correspondingly, battling is often credited primarily or even exclusively to the aggressive tendencies stereotypical of young men, living in suppressed circumstances, which demand some manner of outlet,[84] or treated as "something that is 'healthy and normal' in any social process"[85]; however, such explanations elide the specifically *aesthetic* nature of Hip Hop battling. Rather than being tied to an external goal (say, impressing a particular romantic interest; winning a monetary reward, social power, or some manner of institutional placement; guarding or gaining territory for, or membership in, a gang, etc.) breaking "contests existed for their own sake",[86] simply "to establish who had the suavest, most graceful moves".[87] Isolated from the world outside of Hip Hop, a battle was "a public arena for the flamboyant triumph of virility, wit, and skill", that primarily demonstrated the participants' free and beautiful command over corporeal finitude.[88]

Thus (and third), battling is also explicitly tied to the winning, through aesthetic production, of an increased *consciousness* of one's own creative capacities as well as those of others, or to the aesthetically expressed and grasped *knowledge* of human spirit and its "divinity". As KRS-One notes, one of Hip Hop's central lessons is that "[w]ithout the spirit commanding the body, the body is literally lifeless and without direction", and battling is the culture's central way of increasing this command.[89] Evacuating the previously accepted limits of the body, breakers took conscious control of their corporeal aspects—subjecting them to unnatural, impractical, aesthetic discipline—in a manner that explicitly and beautifully demonstrated a spiritual mastery of their finitude. Battling, many breakers argue, "push[es] individuals to greater achievement" precisely because it "teaches you a lot about yourself and a lot about other people [...] it brings out parts of you. You're never gonna know a person fully until you battle them".[90] Battling reflects more than the mere sublimation of aggression; it sensibly presents humanity coming to spiritual *awareness* of itself as free, in and through disciplinary, yet aesthetic methods of explicitly *embodying* that awareness. Indeed, this is what struck the (probable) first European to visit the Bronx specifically to experience the culture, former Sex Pistols' manager Malcolm McLaren: "I think Hip Hop is being in control of your body; that's the whole art of it, actually understanding that *you're bigger than you are*".[91]

This, then (and fourth), implies an alteration of our relationship to the surrounding world. Battling must take place within a circumscribed, and specifically aesthetic, context; however, as the competitive, experimental interaction of embodied subjects striving for spiritual supremacy, a battle always courts the risk of tipping into the mere contest for dominance; and, indeed, many early b-boy battles did descend back into gang-like violence. Thus, maintaining the aesthetic, and therefore spiritually liberating nature of battle implies "a strategy of setting clear boundaries with an opponent and then taking the most aggressive possible position while staying within those boundaries".[92] Thus, as Hegel suggests, while "the symbolic work of art is always more or less *limitless*", defined as it is by an unclear and implicit message endlessly searching for its appropriate form, classical art's discernment of "the shape adequate to spirit" implies that one must "impose *limits* on [their] productive activity" to ensure that precise, clear, and beautifully idealized forms of individuality are presented (647/I, 286, emphasis added).

In Hip Hop, this limit-setting space is called the *cypher*, which combatants view "with an almost mystical reverence, befitting its status as the most authentic, challenging, and raw environment" for aesthetic battling.[93] A cypher is typically a circle, formed by the crews participating in a battle and/or the engaged witnesses to it; it can appear anywhere, at any time, save that it also requires the presence of a DJ providing breakbeats to which breakers dance (or, alternately, MCs rhyme; and, of course, DJs would also battle within the broader cypher of the party as a whole). This means that anywhere where a DJ plays, and a crowd gathers to take part in or witness a battle, is "the" cypher, which is something like a portable and transient, but nevertheless always self-identical and sacred, temple of Hip Hop. Rather than a spectacle for neutral observation, the cypher is constituted by an aesthetic community engaging in "a collective enterprise that mixes improvisation, competition, and mutual support, where everyone is presumed to be an insider simply by virtue of being there".[94] The cypher constructs a kind of ritual space (of course, in these early years, often within walls already transformed by graffiti into a kind of public temple, which was moreover enveloped in the overpowering sound of a stereo system) that both shuts out the external environment of pervasive violence, survival needs, and economic desires and holds combatants within a space carved out for specifically aesthetic, competitive self-presentation and thus within "which heightened consciousness exists".[95] It both excludes the merely determined aspects of desirous life and draws out that within the competitors which can "demand (or attempt to demand) the attention of everyone present",[96] ensuring that a battle "is presentational, confrontational, and communal".[97]

Set against an opponent in battle within the cypher, the forms of presented character (fifth) necessarily emphasize *control, precision*, and *poise*. In the cypher, breakers find themselves constrained by the size and physical location of the circle, the pressure of audience judgment, the breakbeats selected by a DJ, as well as the unpredictability of an opponent's moves. Movements too broad or sloppy risk not only displeasing, but actually injuring a crowd, just as memorized, heavily choreographed routines are not only ill-fitting to certain spaces, but are easily trumped by dancers more responsive to new beats, the actions of previous dancers, or interactions with the assembled cypher. Thus, for breakers it is the "development of discipline and self-control [that] gives an individual more options", aesthetically demonstrating that the "more self-control one has, the more freely and confidently one can move in a constrained environment".[98] A battle thus demands "that one be intense yet totally in control", focused primarily on ideal self-presentation in the specific context of this battle, within this cypher, facing this opponent, during this break.[99]

What is therefore valued above all in breaking is *the sensible demonstration of complete and consciously self-determining control of the human body in the communal sphere*, no matter how seemingly risky the moves, or uncomfortable the situation; this aesthetically presented form of calm self-control, then, is "perhaps the single most significant aspect of the overall b-boy persona".[100] All of a breaker's moves—no matter how seemingly impossible, how devastating to one's opponent, or how impressive to the assembled crowd—must feed the ideal image of total, free self-control. As late 1970s Bronx b-boy, Mr. Freeze, notes, in battle "it's not about just doing something for yourself; everyone [in the cypher] has to understand what you're doing. I wanted you, I wanted everyone to know what I was doing to you. That was, you know, the foundation of this dance".[101] Just as in Hip Hop adornment what is key is "being able to be presentable and fashionable" despite the grinding poverty around you, within the cypher it is of prime importance to appear *untroubled* either by the difficulty of one's moves, the prowess of one's opponent in battle, or the unique pressures of the ritual environment; breakers thus "must make extensive efforts to preserve [their] appearance, while at the same time appearing unconcerned" with doing so.[102] Hip Hop's infamous "cool" style—which eventually became exemplified by the "'bboy stance' (raised shoulders, arms crossed tightly, head often tilted to one side) which [...] all party goers adopted" as a mark of cultural inclusion[103]—comes precisely from Hip Hop's core aesthetic of idealized self-control, wherein one "should not only be prepared to battle at all times, but [one] should look it" as well.[104] From the entry into the jam to the fevered pitch of battle, breakers must present a calm and dignified ease that cheerfully and tranquilly rises above all struggle, pressure, and effort to palpably present an idealized human form untroubled by any external or internal distress, which reflects the will to "expunge the difference between the spiritual and the purely natural" (434/II, 21), by sensibly displaying a "serenity and bliss which even in misfortune and grief do not lose their assured self-repose" (436/II, 24). Thus, while the human body is the only appropriate figure for classical art, it is nevertheless

> Only *flawless* externality, from which every blemishing trait of weakness and relativity has been obliterated and every tiny spot of capricious particularity extinguished [that] corresponds to the spiritual inwardness which is to immerse itself in it and therein attain an embodiment. (483/II, 83, trans. modified, emphasis added)

Thus, if classical art presents a "perfect plasticity" of the human form through its varied and seemingly superhuman shapes and movements, these nevertheless all point to a "concentrated individuality" which "has pulled itself together out of the variety of appendages, single actions and events into the one focus of its simple unity with itself" (481/II, 81). In classical sculpture, for Hegel, nothing is trivial or capricious, and the "manner in which the different limbs, in every situation of rest or movement, are posed or laid [...] must be expressed most precisely" (725/II, 380, trans. modified). Above all, in order to distinguish the idealized body from the merely natural and desirous one, any presented "posture must appear entirely *unforced*, i.e. we must get the impression that the body has adopted its position of its own initiative, because otherwise body and spirit appear different" (740/II, 399, emphasis added). Thus, regardless of the character in question, their Ideal presentation must appear "without any disturbance of the divine repose" (766/II, 430), for in "true liveliness we find at the same time the breath of grace wafted over the whole" and it is precisely this "[g]race [that] is an appeal to the [..] spectator" (617/II, 250).[105] Consequently,

> we may place this serene peace and blessedness, this self-sufficiency in its own determination and satisfaction at the pinnacle of the fundamental characteristics of the Ideal. The ideal art-form confronts us like a blessed god [for whom] there is no final seriousness in distress [for] even in [such] seriousness[,] cheerfulness or serenity remains its inherent and essential character. This force of individuality, this triumph of concrete freedom concentrated in itself, is what we recognize [...] in the cheerful and serene peace of their shapes. (157/I, 208, trans. modified)

This is, of course, precisely why Hegel identifies the Ideal with sculpture, within which a breaking of natural limits can be presented alongside the blissful ease of a spiritualized subject.

It is perhaps for this same reason that (sixth, and finally), while breaking quickly established a kind of standard progression for the routine of a dancer (entering the cypher while up-rocking, dramatically dropping to the ground, athletically performing a flurry of "floorwork" moves on one's hands and feet, etc.), this progression soon emphatically featured "the *freeze*, a concluding pose that punctuates the dancer's statement".[106] While among the most kinetic dances in the history of the art form, breaking nevertheless differed from the previous dances upon which it drew by highlighting, as its consummate moment, *sustained and tranquil immobility*, usually in a pose that emerged organically from one of the strength- or spin-based moves, but which was designed to present the dancer's body in a form that seemed impossible to achieve, let alone hold.[107] In fact, some breakers, like the tellingly named Mr. Freeze, recall that, when this aspect was first introduced, "everybody was completely mesmerized by it […] and it was at that instant [that] breaking, b-boying started for me".[108] Breakers, in closing each routine with a jaw-dropping freeze, "monumentaliz[e] themselves into *statues*",[109] emphasizing the fact that they are "ris[ing] to individual spirituality [by] contract[ing] into fixed shapes" (456/II, 49).

Thus, while the movements of breakers both developed and fulfilled a "specific set of aesthetic expectations for how [human] personality should come across to spectators: 'colorful', 'exaggerated', 'vibrant', 'larger than life'", the all-important freeze momentarily raises dancers nearly beyond the living human to "actually *become* visual art",[110] and in process "wrests from momentary existence" merely determined finitude "and in this respect too conquers nature" (163/I, 216). Paired with their chosen name, cool style, and skilful self-control, in "the freeze, the dancer […] took on an alternative identity […] Dancers would freeze-pose as […] super heroes, business men, GQ models" or other larger than life forms, and in battling would put their characters to the test of public scrutiny.[111] In the sacred ritual of the cypher, then, the breakers *were* their idealized, sculptural characters, or those "persons who belong to art", precisely because they explicitly, consciously and sensibly unite their merely human and particular finitude with their spiritual and universal freedom in aesthetic contest undertaken solely for communal celebration of the self-determining and blissfully serene beauty of humanity.[112] This explains why Bronx b-boys like Doze Green argue that breaking was "really about the heart, it was really about the core of your existence",[113] for it is this immediately sensible "divinity" which forms the essence of Hip Hop as both a culture and an identity. In this way, Hip Hop vividly recreates Hegel's "classical ideal of beauty [through the sensibly] clear self-expression of spiritual freedom in and through *bodily* form".[114]

As noted above, these kinetic sculptures in battle represent not only the idealized self-presentation created by the artists of the Hip Hop community, but moreover the object of both adulation and critical judgment for the assembled "crowd, who collectively judge[d]".[115] The same was true, of course, for DJ battles, wherein two or more DJ crews would set up in the same park, battling primarily for "bragging rights"; these contests were similarly "not so much about defeating rivals as they were about demonstrating power" despite the various forces that restricted the participants.[116] Just like the breakers, then, they sought to exhibit self-control in the harshest of self-imposed conditions, and to remain visibly "cool" while doing it; thus, in battles, DJs "would raise the bar by spinning on their feet in between beats, moving the crossfader with their hands behind their back or under their leg or with their elbows or nose", all while keeping the beat on time, and making it seem effortless in process.[117] Victors were decided by who could draw and retain the most dancers and thus assemble the largest cyphers, essentially linking DJ and breaking battles in one ritual ceremony enveloped by revolutionary sounds and tagged walls.

THE RELIGION OF ART

If there is one thing the above should make clear, it is that Hip Hop parties were emphatically *not* spectator events, divided into active performer and passive audience, akin to modern forms of romantic entertainment or aesthetic contemplation; rather, to participate in a battle or a cypher was to perceive, cognize, and embrace the value of style, character, prowess, skill, innovation, and repose that idealize the human form as "divinely" self-determining, whether in the blissfully contorted body of a breaker or in the smooth and original cuts and tricks of a DJ. Thus, the crowd participation essential to the success of a cypher demanded that the audience, as much as the breakers and DJs, *completely immerse themselves in and commit themselves to* the new culture in order to appropriately judge; in process, the dance party crowd was transformed into a *spiritual community* grounded in the "divine" essence of Hip Hop.[118] This, especially early on, was palpably clear, as the parties were mainly attended by active or would-be breakers, DJs, MCs, graffiti writers, and their intimate comrades. As eventual Rock Steady Crew leader Crazy Legs recalled when Tricia Rose asked him about the

> communal atmosphere between writers, rappers, and breakers in the formative years of hip hop: "Summing it up, basically going to a jam back then was (about) watching people drink, (break) dance, compare graffiti art in their black books. These jams were thrown by the (hip hop) DJ.... It was about piecing while a jam was going on".[119]

Hip Hop parties might, thus, best be described as communal aesthetic *ceremonies* where participation was mandatory and the audience was as integral to the success of a party, and development of the overall culture, as the work of the new artists themselves.[120]

Hip Hop, then, was less something one *did*, than the very content of one's personal and communal *identity*.[121] For example, the early breakers and DJs quite consciously "developed a skill of battling [primarily] because reputations were made and lost in those battles", reputations which extended beyond the specific cypher to the nascent community as a whole.[122] As the preceding account of experimentation, style, character, and commitment reveal, the idealized self-presentations were not "put on" in battles, but actually formed the communally enacted identities of the emancipatory artists of the South Bronx. Battling was, thus, a matter of *honour*, and demanded an *earnestness* of presentation, or *authentic commitment* to the aesthetic Ideal embodied in Hip Hop precisely as a duty to oneself and one's community. As b-boy Freddy Love explains, in a battle "[w]hat's at stake is a guy's honor and his position in the street. Which is all you have. That what makes it feel so important, that's what makes it feel so good".[123] Such reputations, as we have seen, could only be earned for artistic innovation in the evolving tradition of battling, and thus demanded total immersion within and study of the culture in order to ensure the uniqueness of one's character or moves. Those unserious about their art, or who treated it as a mere gimmick or fad, were easily eliminated from competition, and sometimes even from the nascent community itself, which defined membership through artistic achievement, skill, knowledge, and commitment.

Thus, as with graffiti, "a certain unwritten moral code"[124] firmly guided breaking and DJing, and was communally enforced in the cypher and the community; the central and most strictly enforced rule outlawed "biting", or stealing someone else's style, moves, or character as your own, as this degraded the free creativity manifested in Hip Hop to merely unfree imitation. All of Hip Hop's elements demanded intimate historical knowledge and innovative contribution, which grounded the essentially collective and self-surpassing ethic of the culture. Now, however, these rules were enforced not only by the artists themselves (as suited the subterranean world of competing subway writers), but also by the community that supported them (the cypher who could grant victory in a battle to a non-biter, but also spread word around the community about the "wackness" of a particular performer, party crew, or occasionally impose less savoury forms of collective discipline, etc.). This, in turn, implied a kind of ethical responsibility for the audience, who needed to know not only the historical canons of breaks and moves (in order to distinguish innovation and creative re-deployment from mere imitation or plagiarism), but also the aesthetic principles upon which battlers were to be judged (which often demanded participation in one of the four aesthetic elements, but at a minimum required continual and earnest immersion in the culture built around them).

Because the judgments of cyphers helped both define and enforce the morality that grounded the Hip Hop community as it came into Ideal shape, the aesthetic, moral, and subjective code of the artists dispersed into and throughout the community, as the ground of their social subjectivity. For artists and audience alike, an engagement in and commitment to the culture itself became the principle of collective and individual existence; thus, as KRS-One argues, Hip Hop from its inception has been "united by an agreed-upon set of principles, elements and folklore unique to [the] experience" of those who lived it as their aesthetic and ethical culture.[125] Just as, for Hegel, "in Greek ethical life the individual was independent and free in himself, though without cutting himself adrift from the universal interests present in the actual state and from the affirmative immanence of spiritual freedom in the temporal present" (437/II, 25), so in Hip Hop the individuality of style and character was essentially united with an allegiance to one's community, its evolving tradition, as well as its ethical laws. As Schloss puts it:

> The art that [the Bronx breakers and DJs] have created gives each individual an opportunity to define and express a persona, while the standardization of the form [via principles and rules] allows each individual's story to be connected with all the others. This gives rise to a rich, almost three-dimensional social mosaic where each individual's expression also contributes to the beauty of the collective. This relationship and the sense of community it creates thus become self-reinforcing.[126]

This echoes Hegel's account of the classical "religion of art" which, while founded on idealized self-presentations, nevertheless demands a fundamental *integrity* of all participants in the assembly and community. Deprived of the stable institutions of the modern state, in the "Heroic age" or "pre-legal era", individuals confront the fact that "right and order, law and morals, proceed from them and are actualized as their own individual work which [thus] remains linked with them" (185/I, 243–4). The classical artist thus "has linked himself with the object completely [*ganz mit dem Gegenstande zusammengeschlossen*], and has fashioned the artistic embodiment [*Kunstverkörperung*] out of the inner life of his heart and his imagination" (291/I, 376, trans. modified), and these "heroes" must be in *earnest* in their work, for the very ethical foundation of their community rests upon their creations, whose effective message is that all are "answerable for the entirety of [their] act[s] with [their] whole personality" (A, 188/I, 246). Art's highest vocation, then, both depends upon and clearly reveals heroic subjectivity as the foundation of the developing community, and it falls to all to cognize, celebrate and ensure the culture's continued existence and development. It is just because classical art's "value lies in its ethical substance and function" within a unified community of artists and their participatory audience that the Ideal manifests as a "religion of art".[127] The young community in the South Bronx, radically abandoned by the state and left to fend for themselves in a virtual state of nature, "developed its own conventions, stylistic norms, and historical self-consciousness" through the aesthetic and communal presentation of idealized human form in self-determined and -invented skills,[128] which were put on display in collective jams that functioned as "'open air' community centres in neighbourhoods where there were none".[129] Grounded in ritual battles, whose structure both informs and reflects its general moral basis, Hip Hop demands that all participants "completely commit to their choice regardless of the consequences".[130] When KRS-One argues that Hip Hop is "beyond entertainment", this is precisely because it aesthetically presents the "priceless principle of self-empowerment" to a people both in need of, and concretely and collectively discovering, it.[131] Which means, as Schloss argues, that

> what [Hip Hop] offers is an increased consciousness of one's life options and a set of techniques for mastering them. The promise of b-boying is that, through a study of the discipline, b-boys and b-girls can exercise control over the meaning, value, and direction of their lives. This, too, is the promise of hip-hop culture: that artistic power can be ideological power and that ideological power can be the key to creating a place in the world for themselves and their community. [...] Any form of expression that either fails to achieve this goal or—even worse—achieves it and wastes it is arguably at odds with the principles of hip-hop culture. If hip-hop reduces your options, if it pressures you to be something you're not, if it asks you to reject your

own history, if it expects you to judge yourself by someone else's standards, it is violating its own most fundamental principles. The fact that b-boying not only lives by these principles but also continuously tests itself on them is the reason that so many identify so deeply with it. It is the reason that so many b-boys and b-girls view the dance as a discipline to be mastered, a history to be preserved, and a legacy to be treasured. It is the reason that [b-boy] Alien Ness says the following words, and the reason that I know, beyond a shadow of a doubt, that he means them: Man, competitive dance is it. It's been around for ages. B-boying is in our genes. It is in our blood. It is in our system. It has been part of our religions. Things have just been wiped out and stuff like that. But *that's my religion*. That's my culture.[132]

"I Am Hip Hop"

While several early MCs lay claim to being the first to use the phrase "Hip Hop", and there are varied stories as to how it became used locally to refer to jams,[133] there is near-universal agreement that Afrika Bambaataa was the first to use it to consciously name this unified and emancipatory aesthetic culture, under the motto, "Peace, Love, Unity, and Having Fun".[134] It soon passed into common parlance to denote the violence-reducing, youth-empowering, spiritually unified, and ethically organized community of taggers, breakers, DJs, and MCs that emerged from the ruins of the South Bronx. However, KRS-One—exploiting a linguistic coincidence much as Hegel loved to explore terms with multiple, yet revelatory, meanings—notes that Hip (which "according to the English language [...] means to have knowledge of", but which is perhaps derived "from the ancient African hipi [which] means to know or to be aware") Hop (which, in English, "is a form of movement", but in "the Aboriginal American hopi [...] can symbolize peaceful awareness, good awareness or the awareness of peace or goodness") should be more precisely understood as denoting "an intelligent movement—a movement aware of itself"[135]; he thus argues that Hip Hop is best grasped as "moving intelligence, active intelligence, intelligence moving, conscious movement or intelligent movement", aesthetically expressed in the living presentation of Idealized human form as the celebratory focus of a collectively determined, enforced, and lived ethical community.[136]

Whatever one might think of his etymological argument, KRS-One's claim that Hip Hop is a self-conscious form of communal life built around aesthetic achievement is certainly echoed by many of the culture's pioneers.

For example, "the original one-man hip-hop show",[137] Grandmaster Caz from the legendary Cold Crush Brothers, always claimed that "rap is one thing; hip-hop is something else. Hip-hop is the entire culture […] [a]nd the culture is more important than any one of its elements. The culture as a whole […] Hip-hop is my life".[138] MC Sha-Rock of *The Funky Four* similarly recalls that she "basically just lived, ate, slept, and drank hip-hop",[139] just as Grand Wizard Theodore claims, "My everyday life is hip-hop: what I do, what I say, the way I dress, the kind of music I listen to, seeing the graffiti on the walls all the time".[140] All directly echo KRS-One's constant refrain, "I am Hip Hop", which expresses the dialectical manner in which the irreducibly particular acts of individuals came to both reflect and inform a communal process of identity-formation and self-emancipation[141]; and if graffiti writers built its temple, and DJs gathered its community, as Grandmaster Caz notes, "it's such a part of the culture, that those who want to really stay true to the culture [will ensure] that there's always gonna be breakdancing" as its very core.[142]

CONCLUSION: FROM THE CLASSICAL TO THE ROMANTIC

Thus, in much the same way that Hegel argues that art's highest vocation is to unite an ethical community through the self-determined development of a "religion of art", so KRS-One defines Hip Hop as "a unified, self-governing community of peace and prosperity".[143] Its collective ceremonies are grounded in, and sensibly both present and celebrate the achievements of freely self-determining subjects whose art simultaneously embodies their ethical substance and their lived communal existence. However, in both the case of Hegel's polytheistic Greeks and Hip Hop's Bronx partiers, we are still one aesthetic element short. While, for Hegel, the Ideal "sculptural" figure "forms the proper centre of classical art", the very need for clear expression of the import of the communal ceremony demands that "*poetry* complements it by *describing* gods and men […] in their very activity and movement" (455-6/II, 49, emphasis added); similarly, the heroic DJs and breakers who battled in cyphers were, from the start, joined by the MCs who *brought to language* the exploits of Hip Hop's idealized subjects. However, it was also the emergence of Hip Hop's poetic element that not only completed its classical stage, but ultimately led to the community's near-dissolution. The story of Hip Hop's poetic element is thus also the story of Hip Hop's transition into a new set of cultural forms, which both opened up avenues for, and revealed the necessity of, a non-aesthetic manifestation of spirit, marking the decline of the classical Ideal into the fragmentation and contingency of what Hegel calls the *romantic*. It is, thus, to Hip Hop's fourth element, and Hegel's third stage of art's internal development, that we now turn.

NOTES

1. See Fricke and Ahearn, 285–295 for the fascinating story of this essential document.
2. 1982 which, as we shall see, makes it nearly coincidental with the dissolution of "Classical" Hip Hop culture.
3. As Houlgate puts it, sensuous creation "in which the human spirit is fully revealed in and as bodily form, represents, according to Hegel, the purest aesthetic ideal" (*Introduction to Hegel*, 221).
4. Compare Etter, "art will exhibit an ideal of freedom that 'real life' does not, due to the 'contamination' of chance and other exigencies" (45).
5. KRS-One also speaks of graffiti's "effort to brighten up and *electrify* one's environment" as the transformative gesture at Hip Hop's foundation (*Gospel*, 442, emphasis added); and Grandmaster Flash speaks of seeing walls where "colors explode, drip, drift, smash, clash, bleed, and *crackle with energy fields*" (*The Adventures of Grandmaster Flash*, 30, emphasis added).
6. Compare Kaminsky, for whom the classical "Greek artist had to know the kind of human actions and attributes which gave man godlike qualities. The question, therefore, arose: What are those actions and attributes which give godliness to the human form?" (70).
7. Cf. Kool Herc, quoted in Fricke and Ahearn, "Jamaican music was a big influence on me, because there was a lot of big sound systems they used to hook up and play on the weekends. I was a child, ya know, lookin', seein' all these things going on, and sneakin' out of my house and seein' the big systems" (25). Elsewhere, however, Herc denies this influence, suggesting he was too young to actually attend soundclashes. For general discussions of the relations between soundclash and dub culture and the birth of Hip Hop, see Chang, *Can't Stop*, 21–39, or Klive Walker, *Dubwise: Reasoning from the Reggae Underground* (Toronto: Insomniac Press, 2005), 233–256.
8. In my view, the most detailed, expansive and compelling history of DJ culture, especially concerning the varied forms of New York dance music that surrounded Hip Hop, is Bill Brewster and Frank Broughton, *Last Night a DJ Saved My Life* (New York: Grove, 2014). The relationship between the park disco DJs, which emerged from the club scene, and the

subsequent Hip Hop culture demands much more historical and musico-logical research. Bambaataa, for example, was trained as a DJ under his fellow Black Spade member Disco King Mario and—although Bam's emphasis on a shifting collage of obscure breakbeats certainly marks a strong break from his mentor, and his name would seem to belie the point—cases have been made that Herc's discovery may have been made, at least in part, by Mario in 1972. While I think the balance of currently available evidence shows that Hip Hop marks a radical shift from a street scene largely continuous with the disco clubs into a self-contained and -determining culture with its own aesthetic style and rules, it would be hard to deny the influence of the former on the latter. For what it's worth, many of the principal disco DJs, at least from outside the Bronx, give their side of the story in *Founding Fathers* (2009; directed by Ron Lawrence and Hassan Pore).

9. As he would later put it, while at first he "was into [his] graffiti work, [...] that's where [he] graduated from the walls to the turntables", quoted in Bill Brewster and Frank Broughton, *The Record Players: DJ Revolutionaries* (New York: Black Cat, 2010), 168.

10. Chang, *Can't Stop*, 70.

11. Fricke and Ahearn, 25.

12. KRS-One, *Gospel*, 99. Compare Toop, "A B boy classic like James Brown's 'Get Up, Get Into It, Get Involved' [...] is an up-tempo call and response routine between Brown and singer Bobby Byrd. For most whites at the time, this was the most meaningless type of James Brown release, but for those young Blacks still living in areas like the Bronx and Harlem every phrase had a message" (66); and Dan Charnas, *The Big Payback: The History of the Business of Hip-Hop* (New York: Penguin, 2010), "Herc began to spin the songs he knew would drive them crazy. They didn't want to hear the smooth songs [...] played in the discos [...] They liked funk, music that sounded raw and angry like James Brown" (16).

13. Fricke and Ahearn, 26.

14. George, *hip hop america*, 15. Bruce Lee's *Enter the Dragon*, for example, was released in 1973 and was influential on varied New York dance scenes; but, again, the actual extent of these influences is difficult to determine, save that of James Brown, who is cited by all early breakers as a key prec-edent. Much of the scholarship concerning the nature of the dance focuses on the second generation of breaking, after 1976, rather than the earliest dancers who attended Herc's parties. Aprahamian's current research program should help resolve some of these vital and as-yet underexplored questions.

15. Jorge "Popmaster Fabel" Pabon, "Physical Graffiti: The History of Hip-Hop Dance", in Forman and Neal, eds. *That's the Joint*, 57–61 (59). This is an excellent and concise—if not uncontested—history of breaking from one of the finest practitioners and stewards of the art.

16. Fricke and Ahearn, 41.

17. Chang, *Can't Stop*, 79.

18. Fricke and Ahearn, 45.

19. Quoted in Chang, *Can't Stop*, 79–80. Elsewhere, he recalls, "Well the break thing happened because I was seeing everybody on the sidelines waiting for particular breaks in the records" (Brewster and Broughton, *DJ Revolutionaries*, 172). Ewoodzie, 17–8, suggests that this transition happened at the very first party, over the course of the evening as he moved away from reggae. Others contest the idea that Herc began with Jamaican music, given that most of his musical education occurred in the Bronx, and hold that his break-based technique developed more gradually over multiple events. As with so much of early Hip Hop culture, further historical work and debate is needed.

20. Ibid., 78. His "big record back then, and nobody had it then, was James Brown, 'Give it up and Turnit A Loose' [sic]" (Brewster and Broughton, *DJ Revolutionaries*, 170); the rarity of even quite popular records is an indication of the relative deprivation—economically and otherwise—of the Bronx at the time.

21. Ficke and Ahearn, 96.

22. This involves studying the density of the grooves cut into the vinyl. To watch this process in action, see DJ Z-Trip's visit to a record store in the documentary *Scratch* (2001; directed by Doug Pray).

23. Chang, *Can't Stop*, 79. Herc did this with *different* breaks, mixing diverse and often contrasting sequences with each other, although he did (usually unsuccessfully) "try to make it sound like a [single] record" (Brewster and Broughton, *DJ Revolutionaries*, 172); he also only played the breaks a few times in one go before moving back to full records, to please everyone at the party (173). But the breakers, who would soon form the centre of the action, would always wait for the breaks to move, and thus those sections increased as parties inevitably grew. Flash recalls first hearing of Herc through breakers: "'It's his records. He breaks 'em up and takes those motherfuckers apart, piece by piece. My man got everybody out on the dance floor 'cause he was playing the best parts and movin' on to the next jam. No even waiting for the first one to end. I got *mad* tired, I was bustin' so much movement'" (*The Adventures of Grandmaster Flash*, 43).

24. Chang, *Can't Stop*, 79. This break-frenzy, catering to this new form of dance, is the true foundation of Hip Hop DJing. DJ Disco Wiz, for example, recalls, "I gravitated to the breakbeats. Being an ex-b-boy, I

really embraced that. My sets were pretty intense and violent. It was just one breakbeat after another" (quoted in Katz, 28).

25. Although Herc insists that the "term B-boying came in after I started to play, as I called them the b-boys" (Brewster and Broughton, *DJ Revolutionaries*, 167), there are still controversies as to the true origin and meaning of the term, which some claim actually began in reference to the geographic home of those who danced on the break, that is, "B(ronx)-boys", cf. Joseph Schloss, *Foundation: B-boys, B-girls, and Hip-Hop Culture in New York* (New York: Oxford University Press, 2009). The placement of the b-boy name and style at this early juncture in the development of the culture has also been (aggressively, as its title suggests) contested by Thomas Guzman-Sanchez, *Underground Dance Masters: Final History of a Forgotten Era* (Santa Barbara: Praeger, 2012). Because so much of this history remains somewhat unclear, I stick to the mainstream account, here. I have also opted to primarily use the term "breakers", both because it coheres with the fact that the dance was primarily called "breaking" during the period in question, and for its gender inclusivity, which reflects the strong and as yet underappreciated presence of women in early Hip Hop dance. Today, in part due to the backlash against the 1980s coinage of "breakdancing" to spur the fad, "b-boying" is by far the preferred term by practitioners, and thus "b-boy" is often (although this is changing) used to refer to both b-boys and b-girls within the contemporary scene. For an account of some possible differences between b-boy and b-girl styles, see Nancy Guevara "Women Writin' Rappin' Breakin'", in W. Perkins, ed. *Droppin' Science*', 49–62 (58), and for a solid primer on the varied gender issues and contestatory feminist discourses in the wider culture, in particular in rap music, see Gwendolyn D. Pough, Elaine Richardson, Aisha Durham and Rachel Raimist, eds. *Home Girls Make Some Noise: Hip Hop Feminism Anthology* (Mira Loma, California: Parker Publishing, 2007). On gender issues in the first decade more broadly, see Ewoodzie, 139–51; and, again, watch out for forthcoming work by Aprahamian.

26. Fricke and Ahearn, 31.

27. Seeing Herc perform, Grandmaster Flash quickly realized "that in his heart he wasn't about the individual songs. To Herc, a DJ set was one continuous piece of music" (*The Adventures of Grandmaster Flash*, 74).

28. Graffiti writer Phase 2, speaking in the documentary *The Freshest Kids* (2002; directed by Israel). Originally referring to the sudden eruption of something negative (as in, "Why you breakin' on me?"), it quickly came to name the explosive moves that went off during the Merry-Go-Round.

29. Schloss, *Foundation*, 19.

30. Chang, *Can't Stop*, 102.
31. Cf., Trac 2, speaking in *The Freshest Kids*: "All the breaking and stuff was considered underground, until Kool Herc brought everything out into the open, and that was like, say, '74–75. All the underground stuff, all the in-house, all the hallway dancers, and all the house party dancers were brought out to the street, and the more they took it to the street, the more nationalities got involved in it; it was no longer an Afro-American thing". Compare Grandmaster Flash's impressions from his first Herc party: "There must have been a thousand people getting down to his music. Folks from four to forty, sweating and bouncing, breakin' and popping, doing the pancake and getting buck wild. But every single head was doing the exact same thing—bouncing up and down to this guy's jams. This cat the scene locked down! Another thing: nobody was fighting. I mean *nobody* was swinging fists or pulling pistols, and there must have been six different gangs representing that night! [...] That's how it went until six in the morning. No cops breaking it up, no gang fights turning it loose; just everybody doing their thing, having fun, and riding the beat" (*The Adventures of Grandmaster Flash*, 47–9).
32. Speaking in *From Mambo to Hip-Hop: A South Bronx Tale* (2006; directed by Henry Chalfant). Pioneering MC Melle Mel claims that, even as Hip Hop began to move into nightclubs, "You couldn't do indoor parties in the summer [...] 'cus no one would come inside" (Ewoodzie, 93)
33. This division is, of course, somewhat too simple, given Hegel's account of the "inner" contribution involved in hearing, as distinct from, for example, sight. While there isn't room to rehearse the details, here, I discuss this at length in *Hegel's Philosophy of Language*, Ch. 2.
34. *Foundation*, 19, emphasis added.
35. Ibid., 21. Katz highlights the subjective contribution in the very isolation of the break, "Hip-hop DJs (and the b-boys and b-girls they catered to) did not just hear breaks as tantalizing; they heard them as fundamentally incomplete, as fragments that demanded to be repeated" (16).
36. Schloss, *Foundation*, 19.
37. Ibid., 21.
38. Ibid., 19.
39. Speaking in *Scratch*. Robert Farris Thompson, "Hip Hop 101", in W. Perkins, ed. *Droppin' Science*, 211–19, compares breaking to forms of Haitian ritual dance "where *cassé* ('break') stands for the deliberate disruption of the beat of the drums, which throws the dancers into ecstasy" (215).
40. Kaminsky, 74.
41. Frick and Ahearn, 31, emphasis added.

42. Hager, Ch. 3. Grandmaster Flash, for example, describes his first experience with breaking as seeing a friend "shuffling his feet in the strangest way *ever*, sliding backwards like he's walking on the surface of the moon" (*The Adventures of Grandmaster Flash*, 38).

43. Thompson, 218. He also takes up the aforementioned trope of the breakers' "body lightning" (211); many breakers, DJs, and eventually MCs would also refer to their ability to "shock the house".

44. Chang, *Can't Stop*, 118.

45. Schloss, *Foundation*, 11.

46. This, in fact, was the theme of the earliest Hollywood depictions of Hip Hop, where professional dancers come to learn new modes of movement from "street" performers. See, for example, *Flashdance* (1983; directed by Adrian Lyne), or *Beat Street*.

47. Schloss, *Foundation*, 19.

48. Rutter, 31.

49. William Eric Perkins, "The Rap Attack: An introduction", in Perkins, ed. *Droppin' Science*, 1–45 (14).

50. Katz, 39.

51. Ibid., 16.

52. Ibid., 39.

53. Using different breaks back to back and without headphones to cue them, for example, meant that he rarely kept time. His successor DJ AJ, for example, discusses the "severe" nature of Herc's beat mixing in the VH1 series *And You Don't Stop: 30 Years of Hip-Hop* (2004; directed by Dana Heinz Perry and Richard Lowe), and Herc recreates his early technique in first episode of the documentary series *The Hip-Hop Years* (1999; directed by David Upshal).

54. Brewster and Broughton, *DJ Revolutionaries*, 177.

55. Ibid.

56. *The Adventures of Grandmaster Flash*, 72.

57. Brewster and Broughton, *DJ Revolutionaries*, 177.

58. One technique involved adding a headphone output to the two-turntable set-up, so that the break on one record could be cued back to the start while the other played. These were literally glued onto his rig, to which he eventually added a third turntable and finally a drum machine, from which we get the term "beat box"; all of these, of course, would eventually become standard parts of a DJ rig. Much of his earliest gear, however, was gained by "going into the backyards and looking for electronics stuff, and looking for burned out cars, and looking for capacitor and resistors" and other parts to creatively reassemble (ibid., 178). While most scholars credit Flash with the addition of the cross-fader—and some, most famously KRS-One, have even credited him with *inventing* it—in recent

years participants in the original scene have made the case that this gear was not only available for purchase by DJs at the time, but that it was brought to the Bronx by Kool DJ Dee, whose role in the early development of Hip Hop (as with Disco King Mario) demands more research. Flash did, however, inventively find ways to construct such tools from spare parts.

59. Flash vividly explains his early experiments, reasoning and process in *The Adventures of Grandmaster Flash*, 53–81, and there are several excellent DJing tutorials by him circulating on YouTube.

60. Flash also takes, and is often given, credit for the discovery.

61. Edwards, 42.

62. This is *pace*, for example, Rose: "At a time when budget cuts in school music programs drastically reduced access to traditional forms of instrumentation and composition, inner-city youths increasingly relied on recorded sound" (34). Acquiring, to say nothing of mastering, the stereo equipment necessary to become a DJ in the Bronx was far more difficult than sticking it out in what remained of school music programmes, or playing instruments inherited from relatives; and DJs like Flash recall having to buy records based on covers alone, or other non-musical information, in hope of finding breaks no-one else had discovered yet (cf. *The Adventures of Grandmaster Flash*, 65). As Katz notes, there were far "easier ways to get into music" (65), as demonstrated by the fact that "DJs put huge amounts of time and energy into building their sound systems [...] scour[ing] the city's many vacant lots for any bit of abandoned equipment" that could be refurbished, as well as intense effort in learning how to bring them back to life (49), while refusing the remaining traditional instruments on offer to focus on acquiring massive and cumbersome record collections whose tracks would mostly remain un-played, and which would feature many duplicate copies. The prevailing "assumption that necessity was the mother of hip-hop" thus misses the fundamental role played by the essential "*creativity* [and] *agency* of individuals", of which it offers palpable and compelling evidence (65, emphasis added). Roughly the same argument is made throughout both Ewoodzie and Schloss, *Making Beats*, and *The Adventures of Grandmaster Flash* provides a stirring first-person account of the intense, self-determined and dedicated work of the early Hip Hop DJ.

63. Brewster and Broughton, *DJ Revolutionaries*, 177. In fact, Flash is explicit that he *consciously sought* to correct the flaw in Herc's parties: "I noticed the crowd: if they were into a record they would have to wait until he mixed it, because it was never on time. And I didn't understand what he was doing, at the point, because I could see the audience in unison, then in disarray, then in unison, then in disarray. I said, 'I Like what

he's playing, but he's not playing it right' [...] So the thought was to not have disarray, to have as little disarray as possible" (178). In his memoir, he ties this to his other great love: discerning the inner working of electronic gadgets, claiming he doesn't "know which sent me higher—the music or the mystery of how it played" (*The Adventures of Grandmaster Flash*, 8). As I discuss more fully in the conclusion, it is indeed curious that the conscious, aesthetically expressed drive for skilled mastery of one's environment and oneself that is continually both demonstrated and voiced by Hip Hop's pioneers is so frequently elided by scholarly, as well as popular, discourse on the culture.

64. *Ruminations*, 89.
65. Mr. Freeze speaking in *The Freshest Kids*. Compare to Rock Steady Crew leader Crazy Legs, speaking in *Bboy: A History of Breaking* (2016; directed by Marc-Aurèle Vecchione): "The main thing for a b-boy back then was to practice and battle."
66. Toop, 60. Flash describes his lamp-jacking technique in *The Adventures of Grandmaster Flash*, 61.
67. As Cold Crush Brothers DJ Charlie Chase recalls, "We made a lot of mistakes because we were learning on our own—we didn't have any teachers. Like everything else in this business of hip-hop, we learned on our own, nobody taught us" (Fricke and Ahearn, 167).
68. *Gospel*, 499.
69. As b-boy Anthony Colon argues "The main thing is that hip-hop, breaking [...] is about the people" (quoted in Schloss, *Foundation*, 40). Ewoodzie also reminds us "there was no inherent value in the breaks [Herc] played other than that assigned by the audience. In a sense, *the audience made Herc special*" (48, emphasis added).
70. Ewoodzie, 45.
71. More on this in Chap. 6. Evidently, Herc would eventually also pepper his sets with snippets from groups like the Last Poets, although this may have been due to their driving, polyrhythmic breaks.
72. Ewoodzie, 45.
73. *Ruminations*, 89. Compare to Westbrook, who defines Hip Hop as "A culture that thrives on [both] creativity and nostalgia" (64). Of course, many of the key breaks (e.g. the "Hip Hop national anthem", "Apache" by the Incredible Bongo Band) were drawn from contemporary, rather than older, records. They were almost always, however, sonically similar to the funk music found in the record collections of many parents. Flash's memoir details the link between growing up around breaks and seeking them in more recent records, and emphasizes the distance between Hip Hop's soundscape and that of the softer black dance music of the 1970s,

disco: "Disco gets that old feeling running through my muscles and nerves again. My head is spinning with the crazy, romantic fantasy of this late-night scene. Everything about it has me spinning except for one thing: the most important thing of all. The Beats. Disco is most definitely not homemade. Disco DJs play the whole song. Disco DJs don't mess with the beats" (*The Adventures of Grandmaster Flash*, 93).

74. KRS-One, *Gospel*, 580.

75. As Chang summarizes the thought of Afrika Bambaataa, "Consciousness did not come from the unmasking of social forces, but from having a *true reckoning with one's god within*. [...] If you are as gods, Bambaataa seemed to say, then it follows that *you are just as capable as I am to make this new world*." (*Can't Stop*, 106, emphasis added).

76. Ibid., 75. A fuller version of the quote from B-boy MAEZ reads: "Back in the days, you always had a meaning for your name. Like, some kids write a graffiti name, but it has no meaning. For us, we had deep meanings for our names. There was a reason we wrote it. Because of Bruce Lee [and] martial arts, "Master at Eternal Zenith" meant: all the time, you have to be tip-top".

77. Ibid. As Ewoodzie notes, "Hip-hop performers *earned* a name based on their role at parties" (137, emphasis added).

78. Compare to the discussion of gold chains in later rap fashion in Paul Gilroy, *Against Race: Imagining Political Culture Beyond the Color Line* (Cambridge: Belknap Press of Harvard, 2000), 199.

79. George, *hip hop america*, 157.

80. Compare the preceding quotes by Hegel to the words of legendary NYC airbrush artist Shirt King Phade, explaining why people gravitated to novel designs by him and other "street entrepreneurs" during the emergence of Hip Hop: "When times are bad, a lot of people tend to gravitate toward art. Art takes your mind to another place", speaking in *Fresh Dressed* (2015; directed by Sasha Jenkins).

81. Schloss, *Foundation*, 78–9. For an example, see Popmaster Fabel's description of the manufacturing of the "fat laces" for sneakers in *Fresh Dressed*.

82. Elena Romero, *Free Stylin': How Hip Hop Changed The Fashion Industry* (Santa Barbara: Praeger, 2012), 15. As she writes, fashion in the culture "was like a b-boy battle in the sense that it was a competition to win the title 'best-dressed' like best dancer" (14).

83. Compare Hazzard-Donald, for whom modern "African-American popular cultural creation is [...] driven by a [...] tendency toward embellishment referred to as the 'will to adorn'" ("Dance in Hip Hop Culture", 221), grounded in their imposed social location; she also describes some of the fashion shifts in the early culture (227). Perhaps the best visual

record of the years of Hip Hop adornment (although it tends towards the latter part of the decade and after) is Jamel Shabazz, *Back in the Days* (New York: powerHouse Books, 2001).

84. See, for example, Fab 5 Freddy's comments in *The Freshest Kids*, or Schloss, *Foundation*, 115: "The battle aspect of b-boying has its immediate roots in teenagers' natural competitiveness".

85. Ewoodzie, 77.

86. Schloss, *Foundation*, 116.

87. Hager, Ch. 3.

88. Sally Banes, "Physical Graffiti: Breaking is Hard to Do", in Cepeda, ed., 7–11 (8).

89. *Ruminations*, 82.

90. Schloss, *Foundation*, 107. The second quote is from Phantom, a present-day b-boy, but one affiliated with the foundational Zulu Nation (more on them in Chap. 6). Compare with Banes: "Inside the ritual frame, burgeoning adolescent anxieties, hostilities, and powers are symbolically manipulated and controlled" (9), or Gilroy's discussion of the manner in which Hip Hop's "vernacular arts precipitate and dramatize intracommunal conflicts over the meanings and forms of identity and freedom" (*Against Race*, 179).

91. Speaking in *Beat This: A Hip-Hop History* (1984; directed by Dick Fontaine), emphasis added.

92. Schloss, *Foundation*, 110.

93. Ibid., 99. There are, of course, various possible antecedents for this, but some recent oral histories available in various forms on YouTube (e.g. those featuring first generation b-boy Cholly Rock) suggest that it may have emerged from the "Spade Dance", a stomp-based form of dance which either preceded or was renamed up-rocking, and was performed with individuals entering a circle to show their stuff. Its name derives from the fact that it was initially developed by members of Bambaataa's division of the Black Spades. Then again, in those same oral histories, some people from the Bronxdale projects claim to have been doing backspins and other power moves as early as 1972.

94. Ibid., 99.

95. Perry, 107.

96. Schloss, *Foundation*, 100.

97. Imani Kai Johnson, "Hip-hop Dance", in *The Cambridge Companion to Hip-hop*, ed. Justin A. Williams (Cambridge: Cambridge University Press, 2015), 22–31 (24).

98. Schloss, *Foundation*, 103.

99. Ibid., 78.

100. Ibid., 84.

101. Speaking in *Bboy: A History of Breakdance*.
102. Schloss, *Foundation*, 78–9. Compare Kaminsky's claim that, for Hegel, "great sculpture avoids too much concern with capturing human emotions", all the better to emphasize "permanent rather than accidental or momentary traits in the human personality" or the "permanent core of man" (72–3).
103. Ewoodzie, 48.
104. Schloss, *Foundation*, 84.
105. That is, "genuine art, for Hegel, does not present us with things as they are in ordinary experience, it idealizes them by investing their natural form with grace, balance and proportion which are not encountered in such a pure form in nature itself" (Houlgate, *An Introduction to Hegel*, 214).
106. Schloss, *Foundation*, 86, emphasis added.
107. Cf., e.g. Thompson, "the way some spins dissolved into the freeze could be truly magical" (218).
108. Speaking in *Bboy: A History of Breakdance*.
109. Chang, *Can't Stop*, 118 (emphasis added). This is not, of course, to suggest it was the only dance that thematized frozen movement; it does, however, seem to be unique in making it a necessary and consummate aspect of a routine that was necessary to count as an example of the dance. See Hazzard-Donald for discussion of some of its likely historical antecedents.
110. Schloss, *Foundation*, 74. Thus, the common appellation of breaking as "physical graffiti", explicitly made, for example, by Banes and Pabon, implied by KRS-One (e.g. *Gospel*, 114) and reflected in Afrika Bambaataa's naming of his own form of b-boy fashion "Wild Style".
111. Rose, 47–8.
112. As an unnamed b-boy puts it in *The Freshest Kids*, "B-boying is like the ultimate body expression of Hip Hop. Not only do you have your feet moving, your arms moving, every single part of your body, your head, your neck, [but] also your character".
113. Speaking in *Bboy: A History of Breakdance*. As Grandmaster Flash puts it, there was a specific personal "attitude you had to have if you called yourself a b-boy. You had to be ready to battle at the drop of a hat, whether you were in the street, in a park, or at a jam, and you had to be on your shit if you dared to compete" (*The Adventures of Grandmaster Flash*, 39). In the conclusion, I discuss some misconceptions about "Hip Hop attitude" that have emerged since the era of recording.
114. Houlgate, *An Introduction to Hegel*, 233 (emphasis in original).
115. Banes, 10.
116. Katz, 48.

117. Ibid., 57. Flash recalls "I could do anything once I was in that magical zone. I could spin around, cut with my hands behind my back, hit switches with the top of my head, kick off my shoe and throw the cross-fader with my feet" (*The Adventures of Grandmaster Flash*, 110).

118. As a minor but instructive example, see *The Adventures of Grandmaster Flash*, 63–4, for a tale of local gangs robbing a downtown disco primarily to get better turntables to donate to their favourite DJ, despite never having met him previously.

119. Rose, 35.

120. As Sal Abbatiello, manager of one of the first nightclubs to host Hip Hop events, remarked regarding his early exposure to the culture, "I'm leaning on the wall, observing the crowd, how the people who weren't dancing were involved with the music as much as the people who were dancing. It was bringing people together: people were talking to strangers, smiling across the bar at someone, all doing the same thing" (Fricke and Ahearn, 180).

121. Cf. KRS-One, "A Jam was a time to either show-off your own unique talents or watch the unique talents of others. A Jam wasn't just about a crowd of people listening to a DJ (or, years later, to an MC), a jam was a community event—a social gathering. It was a time and space where the young neighborhood school kids as well as the young outcasts, the outlaws and young revolutionaries would all come together to exchange ideas, street products, plans, gossip and of course talents. [DJs like] Kool Herc […] were [thus] also activists in their community and their free service to their community is what caused Hip Hop to exist" (*Gospel*, 94–5).

122. Fricke and Ahearn, 339. Compare to Crazy Legs, speaking in *Bboy: A History of Breakdancing*, "That's what we live for, man: […] to create, to battle, to get some props".

123. Quoted in Banes, 11.

124. KRS-One, *Gospel*, 742. Compare Schloss, *Foundation*, 117. A longer list of Hip Hop's ethical rules can be found in Wimsatt, *Bomb the Suburbs*, 54, although the code, obviously, is internally contested and evolving. Ewoodzie, for example, provides evidence for "the unwritten rule that crews had to play with their own equipment. They could borrow from other crews, but renting professional equipment was out of line" (117); a rule which dropped from the battling tradition once clubs entered the scene.

125. *Ruminations*, 154.

126. *Foundation*, 92.

127. Etter, 6.

128. Schloss, *Foundation*, 18.

129. Rose, 22.
130. Schloss, *Foundation*, 109.
131. KRS-One, *Ruminations*, 207.
132. *Foundation*, 150–1, emphasis added. Compare to his discussion of "breakdancing" vs. the "b-boy lifestyle", ibid., 61–3. In many ways, the remainder of this book is an effort to account for the tensions described in this passage, as they manifested themselves within the culture as a result of its co-option by mainstream forces; and breaking was certainly the element that suffered the most from becoming a "fad".
133. Cowboy, from the Furious Five, is now generally credited with originating it, although some still give credit to Lovebug Starski. Many pioneers claim that it was original a derogatory term, meant to emphasize that the party culture was just a "kids' thing" that was effectively a waste of time, as in "Why are you bothering with that 'hippity hop stuff'?"
134. Cf., Chang, *Can't Stop*, 105. These are also sometimes called the "four core principles" of Hip Hop, alongside its "four core elements" of aesthetic creation.
135. *Gospel*, 71; 73. As he extends it later, "This is the meaning of our movement. VICTORY OVER THE STREETS! There it is" (529). Compare Asanti, 24–26.
136. *Gospel*, 70–1.
137. Hager, Ch. 3, citing the fact that Caz was the first to master all four elements, in most of which he also paved new ground.
138. Fricke and Ahearn, 337–40.
139. Ibid., 109.
140. Ibid., 340.
141. *Ruminations* and the *Gospel, passim.*
142. Speaking in *The Freshest Kids.*
143. *Ruminations*, 204.

CHAPTER 5

MCing, or the Romantic Stage of Art

PROLOGUE

Having contingently attended a party at the Harlem World disco club, which had begun to host Hip Hop nights, soul singer Sylvia Robinson became enthralled with, and instantly saw the commercial potential for, what appeared to be an entirely new musical form; she quickly resolved to put it to wax, launching her own record label in process. She initially approached some of the dominant DJ crews of the Bronx (including Grandmaster Flash and the Furious Five), but was greeted by immediate refusal. Hip Hop, after all, was not just a kind of music, but a complete and diverse *culture* of live aesthetic performance that centred on DJs and breakers, in addition to crowd-responsive and -motivating MCs, and which was also intimately connected to the immersive world of graffiti. The ceremonial nature of Hip Hop, most felt, would simply not transfer to record.

Searching for talent to record, she stumbled upon a pizza place in New Jersey, where "Big Bank" Hank Jackson, then manager of Bronx MC and DJ Casanova Fly (who would soon change his name to Grandmaster Caz), was rapping along to a tape of his client rocking a party. Hank was invited out to her car to audition, where he recited Caz's lines over Chic's then-popular disco record "Good Times". Two passers-by—Guy "Master Gee" O'Brien and Michael "Wonder Mike" Wright—also approached Robinson, boasting of their own lyrical skills; they auditioned on the spot and were quickly added to the fold. Despite the fact that none of them had any direct involvement in the Bronx's aesthetic culture, they promptly signed

© The Author(s) 2018
J. Vernon, *Hip Hop, Hegel, and the Art of Emancipation*,
https://doi.org/10.1007/978-3-319-91304-9_5

to the newly formed Sugar Hill Records, which assembled a live band to mechanically play an imitation of the "Good Times" riff to mimic a break-beat, as the three newly minted "rappers" recited rhymes. While Wonder Mike and Master Gee performed original, albeit generally derivative and rudimentary, material, Hank stuck to his successful tactic of reciting Caz's routines (as well as some lines taken from Funky Four/Furious Five member Rahiem), right down to introducing himself in his opening line as his client ("I'm the C-A-S-A-N the O-V-A, and the rest is F-L-Y"). While clearly plagiarizing, Hank subsequently secured at least implicit permission to do so from Caz, who, like most, was sceptical that Hip Hop could become a recorded music, but also was hopeful that, if anything did come of it, having a manager with links to a record company would open up doors for him and his crew.

And doors certainly were opened, although not for Caz or most of the other pioneers. "Rapper's Delight" by the Sugarhill Gang took the country and world by storm, topping the charts in several countries and breaking the top 40 in the United States.[1] Hank spent the subsequent years alternately denying the lyrics were lifted, or claiming that he co-wrote them with Caz, who never saw a dime from his authorship. While the record bore no connection to graffiti or breaking, featured no DJ, and sounded precious little like anything previously heard in Hip Hop music, it instantly vaulted the final artistic element of the South Bronx's aesthetic and emancipatory culture from the obscurity of the block party into the pop mainstream. In process, however, it propelled the fragmentation of the aesthetic elements, not only from each other, but from ethical community which they had collectively helped to build.

BACKSPIN

Given the omnipresence of Hip Hop's poetic element in contemporary culture, it will no doubt appear somewhat odd that MCing has, as yet, received no explicit treatment here; however, as Grandmaster Caz reminds us, "the Hip Hop movement started with Kool Herc. Actual rap didn't start until later. It was deejaying and breakdancing at first. Not everybody even had a mic. It was just about your beats".[2] Caz, by distinguishing MCing from the early block party culture, implicitly articulates the overarching argument that guides this book; that Hip Hop culture arose in temporal stages, characterized by the sequential emergence of its different aesthetic elements. However, before we explore its final aesthetic stage and element, it may be best to remember how we arrived here.

We began with the symbolic stage of graffiti, or the impulsive, omnipresent, and transformative work of taggers which "architecturally" converted the crumbling and burning South Bronx into "a beautiful artistic enclosure for spirit [by] picturing the inner meaning of spirit in an adumbrative way in its external sphere" (624/II, 258, trans. modified). This transformation was expressive of the emancipatory freedom essentially possessed by the excluded citizens of the region, but in a manner that remained partial and implicit. Symbolic graffiti's contribution to the Hip Hop community's development thus consisted in working "*from* spirit, to prepare *for* spirit in its living and actual existence, an *external* environment pursuant to art" (888/III, 131, trans. modified). On its own, then, graffiti was "incomplete" (888/III, 131); it preceded Hip Hop as a broader cultural movement, which explains why so many early taggers saw themselves as distinct from the subsequent aesthetic community, and why some Hip Hop pioneers distinguish their culture from the antecedent art of graffiti, but nevertheless in its very nature called forth aesthetic and social developments that explicitly built on its foundation, explaining the retroactive inclusion of graffiti into Hip Hop as the broader culture expanded and solidified. If graffiti sensuously indicated the free creative spirit from which it issued by constructing an aesthetic "temple", like every temple, its very form revealed that it "needed a god to live in it" to complete it (959/III, 222).

Kool Herc's discovery of the break gathered these "gods" to the temple, in the form of breakers and DJs, who placed "spirit before us in plastic beauty [by giving] to the material [art] uses for this purpose forms which by their very nature are not alien to the spirit but are the shape immanent in the selected content itself" (959/III, 222). This plastic beauty is the human body in idealized, self-determining form, explicitly manifested through the visible performance of feats of human skill and statuesque, yet vibrant corporeal movement; the presentation of these bodies palpably contested not only the "natural" situation of the repressive and crumbling borough within which the Hip Hop community lived, but the merely received limits attached to the bodies of uniquely alienated teenagers. What defined the temple of Hip Hop was not the life *outside* the block party, but the idealized forms of sensuous presentation attained *within* it, where breakers and DJs went by self-created names, and executed self-determined forms, all in a manner that intentionally foreclosed presentation of both the wider struggle of eking out an existence in Little Vietnam, as well the personal struggle of mastering one's moves or equipment. From one's own body, to their immersive environment, to the area's remaining power grid, South Bronx block parties made palpable the fact that those who endured an effective return to stateless social conditions not only *could*, but actually *had*, freely transformed both themselves and

> the whole external world [into] an accessory, as the ground and means for higher ends, yet as a ground and an environment over which that harmony and independence is diffused and comes into appearance only because each and everything produced and used by human hands is at the same time prepared and enjoyed by the very individual who [uses] it. (261-2/I, 339, trans. modified)

What we see represented at every turn by the self-determining artists of the Bronx, are the "chief characteristics" of the classical Ideal, "blessedness and independence, satisfaction, tranquility, and freedom" (530/II, 142-3).

Hip Hop was emphatically *not*, then, a form of mere *spectacle* or *entertainment* that competed with others available in the popular sphere for audience attention; as DJ AJ recalls:

> In the South Bronx we really had nothing to do. There wasn't no movie theaters—everything we did was like something just to make a little bit of excitement in the area. [...] And when people seen Kool DJ Herc, it was like some excitement, and it drew a crowd.[3]

Radically isolated from the economic, political, and artistic opportunities available in the broader modern world, the citizens of the South Bronx "reach[ed] within [them]selves to pull out something creative, and when hip-hop came to the front, it appealed to every kid" because it was the primary form of aesthetic expression and appreciation available to them. For its creators and adherents alike, there "was no right or wrong" standard set which everyone had to follow; rather, "everything that was done was somethin' new" and thus the structuring and subsequent proliferation of the cultural norms, or the solidification and expansion of the ethical community, were autonomously determined within and by the Hip Hop community itself.[4] Hip Hop's "public" was thus not a passive audience witnessing a spectacle, but an active, essential, and determining component of the artistic culture; they physically formed the cypher, decided winners in the battles and determined, carried forward and held other participants to the ethical standards developed in the nascent community. Thus, just as for Hegel the "supreme end in Greece was [...] the body of the citizens, and their ethical and living patriotism [for b]eyond this interest there was none higher or truer" (510/II, 117), so the collectively determined aesthetic of Hip Hop culture marked the "discovery of a way [for South Bronx residents] to distinguish themselves in a very *direct, self-contained, and totally controllable way.* They [only] needed simple tools to make their art and they *made their own decisions about what made it good*".[5]

And, as Grandmaster Caz suggests above, this self-contained and self-determining Hip Hop community was essentially complete *prior* to the emergence of "rapping", at least as first presented to the world at large through "Rapper's Delight". In this chapter, I argue that what was initially called "rap music" emerged precisely at the point at which art had completed its job of emancipating its practitioners from the most radical form of their social abandonment and facilitated (what should have been) their rightful inclusion in the institutions of the surrounding state. In process, the MCs of the South Bronx (as well as their followers from other boroughs and cities) will guide us through the development of *poetry* as spirit's aesthetic self-expression in words.

Of course, as Afrika Bambaataa reminds us, in a certain sense, the poetry of:

> Rap has always been here in history. They say when God talked to the prophets, he was rappin' to them. You could go and pick up the old Shirley Ellis records, 'The Name Game,' 'The Clapping Song,' Moms Mabley, Pigmeat Markham, when he made 'Here Comes The Judge.' You could pick up Barry White with his love type of rap, or Isaac Hayes. You could get your poetry from Nikki Giovanni, Sonya Sanchez, the Last Poets, the Watts Prophets. You could get your militancy message rap coming from Malcolm X, Minister Louis Farrakhan, Muhammed Ali. A lot of the time, the Black people used to play this game called the Dozens on each other, rappin' about your mama or your father, and stuff. And you could go back to the talks of Murray the K, Cousin Brucie, and all the other radio stations that was pushing the rap on the air or pushing the rock and roll. So rap was always here.[6]

This list can be extended to include antecedents from the "rapping DJ" scene—built by performers like DJ Hollywood and Eddie Cheeba—that developed in New York's disco clubs in the mid-1970s; the "raunchy" street vernacular records of the 1970s, like the *Hustlers Convention*[7]; the early musical comedy "party records" of Rudy Ray Moore and Blowfly; and could even be extended all the way back to the West African *griots*. All of these, of course, would eventually (and correctly) be cited as inspirations for what would come to be called "rap music". However, given the rich variety of African-American, or even local New York, poetic traditions upon which artists could (and eventually would) draw, perhaps the most striking aspect of poetry's *emergence* in Hip Hop culture is how *little* they appear to have influenced the work of the culture's earliest MCs. In fact, the characteristics that would ultimately become synonymous with "rapping" (intricate rhyming patterns, first-person narratives grounded in subjective or dramatized experience, evocative descriptions of living conditions, vivid declarations of social protest against the broader world of racist policing and late capitalism, etc.) were remarkably *absent* at the dawn of the culture's final aesthetic element. As 1990s MC Abstract Rude would later claim, while "poetry is old as dirt [...] rap is dated back to the early '70s", for it emerged from the quite specific, local, self-contained circumstances in the South Bronx.[8] Grandmaster Flash would go so far as to claim that the "new DJ culture that guys Herc and Bam and I were creating [gave] birth to a *new* form of expression" that could even be called "a new life-form down here on earth [...] the MC".[9] Thus, we must not only account for the emergence of poetry, as a supplement to the aesthetic community of Hip Hop, but more precisely for what appears to be the *re-emergence* of poetry in a form of aesthetic expression unique to Hip Hop, operating at a *remove* from the refined forms of speech which already dominated literary culture, musical lyrics, and political discourse in post-Civil Rights America. That is, we must explain not only why Hip Hop supplemented itself with poetry, but why this poetry reverted to the earliest and simplest—rather than adopting the more refined and habitually familiar—forms of aesthetic language, in order to found a novel form of poetry that both emerged from, and eventually broke with, the previously developed aesthetic elements.

THE EMERGENCE OF POETRY FROM THE CLASSICAL IDEAL

While not every DJ in early Hip Hop had a mic, Kool Herc certainly did. As Grandmaster Caz recalls, "MCing evolved from the DJ having a microphone to make announcements; to announce when the next party was going to be; where the next party was going to be; who was going to be at the party; [...] to acknowledge members of the group, members in the crew or people in the audience",[10] and Herc needed a mic for such announcements to be heard over his legendarily loud sound system. Almost from the start, however, he also embellished his announcements with echo effects, braggadocio, and evocative descriptions of the general party atmosphere. While Herc's vocalizations, combined with his upbringing, might appear to directly spring from the vocal "toasting" that accompanied the dub rhythms of the open-air soundclash culture, Herc actually denies the influence, instead citing records in his collection (esp. those of James Brown and Lightnin' Rod) for the inspiration.[11] However, Herc's lines—such as "You never heard it like this before, and you're back for more and more of this rock-ness. 'Cause you see we rock with the rockers, we jam with the jammers, we party with the partyers"[12]—show none of the narrative storytelling, or even the rhyming structure of the *Hustlers Convention*, nor do they display the kind of political potency, rhythmic impact, or contagious repetition for which Brown was rightly famous; rather the "Kool Herc style at the time was basically freelance *talking*, not necessarily [even] syncopated to the beat".[13] Because he was often too busy cueing breaks or adjusting his system to get on the mic, friends often took over hosting duties; however, they would similarly "just get on there and say his name, haphazard, no real talent being displayed", taking up Herc's style as Hip Hop's own poetic foundation.[14] Thus, the earliest MCs like Herc's (and arguably Hip Hop's first standalone) accompanying poet Coke La Rock,[15] or others like Timmy Tim and Clark Kent "said phrases; they didn't say rhymes. They would say, 'On down to the last stop.' 'More than what you paid at the door.' Stuff like that".[16] Nevertheless, Herc recognized that even uttering seemingly haphazard and fragmented phrases was the MC's manner of "throw[ing] out his poetry" into the ritual mass.[17] All of which, of course, raises the question: what exactly is poetry, and under what conditions does it emerge to play a central role within an aesthetic community?

Hegel defines poetry, in its most general sense, as simply "the art of speaking [*die redenend Kunst*]" (960/III, 224, trans. modified), and as such, this art form poses special problems. *Prosaic* speech, after all, is a constant feature of our everyday life; every action, object, or situation that poetry can express not only *can be* expressed prosaically, but within post-1960s modernity likely *had been* in some way expressed, and thus these treatments form part of our merely given situation. While Hegel does make some (undefended, and rather implausible) claims about poetry being "older than skilfully elaborated speech" or "the original presentation of truth", these concern a postulated "primitive poetry" that would have been "composed before ordinary prose had been skilfully developed"; the core problem of poetry in the situation under consideration here, however, concerns a "period when prosaic expression had already been completely elaborated" (973-4/III, 240-2). In such a time, speech as habitually spoken and heard describes "the field of externality and finitude" where "every particular either appears [...] as independent or is brought into a mere relation with another" and which, therefore, "has nothing to do [...] with the essence of things" that gives these particulars their unifying significance (975/III, 243). In such a situation, language as habitually spoken expresses a merely given, inflexible, and thus essentially *inhuman* world; one which is there to be *understood*, but one in and through which we do not truly understand and experience *ourselves*.

By contrast, poetry, as the *art* of speaking, finds its focus not in externality as given and determin*ed*, but in free humanity as creative and determin*ing*. For Hegel, poetry's "proper subject matter is [the] *spiritual interests*" manifested through the actions, creations, and words of self-determining individuals, as well as through the external world as reflective of, and infused by, free spirit (972/III, 239, emphasis added). Thus, in poetry the

> entire external sphere only enters in so far as the spirit finds in it a stimulus or some material for its activity; thus [finitude] enters as a *human* environment, as our external world which has essential worth only in relation to the inner realm of consciousness. (972/III, 239, trans. modified)

Just as prosaic treatment serves to objectively *describe* the world as given, inflexible, and external, so poetic speech seeks to evocatively *express* a world that is freely created, and thus self-referring; as such, an alienated community produces and embraces poetry *subsequent to the aesthetically self-determined transformation of both themselves and their world*. Poetry both expresses and presupposes a fundamentally human environment forged by and reflective of a community of free individuals, and thus can only arise *after* the preceding symbolic and classical arts have done their job, or "once, in the midst of his practical activity and need, the individual moves to collect and communicate their thoughts [*zur theoretischen Sammlung übergeht and sich mitteilt*]" in language (974/III, 241, trans. modified). This helps to explain why MCing, despite utilizing the most immediately available means of creative expression, and eventually becoming the most popular art form to emerge from the culture, was the *final* aesthetic element Hip Hop developed.

It also, however, helps to account for the marked *distance* between the initial poetry of Hip Hop, and the previously developed traditions of artistic speech cited above. While these extant forms of aesthetic expression would *eventually* (which, on Hip Hop's compressed timeline, means within a matter of months) inform the poetic style of rappers, the forms of language found on records, books, or in the rhetoric of the Civil Rights and Black Power movements, were nevertheless *a part of the merely given world* surrounding the isolated South Bronx. While the culture's earliest poets were, of course, uniquely alienated teenagers with somewhat limited access to media, they assuredly would have been intimately familiar (through their parents, churches, radio, school, and other sources) with these forms of creative language; however, they also formed one small part of the larger realm of merely given and restrictive externality out of which the Hip Hop community had been liberating itself through its painting, dance, and music. As Hegel argues, in a situation where the previously given forms of expression, or "*prose* has already drawn into its mode of treatment the entire contents of the spirit and impressed the seal of that treatment on anything and everything, poetry has to undertake the work of *completely recasting and remodelling* [*so muß die Poesie das Geshäft einer durchgängigen Umschmelzung und Umprägung übernehmen*]" language so that it reflects the subject freshly liberated from external determination (976/III, 244, emphasis added). In order to remain *free* and thus *artistic* expression, poetry's task is to "tear itself free from adherence to the ordinary contemplation" by "transform[ing] the prosaic consciousness' ordinary *mode of expression* into a poetic one" in order to "preserve the appearance of that [...] original freedom which art requires" (976-7/III, 244-5). And the earliest MCs, by developing linguistic resources specific to their unique culture, brought to Hip Hop poetry a freely created, self-contained, and self-determining ground upon which to build more refined and varied forms of artistic speech.

Because it is distinct from merely descriptive, or otherwise prosaic speech, at its core "poetry is actual *speaking*, the audible word, which in its temporal duration as well as its real sound must be shaped" by the poet (1001/III, 275, trans. modified); we find this in Hip Hop culture's exclusive focus on the *spoken* voice of a *physically present* poet. According to Hegel, poetry progresses through distinct stages—which he labels the epic, the lyric, and the dramatic—each of which is linked to a distinct content and form. Each of these stages, I aim to show, corresponds not just to the formal varieties of poetic expression one finds MCs sequentially employing, but to a specific, evolutionary shift in the import of Hip Hop's poetic element. They also, however, chart the gradual separation not only of poetry from the preceding art forms which made it possible, but from the community which originally expressed itself through them. The history of Hip Hop poetry, in other words, is simultaneously the evolution of the art of MCing into arguably the most varied, popular, and potent form of aesthetic language in the contemporary world, as well as the supplanting of Hip Hop culture by what we now call rap music; a transformation of which "Rapper's Delight" was less the determining cause than an undeniable— and arguably inevitable—symptom. Before we "get on down to the last stop", however, let's take a closer look at the original poetry and poets of what was then, still, the unified and isolated Hip Hop community.

"GRANDMASTER, CUT FASTER": THE EPIC POETRY OF THE FIRST MCS

While we normally associate epic poetry with lengthy, narrative sagas detailing real or mythical events of great import to a nation, Hegel reminds us that the "Greek 'ἔπος' and the Scandinavian 'saga' both mean 'word', and what they state in general is what that thing is which has been transformed into the 'word'" (1040/III, 325).[18] Thus, while generally using predictable examples of epic poetry, he more pertinently isolates the foundation of poetry in the process through which a newly artistic people "extract[...] from the concrete world and its wealth of changing phenomena something [...] and express[... it] independently" (1040/III, 325). The epic stage of poetry is thus defined less by the presence of particular forms of narrative content, than it is by the poet's striving to *aesthetically express in language the spiritual world in which she finds herself at home*, or the linguistic "representation of a national spirit of a particular people at an early and definitive stage of its development".[19]

According to Hegel, the "most elementary" form of poetry is thus the "epigram" whose essential characteristic is to serve, "as it were, as a spiritual hand pointing to something" in the poet's surrounding environment (1040/III, III, 325, trans. modified); it does not simply name or describe something present to hand, but uses language to aesthetically celebrate something as a site for spiritual reflection. However, in this elementary form of epic poetry, the "author is not yet expressing his own concrete self" as a free subject; rather one begins the process of poetic expression by simply "look[ing] around" and introducing to "the place which he sees confronting him, and which is claiming his interest, a compressed explanation concerned with the kernel of the thing itself" (1040/III, 325-6). Here, the poet searches her surrounding environment for contents suited to aesthetic commemoration, which are then "concentrated into epic phraseology" (1040/III, 325). The epigram moves beyond prosaically naming an object precisely by linking it to the very spirit of free creation which defines a fundamentally human environment. These early expressions of objective, but spiritually infused content, are quickly followed, Hegel argues, by "maxims" or "apophthegms" [*Sittensprüche*], wherein, rather than simply trying to capture something from their environment in poetic words, the artist "expresses [her] idea of the object" as an expression of what an ethical community's poets take to be "of intrinsic worth [or] what is decent and honorable", in search of a "vision of what in the spiritual sphere forms the fixed foundations and stable bonds of human action and knowledge" (1041/III, 326, trans. modified). Epic poetry spiritually captures elements of the aesthetically developed situation in creatively modified language, and thereby subjectively declares what is good, true, or honourable within it to the unified community. And this is precisely the process we find in the work of the first "generation" of MCs.

For example, as Bambaataa remembers, "Herc took phrases, like what was happening in the streets, what was the new saying going around the high school, like 'rock to my mellow', 'to the beat y'all', 'you don't stop', and just elaborated on that".[20] That is, Herc searched his local, aesthetically transformed environment for objective content (in this case, the unique and omnipresent slang of the South Bronx) for phrases suited for creative capture by the living poet at a block party. He would then truncate, extend, or otherwise alter these phrases into expressions reflecting the environment of, and occurrences within, the party at hand. For example, he used the local appellation "my mellow" and his echo effects box to shout out favoured partygoers (as in "This goes out to my mellow Wallace D....D....D.."), or adding catchphrases (like "You never heard it like this before") to his party announcements.[21] Many early MCs would just recite the names of their assembled friends, frequent partiers, or just "people who were down", supplemented with jokes about people being double-parked, avoiding parents looking for them, or other references to the surrounding realm, but quickly developed similar phrases based on or akin to Herc's lines.[22]

The poetic capture of surrounding externality, however, was not strictly or even primarily limited to the modification of prosaic slang, or shout outs to contingently present friends or devoted Hip Hop heads. While it may be slightly inaccurate to claim that the art of MCing "started out with rappers talking on the microphone about the skill of the disc jockey",[23] this kind of poetic tribute was certainly an early and central task of Hip Hop's earliest poets. It was likely Grandmaster Flash's accompanying MC Cowboy who "was the first MC to talk about the DJ" and their skills,[24] but from their earliest involvement in parties, MCs helped secure, and in some cases created, the "god-like" status of DJs, as well as breakers, in the South Bronx, precisely by linguistically expressing their heroic acts of creation. Because jams often consisted of battles between DJ crews, and because battles were won by attracting breakers to one's beats, it should be unsurprising that a key task of the MC was both to "hype" the powers and beats of the DJ, as well as to call forth the hottest moves from the assembled dancers. Thus, to be an "epic poet" in early MCing meant being "concerned to honour the hero whose fame he spreads" (1130/III, 440), as when Coke La Rock would call Herc the "man with the master plan from the land of Gracie Grace", or Cowboy and his comrades would shout "Check out the mix of the greatest of them all", "One, two, this is for you, you, and you/Three, four, cuts galore", or "Grandmaster! Cut Faster!" to accompany Flash's displays of skill.[25] Thus, just as "Homer and Hesiod gave the Greeks their gods" (1047/III, 335), so MCs like Thee Kidd Creole and Coke La Rock gave Hip Hop its founding pantheon; and as the presentation of idealized human form "places the gods in their genuine shape before sense-perception [and thus] forms the proper centre of classical art", it comes to pass that "poetry compliments it by describing gods and men in a way distinct from the self-reposing objectivity or sculpture or by [linguistically] presenting the divine and human world in their very activity and movement" (455-6/II, 49).[26]

However, if Hip Hop poetry begins with epigrams concerning the activities of the assembled participants and officiants in the ritual mass, keeping the show rolling necessitated the use of exhortatory apothegms. For example, when Grandmaster Flash perfected the combination of his "quick mix" theory, and began to deploy it in his parties,

> The reaction was not what he had expected. [Flash recalls] "The first time I did it, the crowd just stood there, just watching me. I was hoping to get 'Whoa yes, I love it!' But it was like, no reaction, no movement. Just hun-

dreds of people standing there." [...] It was a lesson. You could be smart, you could be good, you could be scientific, but being smart and good and scientific wasn't going to rock a party all by itself." [...] He was going to have to win crowds over to his new style.[27]

Flash, thus, "set his mind to theorizing the rest of his show" to determine how best to keep the crowds active while he performed his new feats; he quickly "realized [he] needed vocal accompaniment to help spark this concept", as MCs could use evocative language to urge the crowds to stay involved and breakers to keep dancing despite the spectacular new trick to watch.[28] Thus, his first MC Cowboy—who Flash claims was so charismatic and compelling on the mic he "[c]ould have told [the crowd] to jump off a bridge and they would have done it"[29]—pioneered Hip Hop's use of such phrases as "Throw your hands in the air, and wave 'em like you just don't care", "Clap your hands everybody", or "Say Ho", to keep the crowd pumped and bodies moving[30]; and, as Funky Four MC K.K. Rockwell recalls, one primary role of the MCs was to specifically "talk to the b-boys—'B-boys, are you ready?'", in order to prepare them for athletic display when a break like "Apache" or "It's Only Just Begun" was about to come on, continuing the participatory nature of the party. This, of course, also aided their DJ in battle by drawing dancers and cyphers to their side.[31] Thus, drawing out, commenting on, and encouraging both the actions of breakers and the involvement of other partiers was one of the most fundamental jobs of early MCs, as participation in the ritual mass of the block party grounded the honour code of Hip Hop.

Keeping the party going was not simply required to affirm the rep of a DJ. While the block party emerged as an antidote to pervasive street violence, it was not (contrary to the often idealized story of Hip Hop) as though the conflicts and habits that previously dominated the area had been totally eliminated.[32] A party that failed to sustain enthusiasm meant a restless crowd that might direct their energy into less communal and productive pursuits. Thus, MCs were required not only "to help [the DJ] get the crowd involved but also to control them when they got too restless".[33] This is why the culture's first poets are called MCs, rather than the later appellation "rappers"; they were the *Masters of Ceremonies* who presided over and ensured the smooth, participatory flow of Hip Hop's ritual mass.

And, finally, it is important to note that, while it is true (as the examples above indicate) that early MCs would "maybe, recite a string of rhymed couplets to show off individual verbal artistry", rhymes were by and large *absent* from the poetry of the earliest MCs.[34] Initially, they chose to "celebrate the DJ's skill and the prowess of the MC crew, [and] encourage group participation [etc.] with *repeated catchphrases*".[35] This meant that the overall emphasis of the first MCs was not on rhyme, but on *rhythm*, and it is precisely rhythmic, rather than rhyming, language that Hegel associates with poetry's emergence from prosaic speech. In the epic, the emphasis is on "the sound of syllables in their *temporal duration*" or on the "measurement of longs and shorts, of rhythmic emphasis and the reverse, and of the various sorts of enlivenment in language, without being governed by that intonation through which alone the *spiritual* sense of a word or syllable receives its emphasis" (1026/III, 308, trans. modified). It is this discovery of evocative rhythms within the "natural length and shortness of syllables" (1027/III, 309) that we find, for example, in the contrast between the staccato opening syllables and the extended, closing vowel sounds in the well-worn phrase "B-Girls are you readyyyy", the contagious joy found in Cowboy's repeated, punctuating use of the meaningless syllable 'Ho!!!', or The Kidd Creole's creation of the now ubiquitous alliteration "Yes, Yes Y'all!".[36] If poetry begins by concentrating the human world into epic phraseology radically divergent from previously given forms of speech, then it is unsurprising that—despite the many refined forms of poetry available for adoption—unlocking the potential in the natural rhythm of words to move, calm, or draw crowds was the skill of the earliest MCs, who focused on individual phrases, rather than rhyming couplets, precisely because they were (re-)discovering the very nature of, and communal need for, living, spoken poetry in the new aesthetic culture.

Thus, MCing emerged through the use of varied forms of linguistic rhythm to point a spiritual finger at the aesthetically and ethically significant features of the participatory and ritual atmosphere of the block party, drawing ever more attendees into active roles in varied forms of reciprocal interaction between the MCs, DJs, breakers, and cyphers. Of course, because "the performance was thought of as a three- to four-hour continuous set", and could stretch to two or three times that length, with partiers coming and going throughout the night, "MC performances did not narrate a complete story",[37] as in the later developments of epic poetry that occupy much of Hegel's account. But these epic MCs did lay down the rhythmic bed upon which later poets would develop such skills by linguistically capturing an environment infused with the spiritual ethos of Hip Hop, and in a manner that ensured the continued flow of the violence-quelling and community-building block party against potential intrusions contrary to its collectively enforced ethic.

As we saw in the previous chapter, however, central to this ethic was the commandment not to "bite" the work of another artist, and MCing was thus guided by the same demand for self-surpassing creativity that guided Hip Hop's other aesthetic elements. While many of these epic phrases were retained as Hip Hop poetry developed, they could not simply be repeated without modification or addition, as no MC would be accepted by a crowd if they were perceived as plagiarizing another's creation, and one could only win recognition in the culture by developing new skills in their chosen field. To have standing as a true Master of Ceremonies, a poet thus needed to continuously *recreate* Hip Hop's poetic language, and it was this internal pressure that pushed MCs forward from the fragmentary, rhythmic epithets of the epic to refined, rhyming *lyrics*.

From Epic to Lyric Poetry

As with the previous elements, what motivated the MCs was the *competition* with others to earn the acceptance of the breakers and the crowd. This demanded continual innovation in poetic expression, as only this adhered to the fundamental and self-surpassing ethic of Hip Hop's aesthetic culture, forged through combative displays of aesthetic self-mastery. As we have seen, this initially took the form of embellishing, adding forms of intonation, or modified rhythms, and so on to phrases used by others in a form that distinguished the usage as belonging to one particular MC; and this reflects, in a sense, the development of what Hegel refers to as the "epigram [that] adds a [subjective] feeling to [epic] expression" (1116/ III, 423). While this shift seems subtle to the point of being trivial, it ultimately affected not only the form and content of poetic language, but the nature and role of the poets themselves.

First: language. Because the meaningful contents MCs were called upon to express during parties were all roughly the same (who and how great the DJ is, the breakers should prepare for the coming selection, the declaration of victors in battle, the where and when of the next party, etc.) the only way individuals could stand out as unique was to focus on the *form* of expression. An MC needed to *stand out*—not only within a raucous party environment, but more importantly as a non-biter within the overall culture—and thus faced the "task of emphasizing the *sensuous element*" of their expression (1028/III, 310, emphasis added); that is, a poet's language had to "strike out more materially and be coarser, if only to get attention at all" (1028/III, 310). For Hegel, this accounts for the shift away from the epic's focus on rhythm, to poetry's dominant focus on *rhyme*. Rhyme "is a thumping sound that does not need [a] finely cultivated [...] ear" (1028/III, 310), and as such intrinsically draws attention to itself as linguistic *form*, as distinct from the *content* conveyed through it. As Hip Hop's earliest poetic contents (and even some of its specific catchphrases) became repeated sufficiently to become a habitually expected given at jams, its poets—in order to stand out both *from* prosaic speech and *as* original creators of poetic language—moved from the epic to the lyric, or from an emphasis on the rhythm of spiritually meaningful language to focus on the sound of "syllables independently of their meaning" that could be placed into ear-catching rhymes, thus becoming "engrossed more deeply in playing with the now independent sounds and notes of letters, syllables and words" (1023/III, 303-4).

We see this transitional process in the art of MCing in the recollections of Grandmaster Caz: "I would make an announcement this way, and somebody would hear me, and then they'd go to their party and they add their little twist to it. Then somebody would hear that and they add a little bit to it. I'd hear it again and take it a little step further 'til it turned from lines to sentences to paragraphs to verses *to rhymes*".[38] Rhyming, then, was both an *inevitable* and an *internal* development in MCing, and once it arose, its ear-catching sonority, paired with Hip Hop's competitive ethos, meant it quickly spread to poets seeking to make an impact in the developing artistic field. According to The Kidd Creole,

> When we first started rhyming, Flash would have guys on the microphone who'd just get on there and say his name. [...] And [then] my brother [Melle Mel] ... I don't know, somehow or another he got in his head that he was going to make up his own rhymes, and that's what he did. And when he did that, it spurred me to do it. [...] *There was no real outside force that made us write rhymes*, because [at first] *nobody* was writing rhymes. So it was self-motivation. After a point, *everybody* started writing rhymes. My brother and I first started writing rhymes, and then everybody in our neighbourhood *who wanted to do the same thing* started writing.[39]

Rhyme supplants rhythm—and simultaneously, Hegel will argue *lyrical poetry* replaces the epic—precisely because rhyme better distinguishes a specific poet's language from previously given speech; not only as found in

MCING, OR THE ROMANTIC STAGE OF ART   143

prosaic language, but as inherited from the work of earlier and competing poets. In Hip Hop, rhyme allowed a poet to stand out more vibrantly not only as creative, but as adhering to the rules, and contributing to the development, of the overall culture.

Of course, because rhyme is primarily concerned with the *sound* of language, and because the phonemes that could be associated with the standard content of epic MCs presented a limited sonic palette, lyrical MCs could not pursue their art without liberating language "from domination by the accentuating and overpowering *meaning*" of the words (1028/III, 310, emphasis added). While many early rhymers stayed within the 'traditional" roles of the MC, other poets quickly freed themselves from this restriction, and began employing every available linguistic resource to construct their unique routines. And it was at this point, "[o]nce innovation in rap began to perpetuate, [that] the parallels between rap and spoken word poetry became more pronounced, and instances where the two cross over became more plentiful".[40] Initially, however, this influence was felt in ways that were focused primarily on *sound*, rather than meaning. Chief Rocker Busy Bee, for example, introduced the kind of scat singing often heard during the era of early rock and roll ("ba bah-ba bah-da-dang-a-dang-diggy-diggy"), fulfilling the Hegelian expectation that "wholly senseless gibberish, tra-la-la, singing purely for the sake of singing, prove to be a genuinely lyric satisfaction" for rhyming poets (1122/III, 429). In fact, the very phrase "Hip Hop" apparently originates from a "scat routine" of Cowboy's, derived from marching chants that he used at a party held to send a friend off to the army (likely emerging from something like "Left/Right, Left/Hop, Hip/Hop").[41] Another MC from Flash's crew, Rahiem performed a bragging routine (that would actually wind up in "Rapper's Delight"; the part that begins "I'm Imp the dimp, the ladies' pimp") that was derived from a traditional rhyming-game famously recounted in the autobiography of H. Rap Brown. Early verses like Kidd Creole's "He tried to rock the spot/with a cheap cheap rhyme/the rhyme was a joke/the sucker went broke/and he died and went to heaven in a little row boat"[42] drew from a variety of sources, including the local slang used by early MCs ("rock the spot"), nursery rhymes and pop songs (the rhyming structure, as well as "went to heaven in a little row boat", which could have been gleaned either from childhood skipping songs or the Shirley Ellis song based on them that Bambaataa frequently played in his sets), the sonorous pleasures of repetition ("cheap cheap") and consonance ("rock/rhyme"), and the combative nature of Hip Hop battles ("the sucker [...] with a cheap cheap rhyme"); it never, however, adds up to anything like a clear message, or reference to anything specifically occurring within the surrounding party. Rather, it functioned as an *independent artwork*, developed for the *auditory appeal* of its language alone, written *outside* of the party atmosphere and able to be employed *at any time* within it. Thus, by contrast with the epic's grounding link to the immediately surrounding world and culture, lyrical "rhyme is an isolated, emphasized, and exclusive sound" (1028/III, 310), through which

> poetry *cuts* itself free from this importance of the material, in the general sense that the specific character of its mode of sensuous expression affords no reason any longer for restriction to a specific subject-matter and a confined sphere of treatment and presentation [to become] the *universal* art which can shape in any way and express any subject-matter capable at all of entertaining the imagination. (966-7/III, 232-3)

Which means, secondly, that when lyricism "free[s] art from the concept presented" (604/II, 234) by liberating poetry from the need to preserve and express the assembled aesthetic community, it transforms poetic language into "a free instrument which the artist can wield in proportion to his subjective skill in relation to any material of whatever kind" (605/II, 235); thus, the focus on aesthetic *form* simultaneously leads to a new *content* for poetry. Because MCing demanded original, rather than derivative, aesthetic presentation, each MC necessarily drew upon different linguistic resources to creatively modify the art's epic foundations in order to construct unique rhyming routines. These formal differences revealed that each MC had distinct, idiosyncratically personal interests, skills, and style, not only in terms of the forms of expression they used but also as regards the contents conveyed through them; and Hip Hop's lyricists became quickly recognizable within the community by the distinct phrases, rhyme schemes or "flows", themes, and quirks they brought to their poetry. In Hegel's terms, what is thus revealed through the emergence and development of lyric poetry is the fact that the individual "human being stands in connection with the entire world, and this implies at the same time a wide variety in both the spiritually subjective sphere and also the external [realm] to which spirit relates itself" (521/II, 132). Thus, if epic poetry still served to commemorate the objective determinations of the aesthetic community, lyric art's "interest in the objects is inverted, so that it is the *stark subjectivity of the artist* himself which intends to display itself and to which what matters is [...] a production in which *the producing subject himself lets us see himself alone*" (600/II, 229, trans. modified, emphasis added). Rhyming poetry, then, is intrinsically linked to the *first-person perspective* of the lyric precisely because it frees poetry from its subservience to determinations outside the poet's own creative imagination.[43] Correspondingly, rather than lionizing the gods of Hip Hop and ensuring the smooth and participatory flow of a party, Hip Hop's poets began to celebrate *themselves* as creators with a unique, personal style to express.

Thus, while the classical art of the breakers and DJs sensibly presented an emancipatory community through the aesthetic celebration of idealized human form (which was linguistically celebrated by the earliest, epic MCs), what we might call proto-rap, rhyming lyricism "displays predominantly the *inner heart*" of the poet in her idiosyncratic particularity (254/I, 329). If epic MCing treated the lived actions of a unified community as "something which is unfolded before the subject as an objective and self-contained totality, in lyric, by contrast, the opposite need, to express *oneself*, is satisfied" (1113/III, 418, trans. modified, emphasis added). Or if the "supreme end" of the classical was "citizenship [in the community], and their ethical life and living patriotism" (510/II, 117, trans. modified), the defining content of what Hegel deems "*romantic* art is *absolute interiority*, the corresponding form of its spiritual *subjectivity*, as the grasp of its independence and freedom" (519/II, 129, emphasis added). Art shifts from the classical to the romantic, then, precisely when the *isolated, freely creative, and self-determining individual*, as opposed to the *assembled, idealized, and collectively self-determining community*, is placed at the heart of artistic practice; as Hegel puts it, the "general transition from sculpture [and the classical Ideal] to the [romantic] arts is produced [...] by the principle of *subjectivity* which was breaking into the subject-matter and the artistic mode of its portrayal" (792/III, 11). If art's highest vocation is to raise a *community* from the state of nature to free self-determination through aesthetic practice and participatory appreciation, then its emancipatory purpose is accomplished when the *individuals* who compose that community explicitly grasp, and more pertinently *express, themselves* as free enough to be so infinitely self-determining on their own. And in Hip Hop, it is the *lyrical MC* that facilitates this shift away from the collective and ethical culture of Hip Hop towards individualistic or romantic art.

"HEAR ME TALKING 'BOUT CHECK BOOKS": ROMANTIC ART AND THE RISE OF THE LYRICAL MC

Even though it occurred in a mere matter of months, it would be impossible, here, to provide a complete account of the development of rap lyricism, from the earliest rhyming routines to the dawn of recorded "rap music". However, as with the preceding elements, we can identify several features of this transition, focusing on those that closely align with Hegel's account of the decline of classical art and the rise of the romantic.

First, as we have seen, in lyricism the "proper element of poetical representation is the poetical *imagination*" which is specific to each individual poet (89/I, 123). This contrasts with Hip Hop's classical culture, which was forged through the actualization of spirit in and through the willed transformation of the *body* into beautiful form through feats of skill and honour in contest. Because MCs work in the medium of *language*, they not only manifested their creative spirit in a manner which *did not* demonstrably transform their bodies or surroundings; more importantly, they *could* speak of subjective and situational transformations that *were not*, and even *could not*, be corporeally realized. For example, while many "early MCs generally rapped about having huge amounts of cash, women, and fame" as their presentation of idealized versions of themselves akin to those that forged the classical Ideal, unlike breakers and DJs—who had to sensibly *demonstrate* their idealized selves to themselves and others—all partygoers knew that the "early rappers more often than not lived with their parents, owned no cars, and lived in areas with a median poverty-level income", and thus that they were merely *voicing*, rather than concretely *embodying*, an ideal which was present only in their own creative imaginations.[44] If DJs and breakers had to back up their idealized boasts with lived, corporeal action (Flash had to be the fastest, just as breakers had to invent freezes), having grasped their own possession of the free self-consciousness made explicit by their activity, MCs needed only to find creative ways of giving voice to them, and as such opened up a completely unrestricted range of idealized self-presentations. That is, with the dawn of romantic art, in and through lyric poetry, we see spirit "begin [...] to withdraw into the infinity of its inner life" (509/II, 117), where the imagination can construct any fantastic self it likes.

Which means (second) that, by submitting art to the "principle of subjectivity [which] necessarily implies [...] abandoning the [classical] unity of spirit and its body" via the retreat into inner imagination, lyric poetry simultaneously "makes available a space of free play for the particulars of the variety, disunion and movement of spirit as well as sense" (794/ III, 14, trans. modified). Romantic art, turning away from the idealized body and its lived sphere and towards the subjective imagination of the poet, opens up the fields of both content and form to "anything and everything in which a man as an individual subject can take an interest in" (832/III, 61). This, of course, grants to poetry "in respect of its subject-matter [...] an enormous field, [...] wider [...] than that open to the [preceding] arts", which restrict themselves to either cryptic riddles or idealized human figures and their heroic skills (965/III, 230). But precisely because a poet can expressively "unfold himself in the entirety of their human particular character" (793/III, 12, trans. modified), lyricism quickly forsakes art's focus on demonstrating our essential freedom by sensibly overcoming the restrictions of finitude, in order to grant aesthetic expression to "[a]ny topic, all spiritual and natural things, events, histories, deeds, actions, subjective and objective situations", which suit the poet's whims (965/III, 230). As rhyming MCs developed their art, they not only freed Hip Hop poetry from the "epic" contents still tied to the ritual mass, but more importantly began to celebrate the irreducibly singular and infinitely imaginative *mind of the MC* reciting. While the original job of the MC was to hype the DJ and keep the crowd in controlled and participatory movement, lyrical MCs became (in Hegel's terms) "not so much concerned to honour the hero whose fame he spreads in this way as to make [...] the poet heard" through their speech (1130/III, 440).

In fact, we see this in the very routine plagiarized from Grandmaster Caz on "Rapper's Delight".[45] His verse opens, for example, with the by-then standard linking of the MC ("I'm the C.A.S.", etc.), to his role of hyping the DJ ("I go by the code of the Dr. of the mix/For these reasons I'll tell you why"), however, essentially nothing in the subsequent lines refer to either the mix, or its doctor; rather, as with virtually all early lyrical rhyming, the focus throughout is on the idealization of the MC himself. This specifically lyrical idealization is informed less by the honour code of Hip Hop than it is by the contingently given materialism of the very surrounding society whose abandonment of the Bronx brought Hip Hop into being ("I got body guards I got two big cars/That definitely ain't the wack/I got a Lincoln Continental and..../A sun roof Cadillac"). Of course, in lines that would soon become ironic, towards the end of the verse, Caz also recounts a personal anecdote about the formation of his peculiar character ("From the time I was only six years old/I'll never forget what I was told/It was the best advice that I had ever had/It came from my wise and dear old dad"), in which he ties his current avocation as a lyricist to the honour code of Hip Hop ("[He said] 'whatever you do in your lifetime/Never let an MC steal your rhyme'").

One finds a similar tension between "classical" and "romantic" values in Melle Mel's lyrics on the first single credited to Grandmaster Flash and the Furious Five, "Superrappin" (1979), which combines personal history, the influence of what was then the brand new "rap" recording industry, and fantastical dreams of fame in a few terse lines ("Ever since the time at my very first party/I felt I could make myself somebody/It was something in my heart from the very start/I could see myself at the top of the chart [...] Signing autographs for the young and old/Wearing big time silver and solid gold/My name on the radio and in the magazine/My picture on the TV screen"). Moreover, while the song opens with a nod to the party atmosphere in which the routine was originally performed ("It was a party night, everybody was breaking/The highs were screaming and the bass was shaking"), and a repeated celebration of Flash ("Flash was on the beat box"), and even closes with a reminder of the codes that kept parties under control ("So when you walk through the door, just do me a favor/Be sure to be on your best behavior"), throughout, they nevertheless use the lyrics to *invert* the order of priority stated in the band's name, celebrating the MCs of the "Furious Five *plus* Grandmaster Flash", made more emphatic when Melle Mel dreams of making a living "Rapping on the mic, making cold cold cash/With a jockey spinnin' *for me* called DJ Flash" (emphasis added).[46] Like Caz, Melle Mel and the Furious Five thus articulate lyricism's move away from the epic, and with it from the "heroic" focus of the classical Ideal, to focus on the MC as an individual.

In fact, if one sought to determine the pivotal figure in the transition from Hip Hop culture to "rap music", a case could be made that it was not Sylvia Robinson, Big Bank Hank, or any of the others who ushered in the era of recording, but rather Sha-Rock—by most counts the first female MC, and by all counts among the element's finest and most revolutionary early lyricists—who rhymed with the Disco Brothers and the Funky 4 MCs.[47] While it is commonly presumed that the "MC, true to the title master of ceremonies, has *always been* the front man or woman [while] the DJ originally spun records standing at a set of turntables *behind* the MC",[48] as DJ Jazzy Dee reminds us, in the early days "all the MCs used to stand *behind the DJ*",[49] since they were primarily there to *augment* the already existent participatory party culture, not to be the focal point of it.

In fact, precisely in order to avoid the "stage show" problem identified by Flash above, they sometimes even hid in the wings, all the better to allow their words to keep the dancers and party hot, rather than to attract attention to themselves, exemplifying the Hegelian epic "in which an ideal objective action is depicted while the poet himself remains unobtrusively in the background".[50] However, at least in part to bring focus to their unique possession of the greatest female MC in the Bronx, the "Funky 4 was the first ones that used mic stands in front of the DJ", thus placing the emphasis on the lived presence on the unique MC speaking her mind.[51] As other Bronx crews followed suit, this seemingly small change radically altered the nature of both Hip Hop crews and ritual jams.[52]

In terms of the crew, as lyrical poetry increasingly became the focus of the jam, (third) the DJ moved from being the musical link between the statuesque dancers and the assembled community to being mere musical *accompaniment* to MCs, giving the crew the appearance of a live band, with "singers" and "backing musicians". As Hegel notes, because it necessarily organizes an audible material in terms of its metre and tone, "poetry is, according to its concept, essentially sonorous [*tönend*], and must, if it is to emerge *completely* as art, not lack this resonance, all the more because this is the one aspect in virtue of which it comes into real connection with external existence" (1036/III, 320, trans. modified); and what distinguishes a lyric poem from epic or prosaic speech is the sonorous arrangement of its components in a "system of versification" designed to catch and please the ear. Thus, it is unsurprising that eventually "lyric poetry approaches music" precisely because, as it continues to refine its arrangement of words and syllables into beautiful sound, "its language becomes actual melody and song" (1136-7/III, 448-9). This is why Hegel claims that, "in the matter of external execution" that is its live, first-person performance, "we find lyric poetry *almost always accompanied by music*" (1137/III, 449, emphasis added). With the dawn of the lyric, music is increasingly called upon to provide accompaniment for it, rather than existing on its own, as poetry increasingly becomes song (as found, e.g. in the "singing MCing" on the hooks to the Furious Five's first singles, or in the routines of the legendary Cold Crush Brothers).

Fourth, as their lyrics became increasingly complex and increasingly independent of anything else occurring in the room, the MCs inevitably *became the focus* of the party, precisely because they could be best heard when they were also *watched*. Hip Hop's poetic element, while originally a supplement to the ritual mass,[53] rather quickly came to dominate it in the form of the *show* of rhyming MCs; this radically altered the nature of the assembled crowd at a party, and thus of the party itself. Shifting the MC from complementary officiant to the focal point of festivities now *accompanied by* the DJ transformed the event from a "spiritual thing",[54] to "an *entertainment* thing; it became a *spectacle*, something to look at as well as something to hear [whereas, p]rior to that, the atmosphere at the parties was [...] very much about the DJs" in reciprocal relation with the breakers, both of whom depended upon and drew the passionate support of the assembled community.[55] Thus, while Coke La Rock claims that "everything [he] said really related to the party" and thus was dependent on the actions of the DJ, the look of the environment, and the responses of the dancers and crowd,[56] as Thee Kidd Creole recalls, "when we started writing rhymes, we put sentences together. We didn't really have any concept of crowd response. [...] So after we said our rhyme, we just ... was finished",[57] reflecting the fact that lyrical routines were developed externally to the jam context, and thus were transferable from party to party, moment to moment. With the advent of the lyrical MC, then, DJs were transformed into something like backing bands for what now appeared to be just like a concert, which transformed audience members into passive recipients of a spectacular show; and audience who—precisely because nothing specific was demanded of them any longer—did not need to be informed and committed Hip Hop heads, but could just as well *be anyone, from anywhere*. In Hegelian terms, if the classical era of art demonstrates the essential link between the idealized presentation of corporeal human form and the unified aesthetic community that grasps itself as free spirit therein, romantic art, by contrast, necessitates "a closer connection with the *finite subject*" as particular, and thus intrinsically opens itself to generic outsiders (500/II, II, 106, trans. modified, emphasis added).

The nature of this transition is captured well by the reminiscences of tagger and b-boy BOM5. In the early days, when he was too young to competitively dance, he recalls that the scene still maintained a kind of peaceful unity that was grounded in communal aesthetic performance; however, as he grew up and "started dancing more, you could see everyone would stop and pay attention to the MCs", rather than focusing on the collective jam, as before. When the MCs began to perform, dancers noticed that, "You start losing your circles. People walked away from you when the MCs rocked" to go watch the new lyrical show.[58] This explains why, "[b]y 1977, DJs that weren't already rapping [or accompanied by

MCs] were looking to line up rap crews" to match the new expectations of crowds looking for spectacular entertainment[59]; in process, however, the MC "transitioned from sidekick to star".[60]

Star MCs, moreover, did not make their mark by contributing to the overall cohesion of a collective jam, but through their increasingly elaborate routines, which were performed largely identically from crowd to crowd and, as such, no individual audience member, either by their active participation, or even by their mere presence, could affect the nature of the aesthetic content created and presented. While breakers, DJs, and cyphers both required and mutually determined each other, lyrical MCs required no breakers, and (as demonstrated by the frequent shifting of MCs among crews) could perform with any DJ, for any audience, eliminating the need for battles to earn respect in a cohesive and self-contained scene, thereby transforming the crowd from participatory audience to passive spectator.[61] Thus, even before recording was an option, Charlie Ahearn recalls, "Nobody was dancing. Period! Rap became the focal point. MCs were on stage and people were looking at them", and the party scene rapidly descended from a collective communal ritual "into a [...] passive experience".[62] And this, in part, explains why the rise of the MC as the star of the show was virtually simultaneous to the movement of jams from the open-air blocks of the Bronx to the discos and nightclubs of Manhattan.

"RAPPER'S DELIGHT", OR THE BIRTH OF "RAP MUSIC"

Hip Hop was thus seemingly destined to spread beyond the borders of its birthplace; however, if the move was largely determined by the development of its lyric poetry, various other forces certainly factored in. Even in the Bronx, as Hip Hop's local audience grew, the beat-centric music began to spread to non-attendees (those who had strict parents, e.g. or who were too young to stay out late) in the form of cassette recordings of parties (both bootleg and "official") that were sold and traded among heads, thus separating the creations of DJs and MCs from their lived link with the tagged blocks, breakers, and cyphers. The growing interest in Hip Hop's musical elements, as well as the refinements of lyrical MCing, dovetailed with the great blackout of 1977, during which stereo equipment stores were hit hard, placing better recording equipment in the hands of established acts, but also in those of bootleggers and would-be crews. This, in effect, led the pioneers to seek venues where they would be free from the throng of "toys" seeking to challenge them, at right around the time parties were turning into "shows". The increasing audiences—who began to come from other, less alienated areas of the city—meant that crews could soon afford to rent local halls for their events, moving the jam back indoors where admission fees could be more reliably collected, weapons more easily excluded, and so on. The remaining local nightclubs (like the Black Door club, where Grandmaster Flash eventually took up residency, or Galaxy 2000, where Herc battled crews like the L-Brothers) eventually took a risk on the new party culture.[63] Thus, the move to larger, more established and distant clubs in other boroughs was no doubt a natural growth of the culture at that exact historical juncture.

However, it nevertheless remains true that it is *at the very point* that rap lyricism broke with its ties to the immediately present action at a party and developed into a transferable and independent spectacle that interest in the culture blossomed outside the scene. Attracted by the contagious power of this new lyrical poetry and its music, audiences first grew in other inner city enclaves where mixtapes would flow via family and friends (e.g. in Harlem, followed by regions in Brooklyn, Queens, and Long Island), but quickly centred on a handful of clubs in Manhattan, some of which already employed their own "rapping DJs" who modelled themselves on the radio jocks of the 1950s, '60s, and '70s.[64] Thus, while the participatory community of Hip Hop was a far cry from downtown club culture, the sophisticated lyricism of the MCs of the South Bronx, backed by far more original and talented DJs, could easily be grasped by club patrons as an advance over their "rapping DJs", in terms of both technique and spectacle. Appearing like a cross between a dance party and a concert, and emerging simultaneous to the evolving new wave and punk scenes, clubs that featured Bronx acts—downtown venues like Negril, or uptown ones like Harlem World—quickly learned that they could draw a large and diverse crowd from subcultures across the city. It was in just such a club that Sylvia Robinson heard the sound she wanted to record; she just needed to find artists willing to do it and, perhaps tellingly, she needed to move *outside* the original culture to find them. But when she released "Rapper's Delight", the poetry—but, crucially, not the original music, or its paired dance—that emerged from the culture instantaneously won popularity and acclaim in the heart of the city and country whose radical exclusion of the community that birthed its pioneers initially necessitated Hip Hop.

Thus, while there are early Hip Hop artists who hold that "if the leaders of the street thing that we was doin' had got to do the record first, it would definitely have been something different" than what it eventually became,[65] it is perhaps more plausible to understand the emergence of "Rapper's Delight" as the inevitable result of the internal development already underway in Hip Hop's consummating romantic poetry that facilitated its entry into the surrounding world. In fact, even if we remove all of Hank's lines (and thus those attributable to the culture's pioneering lyricists), and focus only on the words of the two rappers "external" to Hip Hop, we see not so much a break with the lyrical MCs of the South Bronx, but a remarkable continuity. The song's infamous opening hook is forged from a combination of Cowboy's "Hip! Hop!" chant, Coke La Rock's "Rock and you don't stop", and some of the scatting of Busy Bee, with a direct focus on pure sound through alliteration, consonance, and rhyme ("I said a hip hop, the hippie the hippie/To the hip hip hop and you don't stop/The rock it to the bang bang boogie"), which is instantly followed by the lyrical introduction of the rapper as unique individual ("See I am Wonder Mike, and I like to say hello"). Similarly, Master Gee links lines lifted from the invocations of Herc and Coke La Rock ("The beat don't stop until the break of dawn") to his personal introduction ("I'm the M-A-S..."). As with the Bronx rappers, their rhymes primarily sing hyperbolic claims of imagined self ("Well my name is known all over the world"), occasionally lingering over the most banal events of human experience ("Have you ever went over to a friend's house to eat/And the food just ain't no good?"), or simply linking together contingently personal phrases and fantastic claims through their rhyming sonority alone ("Skiddlee beebop a we rock a scoobie doo/And guess what, America: we love you/Cause ya rock and ya roll with so much soul/You could rock 'til you're a hundred and one years old").

Moreover, while the song clocks at nearly 15 minutes, it is remarkable for the absolute *lack of musical development* it contains. The "Good Times" bass riff incessantly repeats with such monotonous precision (even every instrumental percussion break is played identically) that the actual presence of a live band during its recording actually is difficult to discern; however, despite the fact that Hank's lifted lines sometimes at least implicitly hype the DJ, no scratching, back-spinning, or other turntable sound is heard. The music sounds as if it is neither played live, nor manually constructed by a skilled DJ; rather, it just *exists* as that over which the rappers recite, emphasizing the music as pure *accompaniment*. The Sugarhill Gang were the *rappers*, not the anonymous band, isolating the lyricists as rap's spectacular stars. Finally, while the lyrics cajole the listener to move, b-girls and b-boys are never actually mentioned. Obviously having no dancers present at a party to whom to refer or celebrate, their invocations are strictly generic; if there is target audience of dancers suggested, it is not those of the block party, but the downtown disco scene, where one might do the "freak" invoked throughout the song—perhaps between sets by one of the new MC crews recently brought in as special entertainment.

Thus, while their rhymes may have been less creative, their ability on the mic more rudimentary, and their credibility within the culture non-existent, the Sugarhill Gang arguably *consummated* Hip Hop's poetic development precisely by completing the process of *separating* lyrical rap from the culture from which it initially arose, solidifying rap as an independent form of musical poetry, intimately tied to the unique individuality of the MC and ready for mass distribution and acceptance. "Rapper's Delight", much like the "paintings of graffiti" that drained tagging of its cultural unity, consummated (in Hegelian terms) the passage from the classical peak of Hip Hop to its romantic dissolution, wherein, even if its "topics […] remain the same on the whole" (idealized self, partying dancers, self-mastered skills, etc.), poets "exchange the earlier, spirited mode of production for an *ever more spiritless presentation* and a *mechanical external tradition*" by producing "an *imitation* which loses itself in pedantry, in death and frostiness, and finally degenerates into a bad and perfunctory technique" (575/II, 197, emphasis added). As Hip Hop inevitably—for sociological and economic reasons, assuredly, but also for internally developed *aesthetic* ones—"moved on from Bronx sound-system battles and outdoor jams to the drinking age uptown nightclubs, [it] depriv[ed] b-boys and DJs of their competitive setting" in the ritual cypher[66]; in process, it transformed the artist from divine sculpture to idiosyncratic personality, the audience from collective participant to finite spectator, and Hip Hop from communal religion to spectacular entertainment. Taking the themes, style, and essential musicality of lyrical MCing and putting it on a record—playable by anyone, anywhere, at any time—fully rendered the lyric into actual song, thus marking its independence from anything extraneous to the imaginative subject's own rhyming musicality. Moreover, because rap's first record was made by outsiders, it showed that such poetry could now be produced by anyone, from anywhere, for any reason, and in any circumstances. If Hip Hop was the aesthetic and ethical culture of the self-emancipating South Bronx community in the 1970s, rap was a form of musical poetry open to all to embrace and/or practice as their own.

Thus, as Chang notes, in a way "it makes perfect sense that a no-name group using partly stolen rhymes [...] would have been the first to tap hip-hop's platinum potential" by recording it.[67] Imitating Hip Hop MCing, rather than emerging from the unified culture from which it arose, the Sugarhill Gang "had no local expectations to fulfill, no street reputations to keep, no regular audience to please, and absolutely no consequences if they failed",[68] and as such were the perfect vehicle for the transition away from Hip Hop culture towards what came to be called "rap music".[69] They were not quasi-gods, whose battles and skills were communally celebrated in ritual masses, or officiating priests who gave voice to a collective and participatory ethos; like the graffiti artists who emerged after 1973 to pursue a career in the gallery system, they were merely finite individuals whose lucky presence in the right place at the right time gave them the chance to make a living within American late capitalism doing something they personally enjoyed, and which raised them from their own (albeit slightly less brutal) poverty and alienation. Produced "[f]ar from the outdoor jams and battles of the Bronx scene where hip hop originated, 'Rapper's Delight' was packaged and designed for travel", and, as such, had no-one to answer to who could hold it to the ethical standards of the culture[70]; and, carrying the culture's name as it spread across the globe, it cut Hip Hop loose from its community base, and allowed any contingent individual access to its elements.

Thus, as Hegel argues, the romantic breaks from the classical precisely when "the moment of *subjective individuality*" in all of its "human weakness, particularity, contingency, caprice, immediate naturalness, passion, etc." permeates the form and content of art (790-1/II, 461, trans. modified). Once lyric poetry turned art inwards to the unique creativity of the individual artist, it was only a matter of time before the culture's form and content would be presented in a manner "perfectly acceptable to folks who had never heard of hip-hop or the Bronx".[71] Consciously designed to appeal to generic spectators rather than informed heads, "Rapper's Delight" might mark the precise point at which Hip Hop's "ideal passes over from loftiness to what is [merely] *pleasing*" (788/II, 457), or from art as the sensuously demonstrable, communally determined liberation from externally determining circumstances to art as a contingent form of sensuous entertainment of both broad and diverse appeal. This would help explain why, in the eyes of many, the emergence of what came to be called "rap music" "began to destroy what hip-hop was".[72] KRS-One, for example, argues that, "[w]hen 'Rapper's Delight' [took off] in 1979, all attention was placed on rap music as a selling tool, not on hip hop as a consciousness-raising tool, as a maturing of the community. When hip hop culture got discarded for the money to be made into rap product, we went wrong from there".[73]

If the initial "response from the hip-hop community was [one] of resentment" that a non-existent crew could be taken seriously as MCs, their financial success and fame nevertheless also fostered in many of the pioneering crews "a desire to get in on the action"[74]; however, this necessitated "pushing [themselves] on a different audience",[75] rather than working to preserve the community that sustained them. One by one, the founding crews sought and (mostly) received record deals,[76] but this new income opportunity generally entailed recording with live bands. This not only allowed record executives to cut the DJs out of the payroll; it allowed MCs, formerly subservient to the headlining DJ, to keep most or all of the money garnered from shows as well. Because rappers were now the focus, "the DJ would have little more to do than keep a beat going", and instrumental records recorded by house bands could be started by anyone, and simply allowed to run much like the metronomic backing on "Rapper's Delight".[77] Rap crews could easily press instrumental versions of their hits, which only required dropping the needle, eliminating the close bond between the MC and DJ. Devoid of purpose and payoff, many DJs thereafter "didn't do too many more parties", retreating to private battles for pride among friends.[78] Thus, as "romantic" rap took root in downtown clubs free of graffiti, MCs abandoned DJ crews while former dancers stood still to take in the spectacle, the unified culture of Hip Hop romantically fell, as Hegel would put it, "asunder into its elements" (575/II, 197).

Of course, this rending of Hip Hop's unity did not occur immediately. Some of the clubs, like The Roxy or Negril used established Bronx acts like the Cold Crush Brothers or Bambaataa's crew, who still tied MCs to DJs, and many of their performances were accompanied by breaking battles, and occasionally would even feature live graffiti demonstrations. Figures like Fab 5 Freddy worked to popularize the culture as a unity of four essential elements, and these efforts eventually culminated films like *Wild Style*, *Beat Street*, and Michael Holman's television pilot *Graffiti Rock*. Thus, in the earliest years of its community's tentative social inclusion, Hip Hop's cultural unity still informed at least some efforts to popularize it in the wake of the explosion of rap music; however, if the self-created and -determining Bronx community "seemed to look like a single culture [...]

whose worldview felt authentic, original, and liberating", its presentation to the generic spectators of the downtown New York scene looked entirely otherwise.[79] Fab 5 Freddy, for example, pushed the cultural unity of Hip Hop largely to secure its acceptance by downtown critics and artists as a viable artistic movement, thus wedding the culture to the surrounding art world and broader society, in which he sought a place.[80] And, rather than expressing the self-emancipation from external determination, these club nights primarily—in what would become an issue which constantly haunted rap music—displayed an alienated people and culture *for the entertainment of socially included spectators*, shifting emphasis towards pleasing a broad and diverse audience, and thus away from collective self-determination.

Predictably, the disciplined battling culture of Hip Hop did not transfer well to alcohol-soaked, cocaine-infused clubs, and contests often led to fights between spectators and novices who failed to grasp Hip Hop's essential ethic; consequently, promoters began to *stage* breaking demonstrations in order to curtail audience participation. At Negril, for example, promoter Michael Holman regularly featured the Rock Steady Crew against a troupe that would come to be known as the New York City Breakers, who were initially selected for their supposed inferiority in order to "fix" the battles; as such, these contest were as consequence-free as "Rapper's Delight", just as the accompanying graffiti demonstrations required no risk and thus had no ethical norms to enforce.[81] Graffiti, having returned to the streets after its first venture into the gallery system, was swiftly re-embraced by the art world during this popular boom, and tags would soon enough be lumped in with other forms of "street art", and treated as part of a broader, post-pop art appropriation of the methods of advertising for "subversive" ends (e.g. the post-tagging and quite distinct work of Keith Haring and Jean-Michel Basquiat). As they crossed into the broader culture, nothing essential held the elements together save the fact that they all emerged from the once-discarded people who were now being exhibited for the entertainment of a passively consuming audience. Nevertheless, in process Hip Hop's aesthetic revolution created forms of social access and economic opportunity for (at least some of) its pioneering artists and tastemakers, as they found the spectacular version of their art forms in high demand. This tension between Hip Hop's sudden social inclusion and the loss of its cultural authenticity is perfectly captured by the Rock Steady Crew's Crazy Legs:

The Roxy could have also been a zoo. People were able to hang out in the cage with us and feel safe from getting beat up and stuck up, as opposed to coming to the Bronx, coming to a jam. It's like they were allowed to hang out in a cage and party with the animals, you know? […] But on the flip side, it was also us getting into places we never thought we could get into. So there was an exchange there.[82]

Hip Hop Is Dead

As Hager's early Village Voice article reminds us, in the wake of Kool Herc's discovery of the break, for roughly "five years the B-Boys, rappers, DJs, and graffiti writers of New York continued to expand and develop their unique artistic vision in almost complete isolation from the rest of the world".[83] This all changed when the culture inevitably migrated beyond the walls of the Bronx into the clubs of Midtown Manhattan, where its success attracted the interest of the music industry, which opened up ties to the economic and political sphere whose exclusion of the inner city had created its sound, style, and ethos. Indicatively, the record which brought about these opportunities was not only crafted by studio executives and performers from outside the Bronx; it nakedly broke Hip Hop's central ethical principle by "biting" rhymes. Thus *from its very origin*, "rap music" lacked an essential connection with the collective values that emerged in the streets of the South Bronx, while simultaneously *co-opting its aesthetic forms* for use in merely romantic expression.

By then, however, Hip Hop had—against seemingly impossible odds—used the sensuous presentation of idealized free subjectivity to liberate its creators from the very worst effects of the renewed war on poor and minority communities, at their most concentrated point. The move from the classical to the romantic form of aesthetic expression coincided with the raising of the artists of the Bronx to a certain, if problematic and tenuous, form of social and political inclusion within the wider social sphere. One might say that Hip Hop culture lost its essential and cohesive ethos at precisely the point at which it lost its strict necessity, or when the heroes of the Bronx, through their self-created and -determining aesthetic culture, gained at least the possibility of re-securing some form of recognized existence within the surrounding socio-economic state. With a certain irony, it was the development of romantic, lyric rap, which was ripe for co-option by the business of spectacular concerts and recording, that opened up the possibility for Hip Hop crews to move beyond the "necropolis", for it was the ensuing interest of the record companies, clubs, critics, reporters, and bohemians of Manhattan and eventually across the globe that allowed Bronx artists (and, following them, some of the informed heads) a way—at least in part—into the social and economic life of the state that had abandoned them. Economic opportunity suddenly arose, names and photos appeared in papers, international coverage of the local phenomenon began to spread, and the most abandoned people in American modernity suddenly found themselves offered at least some minimal form of inclusion within it, through public engagements, international tours, and regular paying gigs. The cost of this "exchange", however, was to fragment the emancipatory community into a mere collection of independent artists, competing with others in the surrounding sphere for increased status. "Rapper's Delight" was released in August of 1979, and many of its pioneers concur with Charlie Ahearn that "hip-hop is dead by 1980".[84]

However, if Hip Hop as a unified and collective culture "died" with its move beyond the Bronx, this was because it had emancipated the abandoned people of the South Bronx from their radical and unique social abandonment, both *as only art can* and *as far as art, on its own, could*.[85] Having gained, through virtually superhuman effort and astonishing aesthetic creation, a kind of foothold in the surrounding social order, Hip Hop transitioned from the sensible presentation of an oppressed community's actualized capacity for collective self-determination to the romantic expression of the contingent, fragmented, yet self-consciously free individuals living (once again, and only in a very limited way) in a stable, modern state. Like Hegel's classical Greek Ideal, Hip Hop was thus a victim of its own emancipatory power, and "died" just because it had already fulfilled its task of raising its people to their rightful claim to self-determining, socially recognized existence in a modern state; as such, it could safely withdraw "to the past".

Bring That Beat Back: From Rap Back to Hip Hop

Or, at least, it should have been, and it is here that Hip Hop's history allows us to most clearly grasp the fundamental *limits* of Hegel's account of art's progress. As we saw in Chap. 2, the South Bronx was the uniquely intense exemplification of the *generalized* renewal of the assault on minority and impoverished communities in the wake of the gains of the 1950s and 1960s. The rise of recorded rap music from the lived culture of Hip

Hop certainly granted *some* individuals *some* level of inclusion that allowed them to identify with the larger culture, or at least the incentive to try to work within its strictures to secure a place therein. This is perhaps why we see the themes of consumption and individual achievement figure so strongly in recorded rap from its earliest development, and steadily increase as it wins mainstream acceptance. The (actually fairly fleeting) fame and (actually fairly small) fortune that attached itself to the core crews of the original scene who broke through certainly brought the South Bronx and its heroic community back into the spotlight; however, if it was no longer radically abandoned and forgotten, the Bronx nevertheless remained in desperate need of a sweeping economic and political revival. Hip Hop did not *overturn* this situation, nor did it even sufficiently amend it to ensure anything like adequate social inclusion; rather, by bringing some economic and social success to a handful of its residents, it merely brought the most excluded and isolated community in the industrialized world back to a kind of *minimal foothold* within it, on a par with other extremely marginalized inner city communities that were often severely *deprived*, without being totally *abandoned*. The Bronx, in short, shifted from being a "necropolis" beyond the pale of even the worst of inner city ruin in other boroughs and cities to, like the others, being a recognized and condemned social problem whose solutions were as obvious as they were unimplemented.

Even more disturbingly, however, the re-inclusion of the Bronx within the broader state not only introduced to the region a host of problems suffered in other, minimally included pockets of repression elsewhere; it coincided with the demonstrable *intensification* of these issues throughout the regions where rap music and other forms of Hip Hop expression were spreading and gaining converts. For example, formerly devoid of police protection, "beginning in the early 1980s, [Bronx] block parties [...] were routinely interrupted by police", often on grounds that "electricity was being used illegally".[86] In 1979, almost exactly simultaneous with the release of "Rapper's Delight", "an astonishingly disingenuous [...] article by neo-conservative Nathan Glazer provided justification [...] for increasingly hysterical policing and punishment efforts directed against youths of color" in the Bronx and in general, by claiming an implicit "connection between the graffiti-makers and the criminals who occasionally rob, rape, assault and murder" in the sense that "all are part of one world of uncontrollable predators" flouting the law.[87] This would soon morph into the infamous "broken windows" theory that justified the "stop-and-frisk" and carding policies, along with other forms of surveillance and profiling whose toxic effect on Black and Latino life in the United States continues up to the present day.[88] That same year, Vice President George H.W. Bush pushed for a renewal and expansion of the war on drugs, now directly involving the CIA and the military in interdiction efforts. Despite these federal efforts (or, as has been plausibly suggested, because of them), starting around 1983–1984—just as rap music gained MTV exposure, and thus broke into the broader mainstream of American pop culture—a new drug that came to be called "crack" began to flood inner cities across the country (much as heroin had at the peak of the Black Power movement), leading legislators and academics, and even many in the affected communities themselves, to push for heavier penalties for users and dealers, and (of course) even greater surveillance by law enforcement. Thus, as Chang argues, just as Hip Hop dissolved into the quickly spreading art of rap music, "the politics of *abandonment*" that produced the emancipatory culture was swiftly replaced by "a politics of *containment*",[89] through coordinated efforts which explicitly and unjustly sought to *control* the inclusion of its original community, while simultaneously *limiting* the culture's emancipatory effects in similarly affected communities, like those in West Philadelphia and East Los Angeles, where the new form of musical poetry, along with Hip Hop's other elements, began to take root and flower.

As we saw in Chap. 1, while he argues that the art is directed towards the achievement of (inclusion within) modern state institutions as a more concrete and stable actualization of the freedom that grounds both, Hegel nevertheless acknowledges that the emergence of such inclusion accompanies the development of a romantic form of subjectivity that emphasizes individual interest at the expense of collective emancipation. If institutions of right are that towards which the religion of art essentially aims, entrance into them is won through the dissolution of its culture and ethos into fragmented individuals seeking their own arbitrary self-expression and satisfaction therein. This, as we also saw, does not preclude the arbitrary erection of barriers that prevent individuals and groups from attaining full inclusion in the state, as clearly demonstrated in the Reagan-era assault on poor and minority communities, whose policies and effects still maintain their grip on the victims of late capitalism. However, if the Bronx was no longer an abandoned necropolis, this was precisely because it, along with other inner city enclaves, became the target of massive and brutal *state interventions*, whose consequence (whether intended or not) was to *ensure* that its people remained only *marginally included* as a surveilled, disenfranchised, contained, often imprisoned, and effectively permanent underclass; and it is just such a possibility that Hegel's Whiggish optimism about history's forward march steadfastly refuses to confront.

Thus, in a stark revelation of the fundamental flaw in Hegel's analysis of the trajectory of art's emancipatory power, the freest state in the modern world actively re-structured itself in order to prevent liberating entrance into its core institutions to a population that had—through the very aesthetic demonstration of the creative and universally human essence that Hegel demands of a truly free people—just powerfully demonstrated the necessity as well as the justice of their inclusion. While Hegel (briefly) diagnoses the factors that can lead to varied forms of state injustice, he considers them peripheral to achieved modernity and thus fails to recognize the existence of what we might call *repressive inclusion*, wherein the state actively structures itself around the containment and control of a targeted community within its borders. Simply put, Hegel presumes too unified a "we" as his focus, disregarding the exclusion of the poor and marginalized throughout history—in particular in the purportedly free modern empires that then, as now, were largely structured around forms of race-based social exclusion and exploitation—thereby blinding himself to fact that the very struggle for freedom that he locates in our aesthetic and political practices does not form one continuous chain for all humanity; such heroic struggles occur *continuously* within and across states, in diverse forms specific to local communities and their circumstances, even as these struggles take, as I have tried to show, a remarkably similar form, precisely because they reflect *the fundamentally human drive for freedom* and *its essential and foundational link, under particularly destitute conditions, to collective aesthetic creation*. If Hegel compellingly explains why art and art alone can liberate us under specific circumstances and only up to a specific point, he nevertheless remains fundamentally and catastrophically mistaken about the relative justice of the modern state and world, as Hip Hop's birth and its community's subsequent suppression viscerally demonstrates.

Hip Hop, then, *should have receded to the past*, for the same reason it *should never have been necessary*: its community had sensibly demonstrated that the drive for self-determination enduringly and ineradicably lives even among those most radically deprived of full protection and recognition within states where contingencies like race continue to "set insuperable barriers to the inherently justified freedom of the spirit". However, the renewed police war on Black, Brown, and impoverished communities that emerged in the 1980s seemed designed precisely to protect the surrounding state from the emancipatory spirit that Hip Hop evinced, both to its progenitors and to those who began to learn about it through the popularity of its resulting commercial products. Thus, having sensibly raised its community to consciousness of their true essence, rather than receding to its well-earned place in the past, Hip Hop was effectively *forced to endure as a largely aesthetic movement*; its art, even in its era of romantic decline, thus *retained its emancipatory promise and endured as an emancipatory form of expression*, just because more directly political emancipation remained unjustly closed to its community.

If it was to endure as *emancipatory*, however, Hip Hop could not remain in the same forms in which it arose. Just as the problems targeted communities faced in the post-"Rapper's Delight"-era were distinct from those unique to the Bronx in 1969, so the people within them no longer stood in need of *sensible evidence of their essential freedom*. Art could not, by means of sensible expression alone, liberate those who were included, by being confined and repressed, within the most modern of states. The politics of containment demanded a new form of struggle, built on the gains of Hip Hop's aesthetic liberation, but reflective of the fact that direct transition into civil society and state life was precluded for those closest to the edge. Moreover, thanks to the heroic struggle for creative self-determination in the previous decade in the South Bronx, *one of the few avenues for social advancement that remained open was in the newly developed entertainment field of rap music*, which was beginning to be embraced across the globe.

Thus, a tension arose between the economic and expressive avenues within the containing state that rap music opened up for those who still lived on the fringes of the social order, and the potent and essential emancipatory spirit that had been awakened and organized by its founding culture. Rap music, entering the mainstream of American life as Hip Hop's poetic voice, would be torn between an adherence to the aesthetic standards and social expectations developed *outside of Hip Hop culture*, but which facilitated social inclusion for its poets and producers, and the spiritual drive for collective and ethically grounded self-determination *that defined the Hip Hop community*, but which now needed to be compellingly and clearly preached to both its own community and to the surrounding world. As we will see in the next chapter, this tension would produce not only a new form of rap poetry, but a fundamental shift in the direction of Hip Hop culture's self-expression, which moved *away* from its exclusive focus on the aesthetic, *towards* a more universal and direct expression of the need for collective emancipation. That is, if Hip Hop could not yet take its proper place in the past, it could nevertheless only carry forth its promise by supplementing the mainstreaming of rap music with a more explicit articulation of its spiritual core; one that took aesthetic and non-aesthetic forms as the culture sought to resist the worst effects of its appropriation by mainstream forces inaugurated by "Rapper's Delight". That is, faced with the increasingly broad appropriation of rap music and the mounting intensification of the politics of containment, Hip Hop both gave birth to a *new style of poetry* and was compelled to add a *fifth element*; it is to these final creations that we now turn.

NOTES

1. A good discussion of the origin and impact of this record can be found in Chap. 1 of Loren Kajikawa, *Sounding Race in Rap Songs* (Oakland: University of California Press, 2015), whose epigram (19) contains quotes from Flash and Chuck D. on the general scepticism regarding the value and possibility of recording Hip Hop music (although part of the quote attributed to Chuck D. actually comes from disco emcee Eddie Cheeba; see Chang, *Can't Stop*, 130). While "Rapper's Delight" is usually cited as the "first" rap record, cases have been made for both New York/Philadelphia radio DJ Jocko Henderson's novelty song "Rhythm Talk (Ain't No Stoppin' Us Now)" and the New York-based disco troupe Fatback Band's B-side "King Tim III (Personality Jock)".

2. Quoted in Perkins, "The Rap Attack", 6. B-boy and Bambaataa affiliate Afrika Islam similarly recalls that the initial "allegiance was to music and the record" (Fricke and Ahearn, 46), not the MC.

3. Quoted in Fricke and Ahearn, 35.

4. This and the previous sentence, Grandmaster Caz, in Ibid., 339.

5. George, *hip hop america*, 20, emphasis added.

6. Fricke and Ahearn, 75.

7. This collection of classic "prison toasts" was a solo project recorded by Last Poet Jalal Mansur Nuriddin under the pseudonym Lightnin' Rod, and actually proved far more influential on early rappers than his political work with his group (*pace*, e.g. I. Miller, 72).

8. Quoted in Alice Price-Styles, "MC Origins: rap and spoken word poetry", in *The Cambridge Companion to Hip-Hop*, ed. Justin Williams (Cambridge: Cambridge University Press, 2015), 11–21 (13).

9. *The Adventures of Grandmaster Flash*, 103–5.

10. Speaking in *The Hip Hop Years*.
11. "Jamaican toasting? Naw, naw. No connection there. I couldn't play reg-gae in the Bronx. People couldn't accept it", quoted in Kevin O'Brian Chang and Wayne Chen, *Reggae Roots: The Story of Jamaican Music* (Philadelphia: Temple University Press, 1998), 72. There are other instances, however, of him affirming the lineage (e.g. Brewster and Broughton, *DJ Revolutionaries*, 174), although this is in the context of him specifying that his rapping didn't involve rhymes, but was centred on "little short sayings" in a manner similar to toasting.
12. Quoted in Chang, *Can't Stop*, 82.
13. Grandmaster Flash, quoted in Fricke and Ahearn, 74, emphasis added.
14. Furious Five MC The Kidd Creole, in Ibid.
15. Herc and Caz both cite him as the first, as does Nelson George, *hip hop america*, 17. While many histories (e.g. Ewoodzie, 184) imply that he was a subsequent addition to Herc's crew, Coke himself claims to have taken the mic at the very first party on Sedgwick Avenue (interview with Steven Hager, available on his YouTube page: https://www.youtube.com/watch?v=Hqi-_g894ss [Accessed July 2016]).
16. The Kidd Creole, in Fricke and Ahearn, 75.
17. Quoted in Ibid., 29.
18. Knox interpolates some terms to Hegel's text, here, but in a way that strikes me as clarifying, rather than distorting; the original, terse passage is "*Das Epos, Wort, Sage, sagt überhaupt, was die Sache ist, die zum Worte vervandelt wird*".
19. Etter, 125; thus, it "can arise only *after* a people has awakened, but *before* law has become codified" (128, emphasis added).
20. Toop, 69.
21. Speaking in *The Hip Hop Years*.
22. Examples I heard from Grandmaster Caz when I took his bus tour of Hip Hop history. If you're in NYC, a Hush tour, especially with Caz at the helm, is an absolute must for anyone interested in the early years of Hip Hop.
23. Toop, 37.
24. Lil' Rodney C from the Funky Four (+ One More), in Toop, 71; Flash bolsters this by claiming he recruited Cowboy because "I needed a cheer-leader. I needed somebody to tell the crowd who I was" (*The Adventures of Grandmaster Flash*, 103). However, along with the widely accepted claims below surrounding who introduced rhyme into MCing, this is con-tested by Coke La Rock in the interview with Hager.
25. A number of pre-"Rapper's Delight"-era recordings of crews like Flash and the Furious Four/Five circulate on YouTube, some very early routines are recalled in *The Adventures of Grandmaster Flash*, 106–110, and brief

transcriptions of Herc's crew "rapping" can be found in Fernando Orejuela, *Rap and Hip Hop Culture* (Oxford: Oxford University Press, 2014), 59.

26. The epic primarily serves to "describe those events and actions which attain major social significance" within an aesthetic community, yet in a manner that "concentrates more on the actual behaviour [displayed] rather than on the psychological feelings of the individuals involved in heroic action" (Kaminsky, 141; 152).

27. Chang, *Can't Stop*, 113. Compare, Brewster and Broughton, *DJ Revolutionaries*, 183: "If I play the get-down part of 10 records in succession and keep em on time, I'm gonna have the audience in this total uproar. I'm gonna be the man. I'm gonna beat Kool Herc. But when I went outside [to a block party], it was totally quiet. [...] Almost like a speaking engagement". In *The Adventures of Grandmaster Flash*, 82–90, he describes the incident in more precise detail, and credits the mentorship of disco spinner Pete DJ Jones with helping him recover from his initial disappointment.

28. Ibid. Compare Flash, quoted in Toop: "the crowd would stop dancing and just gather around as if it was a seminar. This was what I didn't want. This wasn't school—it was time to shake your ass. From there I knew it was important to have vocal entertainment" (71), or Hager who claims "'emcees' [...] were supposed to keep the crowd dancing by talking over a microphone" (Ch. 3). As Price-Styles argues, the original MCs began with the "intention of encouraging people to dance and raise the energy levels of the crowd" (13).

29. *The Adventures of Grandmaster Flash*, 105.

30. Cf., Brewster and Broughton, *DJ Revolutionaries*, 184: "I [...] put a microphone on the other side of the table and [would] see if anyone could vocalise to this rearrangement of an arrangement [i.e. on time]. And nobody could, until Keith grabbed the mic. Keith Wiggins, who was known as Cowboy. And he wasn't technically good, like he wouldn't go into any thesaurical, dictionarial [sic], heavy words; he was simple. And he was more like *the ringleader of a circus*. So it kind of *averted attention away from me*" (emphasis added).

31. Fricke and Ahearn, 96. While it is chronologically somewhat late in the poetry's development, the circulating copy (on YouTube at the time of writing) of the battle between the L-Brothers and the Herculords at Galaxy 2000 in 1978 provides a good example of this early form of MCing to facilitate the battles of DJs and dancing.

32. As many DJs recalled, "people were going to jams and pulling out guns and shooting up the place; people were getting bum-rushed or being robbed" and thus "You had to bring your gang of people [...] You had to

bring your gang for protection" (DJ Disco Wiz, and then Kool DJ AJ, quoted in Fricke and Ahearn, 90).

33. Orejuela, 64.

34. As DJ Charlie Chase recalls from the first jam he attended, "this one guy, he isn't even really rhyming, he's just blurting out stuff. Maybe every now and again he'll say a little rhyme, one line maybe, and that's it" (Ewoodzie, 155).

35. Orejuela, 65, emphasis added.

36. Creole is given authorship of the phrase by a host of early MCs who took it up and carried it forward in the documentary *The Show* (1995; directed by Brian Robbins).

37. Orejuela, 65.

38. Fricke and Ahearn, 97, emphasis added.

39. Ibid., 74, emphasis added. As Flash claims "Mel dropped *serious* English on the crowd when he spoke. Mel [...] could also get extremely creative with words, writing line after line to make you think. I'd be tripping on something he'd said, and by the time I could get my head around it, he'd have spat three more verses, just as clever [...] *nobody* wrote rhymes like Mel" (*The Adventures of Grandmaster Flash*, 108). This, perhaps, explains why Chuck D., in *Fight the Power: Rap, Race, and Reality*, with Yusuf Jah (New York: Delta, 1997) claims that "The first guy I heard really do rapping right [...] was Melle Mel" (71). While some credit the rhyming shift to fellow crew member Cowboy, there is little dispute among historians of the genre that something changed in the art of Hip Hop poetry when Grandmaster Flash recruited these three MCs, and that everyone seeking entrance or continued relevance in the Bronx scene quickly followed suit. Ewoodzie, in fact, argues that "When Herc and Bambaataa were at the helm, b-boys were the main attraction. When Flash became the star [...] it was the MCs' performances that people came to see" (124), leading to the development of "rapping". More on this below.

40. Price-Styles, 14.

41. I quite like the account of this episode (along with alternative accounts) in Ed Piskor's brilliant graphic novel *Hip Hop Family Tree, Vol. 1* (Seattle: Fantagraphics, 2013), but a more scholarly treatment can be found in Ewoodzie, 128–30.

42. Fricke and Ahearn, 75.

43. As Hegel puts it "it is especially lyric [poetry] that is fondest of using rhymes owing to its subjective character" (1031/III, 314).

44. Ogbar, 45.

45. I rely, here, on the facsimile of the original lyrics in *Written: The Lyrics of Grandmaster Caz* (Godalming, UK: The Lyric Book Company, 2012), 39. This is an essential resource on the early history of rap lyricism by arguably its most influential pioneer.

46. This directly contradicts an anecdote Flash tells from their pre-recording days, when Cowboy objected to Melle Mel's insistence that the Furious Four be expanded (through the addition of Mr. Ness) to the Furious Five by shouting "You ain't the boss of this outfit [...] It's Grandmaster *Flash ... and* the Furious Four MCs" (*The Adventures of Grandmaster Flash*, 108, second ellipses and italics in original). While there is obviously good reason, given the crew's tumultuous history, to read some of his account of these episodes with a grain of salt, it is interesting that Flash's memoir portrays Mel's stunningly unique and revolutionary lyricism as sowing the seed of individualism and self-seeking within the crew and, in some sense, the culture; in part, in fact, because Flash claims it was Mel who initially pushed the group to leave their original label (Enjoy) and sign with Sugar Hill, precisely so they could top the mainstream success of "Rapper's Delight" (cf., 140).

47. After a few name and personnel changes, they eventually became the Funky 4 + 1 (More), best known for their immortal singles "Rappin and Rocking the House" and "That's The Joint".

48. Perry, 70, emphasis added.

49. Fricke and Ahearn, 111, emphasis added.

50. Kaminsky, 141.

51. Fricke and Ahearn, 117. Compare Rutter, "Whereas the epic poet disappears into his work [...] it is privilege and duty of the lyric poet to remain in view" (186). They were also, apparently, the first group to add harmony vocal-laden hooks to their rhymes, increasing the presence of performed song within the poetic field, as discussed below.

52. Of course, other figures and acts have been claimed as crucial to making this shift. Rahiem, for example, claims that "MCs didn't really play a pivotal role in hip-hop until the three MCs that were down with Flash became the Furious 4" (Ibid., 142).

53. As b-boy Trac 2 recalls, "our main priority as dancers was the music; we didn't care about who the hell was MCing" (speaking in *From Mambo to Hip-Hop*).

54. Lovebug Starski, in Fricke and Ahearn, 141. The full quote reads: "You know the way some people go to church to catch the Holy Ghost? That's how I caught the Holy Ghost—at a party. That was my spiritual thing".

55. Rahiem, in Ibid., 142, emphasis added.

56. YouTube interview with Steven Hager.

57. Fricke and Ahearn, 174 (second ellipses in original).

58. Ibid, 117.

59. Chang, *Can't Stop*, 114.

60. Charise Cheney, *Brothers Gonna Work it Out: Sexual Politics in the Golden Age of Rap Nationalism* (New York: New York University Press, 2005), 7.

While Cheney dates this to the post-recording era of the 1980s, my contention is that Sugar Hill Records and their competitors did not *create* the rap star, but merely *packaged* an internal development within the Bronx scene for mainstream consumption; thus one might say that it *completed*, rather than *initiated*, rap's separation from the unified culture of Hip Hop.

61. In fact, MC battles were generally less common than those between DJs and, in particular, breakers. Again, more research is needed on this somewhat obscure timeline, but I've heard members of the Cold Crush Brothers and Fantastic Five claim that the legendary crews only battled once (the Five apparently won, although the Cold Crush still contest it). While MCs would often refer to the inferiority of their opponents' skills, these battles, it should be noted, were strictly for *lyrical supremacy*, and were judged on rhyming and vocal delivery skills *alone*. It wasn't until the infamous 1981 Harlem World MC contest—in which Kool Moe Dee shocked the Hip Hop scene with a supremely lyrical (and often trenchantly accurate) takedown of the more primal, epic style of Busy Bee—that the now-infamous, insult-based form of "rap battling" began. You can find his routine with a quick google.

62. Quoted in Chang, *Can't Stop*, 132. The second quote is Chang commenting on Ahearn's analysis. Grandmaster Flash saw this as an inevitable development, at least once rap records were considered: "I knew that eventually when it became wax I would get special versions of [a single] that only I had, that we would [then] perform. Live. No Vocals. No nothing. Raw track. And we would do it live. And that's what I would have. And that's what we did [i.e. play the instrumental single when the MCs rapped]. We also made *a show* where they would disappear for a while, go off in the wings and I would do my thing. *It was a show. A show.*" (Brewster and Broughton, *DJ Revolutionaries*, 188, emphasis added).

63. Herc claims this starts as early as 1975 or 1976 (Brewster and Broughton, *DJ Revolutionaries*, 171), although as with much of this early history, different dates are suggested in different sources, or even by the same figures at different times. Ewoodzie claims Herc moved indoors in 1974, and there were certainly informal "clubs" operating in the burned out buildings of the Bronx around that time, which may both have helped facilitate this move to legal or quasi-legal Bronx clubs and explain some of the confusion in chronology. Flash claims that when he started his residency at the "rocking hellhole for the b-boy scene" in December of 1976, the Black Door was "far from legal" (*The Adventures of Grandmaster Flash*, 96), while others cite his residency there as one of the key shifts to the broader and established club scene. But 1977 assuredly marks the pivotal year in the shift from the rec rooms and block parties into clubs that became more or less permanent for the established crews and those who sought to join them, even as park jams not only continued but spread to other areas.

64. 80s MC Reggie Reg, from the Crash Crew, recalls that "Hip-hop was in the Bronx for like five years before it came to Manhattan. And the way it came to Manhattan was through the high schools. A lot of kids from the Bronx would have these mix tapes of Flash, Bambaataa, Kool Herc, the L-Brothers. In Manhattan, we ain't heard nothing like that. We was more into what they would call the R&B DJ, like Hollywood, Eddie Cheeba, Reggie Wells. Not the real hip-hop [...] that has a lot of rhymes and stuff. [...] We kind of copied that" (Fricke and Ahearn, 81). Again, you can easily find recordings of Hollywood and Cheeba online, along with routines by the Cold Crush Brothers, Funky Four, and others to compare their distinct MC styles.

65. Cold Crush Brothers' MC Richard Sisco, in Ibid., 195.

66. Chang, *Can't Stop*, 128.

67. Ibid., 129.

68. Ibid.

69. Many agree with Nelson George that the Sugarhill Gang's debut single's "title gave the uptown MCs the title 'rappers', which [...] stuck"; tellingly, "many old schoolers disdain the rap label to this day and continue to favor MC" (*hip hop america*, 29).

70. Sujatha Fernandes, *Close to the Edge: In Search of the Global Hip Hop Generation* (London: Verso, 2011), 1.

71. Chang, *Can't Stop*, 132.

72. Ibid., 133.

73. Quoted in Hess, 32.

74. Toop, 16. Compare *The Adventures of Grandmaster Flash*, 140: "Hank's fronting like he's big shit, but everybody on the street knows he stole his rhymes. Hank ain't the real. But Hank's rocking a fur coat, gold chains, and a big limo".

75. Sha-Rock, quoted in Fricke and Ahearn, 216.

76. Kool Herc and his crew are one glaring exception; his first appearance on record didn't come until the 1990s, when he guested on a solo album by Public Enemy's scratch DJ, Terminator X, called *Super Bad*.

77. Katz, 75.

78. Funky Four DJ Baron, quoted in Fricke and Ahearn, 215. As he puts it elsewhere, "When we went into the studio, and [the MCs] got their first payment of 600 dollars it was, 'Ha ha ... we don't need Breakout and Baron no more. We got our own money. We let our records play for us.' That's how it went. That's how we faded away" (Katz, 76).

79. Chang, *Can't Stop*, 141.

80. "I once read somewhere that for a culture to really be a complete culture, it should have a music, a dance and a visual art. And then I realized, wow, all these things are going on. You got the graffiti happening over here, you

got the breakdancing, and you got the DJ and MC thing. In my head, they were all one thing." (quoted in Ibid., 149). It is perhaps relevant that he was a later generation writer (starting in around 1978), whose best known work was the Warhol "soup can" masterpiece that the city allowed to run, rather than buff, and who began with the intention to "be an artist like these pop artists" (quoted in Fricke and Ahearn, 281).

81. Cf. Crazy Legs speaking in the early 1980s: "if we're gonna battle anybody, we just start a fun battle, 'cause battles, now, usually they cause fights, 'cause these days they don't know how to handle them, so they get jealous, and they get mad when they lose. But, back in the old days, everybody used to still get along, there wasn't no fight when they used to battle, but now you have these new people coming along that try to think they was in the old days, and try to run things. They like to just start fights, even after they battle. But now if we do it, if we battle, we just do *our own little show*, we battle between each other, there's no grudges against nobody because we're doing it for fun, it doesn't really mean that [much] when we go down after each other, *it's just a show for the people*" (speaking in *Rock Steady*, dir. Anthony Ralph, emphasis mine).

82. Quoted in Chang, *Can't Stop*, 177.

83. *Hip Hop*, in the chapter entitled "The Pied Piper of Hip Hop".

84. Chang, *Can't Stop*, 132.

85. This resonates, at least to a degree, with the words of Zulu Nation affiliate, early Chicago MC, and Hip Hop teacher Lord Cashus D in the documentary, *Whatever Happened to Hip Hop?* (2009; directed by Sonali Aggarwal). In the context of a broader conversation about the various forces that may have derailed the culture, he argues that in 1975—that is, right around the period Hip Hop arguably reached its peak as a unified, communal, aesthetic culture through the arrival of DJ crews developing new techniques, and rhythmic and rhyming MCs revealing the power of the word at jams that were still centred around breakers and cyphers—"we were at our power as a Black people, *we could have actually jumped forward in our time.* When Hip Hop came along, that was *our birth for the jump forward*".

86. Usher, 100.

87. Chang, *Can't Stop*, 135. The latter two quotations are from Glazer's article, "On Subway Graffiti in New York", *The Public Interest* 54 (Winter 1979) 3–11.

88. For a compelling account of the origin, evolution, and enduring effects of the "broken windows" theory, see Matt Taibbi, *I Can't Breathe: A Killing on Bay Street* (New York: Spiegel & Grau, 2017).

89. Chang, *Can't Stop*, 136, emphasis added.

CHAPTER 6

Knowledge, or From Art to Religion, Philosophy and Politics

PROLOGUE

In the late 1970s, activist and teacher Daryl Aamaa Nubyahn "noticed kids around [his] block in the Bronx doing rap" and became skilled enough in the art himself to use it as an aid in his vocational training courses.[1] However, he was distressed about the fact that, despite the omnipresence of the appealing form of poetry in his borough, "there was no message" to it; rap seemed to merely be a way for contingent individuals to "soup themselves up [claiming] I'm a movie star, I've got all the women in the world" and so on. The idealized self, of course, originally helped local residents to envision their self-determining agency beyond the restrictions of the Bronx, and thus was core to the culture's ethos; but Nubyahn presciently saw within its *poetic* form the prevalence of the kind of narcissistic, materialistic bravado that would eventually be shorthanded to "bling", and which enjoys a dominant market share in rap music up to the present day. Soon enough, he had the "idea of hooking up rap with political information" to combat the trend and set about writing what would become the first "conscious" rap record. In 1980, under the surprisingly direct moniker of Brother D. with Collective Effort, he released "How We Gonna Make The Black Nation Rise" on the newly formed Clappers label (which thereafter, in an inverse of Hip Hop's musical trajectory, focused on roots reggae). As with other early rap songs, the music was lifted directly from a disco anthem ("Got to Be Real" by Cheryl Lynn, which was used on a few early rap records); the lyrics, however,

© The Author(s) 2018
J. Vernon, *Hip Hop, Hegel, and the Art of Emancipation*,
https://doi.org/10.1007/978-3-319-91304-9_6

harshly excoriated party cultures in general for what appeared to him to be their cheerful indifference to the crumbling blocks and increasing repression surrounding them.[2] Its lyrics paired haunting descriptions of the horrors that continued to plague the region, as well as impoverished and minority communities throughout the country at the dawn of the Reagan era (e.g. "Can't you see/What's really goin' on?/Unemployment's high, the housing's bad/And the schools are teaching wrong/Cancer from the water, pollution in the air") that were designed "To bring the truth right on down to earth" or "educate [the listener] to the real deal", with accusatory lines that demanded a move *away from* the celebratory parties that begat rap into a more direct form of emancipatory education, expression, and engagement, in the Bronx and beyond (e.g. "Space out y'all to the disco rhyme/Movin' to the rhythm but you're wastin' time" and "While you're partying on, on, on and on/The ovens may be hot by the break of dawn"). That is, Brother D., on the one hand, promised to "rap for the people, tell 'em where it's at", using sophisticated lyricism to describe the objective conditions within which the subjects celebrating idealized selves actually lived, while, on the other hand, simultaneously demanded a *less aesthetic*, more explicit, and effective response to those conditions, by exhorting his audience "change the way we behave/[and] sacrifice for our righteous cause", rather than preserving the celebratory religion of art. As its closing couplet chants, the problem posed in the wake of Hip Hop's aesthetic re-awakening of collective spirit demanded a non-aesthetic answer: "How we gonna make the Black Nation rise?/We gotta agitate, educate, and organize!".

As Hager notes, while "it was an explosively effective record, it was far too political to ever attain widespread popularity in hip hop circles" at the time. The leap from the lyrical celebration of self in rap music, or even from the communal ritual of the block party, directly into an explicit and militant form of political discourse and action was simply too great to be of appeal to those whose inclusion into the order of the surrounding society was so tenuous, and who had gained it through the cheerful idealization of the divine self. Nubyahn correctly saw that the emancipatory power of collective spirit was being thwarted by the focus on the contingently individual, self-absorbed subject that largely defined the romantic lyrics of the new rap music; however, as the record's popular failure suggests, the more directly emancipatory spirit of Hip Hop would nevertheless need to emerge *from within the artistic culture itself*, which needed to, as Hegel puts it, "create a living entry for new, contemporary ideas about politics" that spoke to those who remained at the repressed margins of the state (1180/III, 503). If Brother D. correctly posed the problem that emerged in the wake of Hip Hop's "death", his proposed solution would need time to develop; however, his simultaneous use of rap poetry to aesthetically express the objective social conditions that required overcoming, and his explicit distinguishing of the emancipatory freedom, discourse, and movement needed to overcome them from aesthetic forms of expression, presciently identified the fundamental tension that has continuously dominated internal debates about the spirit of Hip Hop in the age of rap music. And some may find it suprising that, in the wake of "Rapper's Delight", the "reality rap" that would soon saturate the market actually found its origin *outside* the Hip Hop community in general, while the more explicitly conscious discourses of collective spirit called for by Brother D. were developed *inside* the original Bronx community precisely in response to it.

RAP, REALITY AND REVOLT: DRAMATIC POETRY

In terms of both the form and content of poetry, in the emergence of commercial rap music from Hip Hop,

> we have seen the general artistic development of the classical gods emerge more and more out of the tranquility of the Ideal into the variety of individual and external appearance, into the detailing of events, happenings, and actions which become ever more and more human. [That is,] classical art proceeds at last, in its content, to the separation into contingent individualization [i.e. the singular mind of the particular MC; and] in its form to the comfortable and the attractive [i.e. art made to please a general audience, rather than to impress a knowledgeable and ethical community]. (500/II, 106, trans. modified)

The emergence of lyricism reveals that "the human being, as actual subjectivity, must be made the principle" of art (519/II, 129, emphasis added), and precisely as "the mundane and human subject" (793/III, 12) for "thereby alone [...] does [classical] anthropomorphism reach its consummation" (519/II, 129). Lyric subjectivity consummates art's work of sensuously revealing the infinite freedom essential to all, by expressing it in a form anyone can grasp as their own; not only despite, but in and through, the constraints of their mundane finitude. By contrast with the classical, in romantic art, "what is further developed is *not* the substantial, the meaning of the gods and their universal element; on the contrary, it is the *finite* aspect, sensuous existence and the subjective inner life, which are to arouse interest and give satisfaction" (501/II, 107, emphasis added). And it is this shift—to an artist who uses their uniquely individual creative resources to please contingent and diverse spectators, or who, rather than "raising an individual over their particularity, [...] lets them remain at peace therein"— that, for Hegel, demands the production of a new form of poetry (500/II, 106, trans. modified).

As we have seen, like the classical religion of art from which they emerged, "epic or [at least early] lyric poems have a public consisting as it were of *specialists*" (1174/III, 496, emphasis added). It was the informed and immersed heads of the Hip Hop scene that the earliest MCs needed to impress, and they did so through displays of innovative language use, as well as creative and continual participation in the established, broader culture. With the move to clubs and recordings, however, the public for rap poetry shifted from the founding cognoscenti of the Bronx to literally anyone, anywhere, and thus an audience "brought together *haphazardly* for the purpose of pronouncing judgment, [which becomes] extremely mixed in character: its members differ in education, interests, habitual tastes, predilections, etc." (1175/III, 496, emphasis added). Lacking a unifying set of collectively determined ethical and aesthetic standards, in such a situation "everyone pronounces judgment out of his own head, and approves or condemns [a work] just as the accident of his own personal views, feelings or caprices dictates" (1175/III, 497). Consequently, the demand for personal satisfaction on the part of the audience gradually begins to dictate the form and content of the poetry produced. Rather than expressing their contingent personality in lyrical songs of self, those who wanted to succeed in the newly emerging form of competition for club and recording gigs were forced to consider how a work would be received by an incredibly broad and diverse (and now, of course, potentially *well-paying*) audience. Thus, rather than speaking her mind, the MC increasingly had to use her idiosyncratic imagination to appeal to, or express, the lives and desires of a broad and diverse audience; and it is precisely this need, in the *Lectures on Aesthetics*, that signals the arrival of *dramatic poetry*.

Dramatic poetry—which, for Hegel, is the consummation of romantic art—only emerges once "the free self-consciousness of human aims, complications, and fates [...] have been already completely aroused and developed in a way possible only in epochs of the [...] later development of a national life" (1159/III, 476).[3] Moreover, because romantic poetry's emphasis on "inner [spirit] expresses itself at the same time in the *human mode*, and the human being *stands in connection with the entire* [surrounding] *world*, [...] this implies at the same time *a wide variety* in both the spiritually subjective sphere and also the external [realm] to which the spirit relates itself" (521/II, 132, emphasis added). If participants in the religion of art hold themselves and their celebrated artists to communally determined standards that seek to improve those internal to the culture, romantic spectators demand to be *pleased as the contingent individuals that they happen to be*. Thus, it is unsurprising that rap poetry, cut loose from the unified Hip Hop community, "opens out into a multiplicity without bounds", just because it must now appeal to an arbitrary collection of fragmented and distinct individuals who come from as far away as records and radio waves can travel (525/II, 138). MCs thus needed to confront the fact that the broader "public [...] will not be content at all to be confronted [...] with the rather accidental whims and moods of the individual tendencies of [...] the lyric poet" (1179/III, 502); rather, they will seek to see *their own* finite interests and expectations reflected therein. Romantic drama thus:

> displays the unity of divine and human subjectivity not simply in general but as *this* man [and thus] there enter here, again, in art, on account of the content itself, all the aspects of the contingency and particularity of external, finite existence from which beauty at the height of the classical Ideal had been purified. (536/II, 150)

If the central topic, and lesson, of classical art is that free, universal spirit is our living essence and thus that actualizing it is our essential task, the central topic of romantic drama is the fact that the finitude of human particularity is the only vehicle for actualizing it, and thus contingent individuality must become a—indeed, the—topic of artistic investigation. Because human finitude expands itself into a "multiplicity without bounds", individuals will grasp the link between their particularity and their universal essence in diverse ways; correspondingly, dramatic poets will tailor their work to one or more of these forms of understanding to target a different potential audience. In other words, once lyrical rap emerged from the classical culture of its origins, it was bound to become dramatic; and once it became dramatic, it was bound to split into a number of subgenres that attract distinct audiences, in a process that we see continue unabated to this day.

We cannot possibly do justice, here, to the diversity of rap genres, even as they emerged from the early years of its recording industry, as the proliferation of themes and styles is simply too great.[4] We will and must, however, examine the emergence of what quickly became the most dominant form of dramatic rap music, and the one that perhaps best exemplifies the nature of romantic drama: what is often called "reality" rap, or the visceral depiction of the experiences of the alienated underclass (i.e. rap music as the "Black CNN").[5] As we saw above, when Brother D. attempted to bring this kind of stark truth to rap music, his moralizing tone and condemnation of the celebratory aesthetic in general placed his work at an extreme distance from both the original culture and the given interests of his potential audiences. This may, however, help explain why reality rap found its first popular expression in the most unlikely of sources.

"That's the Breaks": Dramatic Comedy

Kurtis Blow was an MC and DJ from Harlem and, while he would occasionally cross boroughs for a party, his style was largely derived from DJ Hollywood and the disco scene, rather than the more advanced MCs of the Bronx. Perhaps correspondingly, his primary drive was not to compete for lyrical mastery, but to somehow succeed in the music industry, which was suddenly craving rap music. He studied vocal performance at the City College of New York while also directing the campus radio station, but on nights and weekends, he performed in the clubs of Harlem and Queens. Enlisting (soon-to-be Rush Productions mogul) Russell Simmons as his manager, he was then connected with producers Rocky Ford (a former Billboard writer who longed to put a disco rapper like Hollywood on wax) and lyricist J.B. Moore. After seeing the success of "Rapper's Delight", Ford decided that a *novelty* song—specifically, a Christmas record—would be the perfect vehicle for launching rap even further into the mainstream, and Moore rapidly produced "lyrics to a rapping parody of 'The Night Before Christmas'".[6] Blow agreed to record "Christmas Rappin", adding some of the concluding lyrics to the song, which was eventually picked up by Mercury Records. The novelty hit was of necessarily limited and seasonal interest,[7] but sold well enough that they commissioned a full album, the majority of which was written by Moore and some collaborating songwriters; its breakthrough single, however, was conceived of by the MC himself, who suggested recording something for the b-boys and b-girls.

"The Breaks" began simply from Blow's intention to create a record that would contain a number of extended "get down" passages, so that even in the clubs where DJs merely spun records, dancers would have sections during which they could pull out their best moves. Moore, who had no real experience with the original culture, began to craft lyrics based on the multiple meanings of the title phoneme (thus the bizarre opening couplet, "Brakes on a bus, brakes on a car/Breaks to make you a superstar"), but with a particular focus on the *unlucky* "breaks" one gets in life. Virtually none of the rhymes bore any remote relation to the Bronx scene, save the occasional reminder that the song's "breaks will rock your shoes", which were generic enough to resonate just as well with Manhattan's disco hustlers. The lyrics, however, were recited in a staged version of the call-and-response between MC and audience in the party and club scenes, with a fake audience providing atmospheric cheers throughout, and punctuating Blow's lyrics with the repeated catchphrase "That's the breaks".

For many outside the burgeoning scene, this likely felt like a "safe" version of the party experience that, after the success of the Sugarhill Gang, had been widely discussed in the media; it would thus appeal to outsiders looking for a way into the mysterious culture, allowing them to sing along at the club, at home, or in their car, as though they were themselves a part of the scene. It was also performed over an inviting and mid-tempo disco beat, ideal for more casual dancing, but with enough percussion breaks that b-boys and b-girls might be tempted to the floor. Thus, "The Breaks"—crafted by professional songwriters from within the mainstream industry, interpreting the wishes of a rapper who was both familiar with and respectful of Hip Hop culture—seemed intentionally designed to appeal to a maximally broad array of contingently assembled individuals.

As noted, the crowd's catchphrase emphasized the *bad* breaks one gets, with every call and response section isolating details of everyday life that would resonate with many in an era of generalized economic downturn, but especially with the alienated and contained communities who—even as its popularity expanded—still formed the primary base of rap's audience. Although lyrics like "And you borrowed money from the mob/And yesterday you lost your job", or "He took you out to the Red Coach grill/But he forgot the cash and you paid the bill" have an almost pantomime quality, they nevertheless also affirm the realities of the economically excluded, meeting the expectations for such a voice which rap's emergence had fostered in those with an increasing fascination about a culture alien from their own, while simultaneously echoing the frustrations of those enduring varied forms and degrees of containment. One could either identify with the "life is hard, but what to do?" sentiment in the lyrics or aesthetically appreciate them as that which they presumed the "poetry of the streets" would predictably present. So widespread was this appeal, in fact, that Blow became the first rapper to officially go gold.

In Hegelian terms, what we see here is the broad, yet fragmented appeal of romantic art, in distinction from the specialized, but unified audience for the classical, which is necessarily forged through an emphasis on merely given, particular finitude. The classical Ideal emerges in a community whose restrictive circumstances demand the sensuous presentation of free spirit as "complete in itself, independent, reserved [...] a well-rounded individual that spurns otherness from itself [and whose] shape is its own: it lives entirely in it and in it alone, and may not surrender any part of it to affinity with the merely empirical and contingent" (532/II, 145, trans. modified). Such figures allow a repressed community to sensuously grasp the universal essence within their own contingent individuality as intrinsically and infinitely free. However, when such a consciously free individual—like those in the society surrounding the Bronx, or those freshly liberated from total abandonment within it—albeit into a form of state containment rather than true inclusion

> approaches these ideal figures as a [mere] spectator [they] cannot make their existence [their] own as something external related to his own external appearance; [for] although the shapes of the external gods are human, they still do not belong to the mortal realm, for these gods [do not appear to have] themselves experienced the deficiency of finite existence but are directly raised above it. (532/II, 145)

While classical art aesthetically presents human *perfection*, this idealized presentation, nevertheless, "must be of such a kind that it can express itself completely in the *natural human form*" revealing that, even when idealized, sensuously presented "spirit is at once determined as *particular and human*" (78–9/I, 110, emphasis added). Romantic drama, we might say, is the poetic presentation of the ineluctable fact that particular finitude must serve as the vehicle for infinite spirit, and through its *mundane* form. The emergence of dramatic poetry within a culture signifies that, having liberated its community from restrictive finitude to the limited extent that art can, art now allows one to "take [such finitude] up immediately, *as it finds it*", just in order to aesthetically express their freedom from determination by finitude as it stands (531/II, 144, emphasis added). Thus, in "The Breaks"—which is something like a rap version of "Que Sera, Sera"—we find the poetic presentation of the merely given, radically imperfect circumstances of finite life, alongside an affirmation of our capacity for nevertheless reconciling ourselves to it, through an act of inner will, or the aesthetic presentation of what Hegel will deem the "romantic Ideal". In this, it gives clear presentation to the "task" of romantic art; the presentation of the spiritually "divine as interiority in the externality from which it separates itself [*das Göttliche als Innigkeit in der Äußerlichkeit, dieser selbst sich entnehmend dar*]".[8]

"The Breaks" thus reflects what Hegel calls poetic drama, which presents the lyrical individual, now raised into the self-assurance of inner imagination, and who confronts circumstances within which free individuality finds its chosen aims *thwarted*, rather than actualized; more precisely, it reflects the *comedic* form of drama, for "the comical as such implies an infinite light-heartedness and confidence felt by someone raised above his own inner contradiction and not bitter or miserable at all: this is the bliss and ease of a man who, being sure of himself, can bear the frustration of his aims" (1200/III, 528). While the original Hip Hop community focused on transforming their bodies into sensuous demonstrations of the freedom to overcome merely given restrictions, the comedic drama that emerged from it poetically presents for "our contemplation, in the laughter in which the characters dissolve everything, including themselves, the victory of their own subjective personality which [despite its frustrations] nevertheless persists self-assured" (1199/III, 527). It was precisely this comedic presentation of our immersion in the strictures of finitude as free subjects nevertheless capable of rising above it in "the colorful caprice of [...] humor[...]" that pushed the music into the pop mainstream.[9]

While the lyric celebration of idealized self, of course, remains a strong aspect of rap poetry, ever since Kurtis Blow's breakthrough single, its most popular forms have typically catered, at least in part, to the audience's desire "to see the present itself *as it is*—even at the cost of sacrificing beauty" (574/II, 196, emphasis added). As we have seen, however, "at the stage of romantic art spirit knows that its truth does not consist in its immersion in corporeality"; rather, the reconciliation of the romantic ideal is grounded in the turn *inward*, where the free subject is "sure of its truth [or essence, but only] by withdrawing from the external into its own intimacy with itself" (518/II, 129). This is precisely what makes comedic poetry like "The Breaks" so broadly appealing; it may also, however, help explain why Blow was the first real *solo* rapper, beginning the process that rapidly undermined the *crew* aesthetic of Hip Hop, which formerly had, at a minimum, paired MCs with DJs.

The inward turn of romanticism thus inevitably *isolates* individuals from each other, as they develop intensely *personal* visions that demand aesthetic expression; however, as the romantic develops, "the [very] inwardness and subjectivity" that allows for comedic ease even as our social situation thwarts our aims, simultaneously begins "to dissolve again the accomplished unification of conception and execution in the field of sense" made possible by previous forms of art (967/III, 234). As it becomes increasingly romantic and dramatic,

> art no longer has as its aim the free vitality of existence with its infinite tranquillity and the immersion of the soul in the corporeal, or this life as such in its very own essential nature; on the contrary, it turns its back on this summit of beauty; it intertwines its inner being with the contingency of the external world and gives unfettered play to *the bold lines of the ugly.* (526/II, 138, emphasis added)

Thus, rather than making herself at home in the world through participating in collective, creative, and emancipatory activity, the romantic individual quickly comes to grasp "external reality as an existence inadequate to itself" as free and, as such, *separates* herself from it (518/II, 129); correspondingly, romantic artists increasingly present "the general *cleavage* between the explicitly independent spiritual realm" of subjective freedom and the "external existence" in which the free individual moves and lives (510–1/II, 119, emphasis added). And it is precisely this aesthetic demonstration of the *tragic* cleavage between spirit and finitude, which "begins to awaken thought's *discontent* with the reality which is given to it" (501/II, 116, emphasis added), that finds voice in what is widely considered to be the most influential rap single of all time.

"It Makes Me Wonder How I Keep from Going Under": Dramatic Tragedy

The percussionist from Sugar Hill's house band—former school teacher Ed "Duke Bootee" Fletcher—was also a songwriter, and in 1980 took to the piano in the basement of his mother's house in the New Jersey suburbs and began to write a tune influenced by the reggae explosion of the late

1970s. Its lyrics sought to capture the infamous social alienation from which Hip Hop culture emerged, offering a vivid description of the inner city streets, with an emphasis on both the inescapably containing environment of poverty ("Broken glass everywhere") and—in stark contrast to Blow's comedic caprice—the *lack* of subjective reconciliation to the dearth of subjective possibilities within it ("Got no money to move out, I guess I got no choice"). Above all, its infectious chorus ("Don't push me 'cause I'm close to the edge") indicated a seething rage within the mind of the isolated protagonist; one specifically created by the cleavage between the social situation they were confined within and the free citizen they knew they had the inner capacity to be. Sylvia Robinson instantly saw the commercial and artistic potential in what (given the failure of Brother D.'s record to take off) appeared to be rap's first protest song; having recently managed to buy Grandmaster Flash and the Furious Five out from their first record contract, she thought the pioneering Bronx crew were the perfect fit for it.

Flash and his crew, however, saw things differently. As foundational figures in its "classical" period, they knew Hip Hop was not a protest music; while the foundational role "The Message" played in the development of rap music has led many to hold that "its originating impulse was a fierce disgust with the hypocrisies" of the surrounding world, the culture's early years were, as we have seen, almost entirely devoid of explicitly voiced rage.[10] Original Hip Hop was, in essence and above all, a *participatory and celebratory culture* whose focus was least as much on the dancers and DJs as on the MCs. A slow, nearly un-danceable song which not only emphasized the lyrics, but lyrics that served to remind people of just how awful things were around them and how few options they thus had, was radically foreign to Bronx Hip Hop; Flash, in particular, "felt the song had no energy, [and] that the lyrics would get them booed off stage by their hardcore fans", and consequently, as Melle Mel recalls, "Nobody want[ed] to do it".[11]

Robinson, however, had not just secured the rights to the crew, but to their *name*; it was thus within her power to put the song out with an entirely different group, under their moniker, and since their profile was so low outside the small NYC circle of Hip Hop, few would notice the change. This effectively threatened to deprive the group not only of their potential recording careers, but possibly even their club gigs, as crowds were now drawn by hit records, not by street reputation. Under this threat, in search of a hit, or maybe both, Melle Mel secretly agreed to provide vocals, trading verses with Fletcher and adding some of his own lyrics to its coda—lines directly lifted, in fact, from his final verse on the extended, 12-inch single version of the Furious Five's debut single, "Superrappin", but which took on a new resonance laid over the slower beat, and following the harsh realities described in the opening verses—which made it even more explicit that the inherently free and infinite possibilities of each individual ("A child is born with no state of mind/Blind to the ways of mankind") were in conflict with the strictures of inner city existence to the point of inducing violent rage ("You'll grow in the ghetto living second-rate/And your eyes will sing a song called deep hate"). The remainder of the crew eventually appeared on the record, but only in a skit played over its outro, and the two vocalists on the DJ-less track operate independently, even removing the group interplay that gave the Furious Five their rep in the Bronx. Nevertheless, when finally released in 1982, the record was credited to "Grandmaster Flash and the Furious Five"; it would be their best-selling, most praised and influential, but also final, record.[12] While "The Message" may have hastened the dissolution of what was perhaps Bronx Hip Hop's greatest crew—and while Flash himself still insists that it "isn't a song about the place I came from or the people I grew up with. This isn't anything I helped to create"[13]—it also spawned a form of rap poetry that would ultimately help take the art form global.

In Hegelian terms, in this founding landmark of "reality rap", we find, on the one hand, the presentation of spirit

> related to the external not as to its own reality permeated by it [as in the classical Ideal], but as something *purely external separated from it*, a place where everything goes on released from spirit and independence, and which is a scene of complications and the rough and tumble of an endlessly flowing, mutable and confusing contingency. (586/II, 211, emphasis added)

That is, through the progressive development of romantic art, "the ugliness of genuine evil becomes an element of the external world which may find its representation in art as the context of the spirit's activity".[14] With its richly detailed depiction of the mundane horror of everyday life in the inner city under the politics of containment and its eloquent portrayal of the effect it has on the spiritual self-understanding of its victims, "The Message" brilliantly captures the cleavage between a self-consciously free individual and the containing structures of their situation; but rather than a comedic form of subjective reconciliation to the strictures of finitude, it *tragically* portrays a subject *riled* [*gereizt*] by the present as it exists, by the actual political life of his time [...] and therefore [...] caught [...] in the *opposition* between his subjective inner life and external reality. For in his own interiority he does not enjoy full satisfaction in those mere ideas of true ethical life and therefore he turns outward against the external situation to which he relates himself negatively, with hostility [...] there is [...] present to his mind an inner content which is self-determined and, while he steadily expresses it, he has to do at the same time with a world confronting him, contradicting that content, and he has the task of sketching this reality in the traits of its corruption which is opposed to the good and the true. (511/II, 119-20, trans. modified, emphasis added)

Tellingly, "The Message" contains no references whatsoever to the aesthetic culture of Hip Hop, which had carved out an emancipatory clearing for collective and celebratory achievement within the collapsing walls of the Bronx; for that matter, it does not describe or even really mention any form of community—existent or possible—at all. Rather, reality rap's most influential track vividly portrays the conflict between the broader social and ethical order and the radically *isolated* individuals who live "close to the edge" of its brutally contained fringes.

More precisely, the early verses, written by Fletcher, primarily present the conflict between the protagonist and the society that left him isolated and hopeless ("Got a bum education, double-digit inflation/Can't take the train to the job, there's a strike at the station/Neon King Kong standing on my back/Can't stop to turn around, broke my sacroiliac"), while the fourth verse almost resolves the conflict by giving the victims of the situation a sort of comic reprieve ("They pushed that girl in front of the train/Took her to the doctor, sewed her arm on again/Stabbed that man right in his heart/Gave him a transplant for a brand new start"); this juxtaposition of comedy and tragedy leaves the lyric protagonist "living on a see-saw". This tension continues into the Melle Mel-penned final verse, where the life of the "child [...] born with no state of mind" is seemingly determined by their restrictive conditions ("You'll admire all the number-book takers/Thugs, pimps and pushers and the big money-makers"); however, the tone shifts midway to a focus on the *choices* made by the child growing up within them ("You say 'I'm cool, huh, I'm no fool.'/But then you wind up dropping outta high school"). As it carries on, the verse seems to imply that it is not only the situation but also the *decisions made by the individual* within them that ultimately determine his fate ("Turned stick-up kid, but look what *you* done did/Got sent up for a eight-year bid", emphasis added), as well as the child's recognition of their own role in their demise ("But now your eyes sing the sad, sad song/Of how you lived so fast and died so young"). The tragic subject acted in a manner brutally constrained by circumstance and embodiment, but nevertheless also *acted*; his aims were forged within the confines of a brutally stifling social order, but they were still *his* aims.

In the end, "The Message" leaves it unclear whether the lyricists will, in Hegel's terms, "destroy themselves through the one-sidedness of their dignified will and character, or [...] resignedly accept what they had opposed in a substantial way" (1199/III, 527, trans. modified); however, as the closing skit rises, and the group is forced, without charge or crime, into the back of a police car, it seems apparent that either way their plea to not "push them over the edge" will be unheard, as "eternal substance of things emerges victorious" (1199/III, 527), and the "objective ethical realm [of the surrounding state] asserts its necessity as against the freedom of the subject".[15]

The Lessons and Limits of the Dramatic, and of Art

For Hegel, dramatic poetry is characterized by the complex and varied forms of tragic tension/comedic unity between the objective determination of finitude and the subjective infinity of freedom actualized within it. Like the epic, drama sings of the objective—but now confining, rather than sanctifying—circumstances surrounding distinct individuals; and like the lyric, it consciously affirms those confined to be essentially free from *total* determination by the reality in which they act. Neither completely determined by circumstances, nor abstractly free from them, in drama we see

> the fate which [subjective] passion occasions as a necessary result of [the free individual's] own deed. [...] [Here] the action is not presented to our vision in the purely external form of something that has really happened [...] on the contrary, we see it actually present, issuing from the private will, from the morality and immorality of the individual characters, who thus become the centre as they are in the principle of lyric. (1038/III, 323)

In both the tragedy of "The Message" and the comedy of "The Breaks", we continue to see the inner thought of the lyric, which raises the subject above determination into the infinity of freedom; but this interiority is now manifested "in the execution of purposes dictated by passion" or the embodied, situated will of the individual (1038/III, 323). Grounded in the inner revelations of the lyric, dramatic action "originates in the minds of the characters who bring it about, but at the same time its outcome is decided by the really substantive nature of the aims, individuals and collisions involved" (1158/III, 474). Dramatic poetry presupposes "that the principle of individual freedom and independence, or at least the self-determination to will and freely accept responsibility for their own act and its consequences has been awakened" (1205/III, 534, trans. modified), seeking to act in an objective situation which is in principle amenable to, but in actuality is not truly reflective of, that responsible freedom.

Thus, even more than "The Breaks", and maybe even more than "Rapper's Delight", "'The Message' [was] artificial and marginal by the standards of the culture" by which it was inspired, not just in its depressingly realist content, but because that content was recited over a "beat [that was] too slow to rock a crowd", and as such both discouraged dancing and "boost[ed] the rapper over the DJ", confirming the rapper's role as an *individual dramatic storyteller*, rather than a *collaborative master of ceremonies*, through what was, up to that point, the "grimmest, most downbeat rap ever heard".[16] Rap music's founding "protest" anthem, then, in both form and content marked the complete *inversion* of "classical" Hip Hop as it had developed in the Bronx[17]; nevertheless, it was also perfectly suited to express the tension between the marginal inclusion within the broader society achieved by the pioneers of the culture through their art, and the omnipresent repression and containment that they, and countless others, continued to feel as the Reagan era came crashing in.

In a sense, then, the dual authorship of "The Message" encapsulates the tension of the moment in which it was released. On the one hand, the song's emphasis on the grim realities that plagued the inner city, and thus the understandable rage pervading the subjects who inhabited it, was introduced to rap poetry by an exchange with the surrounding culture (i.e. the lyrics of New Jersey teacher and songwriter Fletcher and the vision of Robinson and Sugar Hill), and as such reflected the perceptions and interests of a general audience *external* to the original Hip Hop community. Its lyrics spoke to varied constituencies outside the areas of industrial blight enduring the transition to, or tightening of, the politics of containment: progressives who found in it an authentic and informative portrayal of impoverished life at the dawn of the Reagan era; curious onlookers searching for something more "street" than "The Breaks", who likely found in it an even safer venue than the Roxy in which to view such life; and, of course, architects of the politics of containment who would soon use such the spiteful rage expressed on such records to justify interventions within, thereby tightening their grip on, the very communities whose lives were being portrayed in them.[18] On the other hand, however, "the raw and angry lyrics [also] laid bare ghetto realities in Reagan's America" in a manner that produced, in many of those living on the fringes of American society, a "close identification with a fabricated product [precisely because it] revealed so many truths" about the political realities faced by many across the nation and globe as the new neo-liberal order took hold.[19] The dramatic emphasis on characters constrained by inflexible and unjust circumstances, yet struggling mightily, if unsuccessfully, against forces and powers inimical to their essence, appealed to many of those (in the Bronx and elsewhere) who experienced, raged against, and wished there was some way to overturn the cleavage that defined their social lives. While it inverted Hip Hop's hitherto developed aesthetic forms as well as its communal and emancipatory message, it simultaneously introduced a "language that allowed [contained and otherwise alienated] young people [anywhere] to negotiate a political voice for themselves in their societies".[20] Thus, while it was a contrived studio creation, "'The Message' came to represent a profound counterforce" to the politics of confinement, emerging from the poetry of Bronx Hip Hop, but applicable to any and all individuals repressed by the determinations of their state.[21]

For all of these reasons, "The Message" was a critical and commercial smash, kicking off a "money-minded craze for gory social realism" among record companies and artists alike, and romantic drama's "bold lines of the ugly" quickly became equated in the public mind with the message of Hip Hop.[22] For example, the breakthrough single by rap music's first real superstars—"It's Like That" (1983) by the Hollis, Queens trio Run-DMC—paired tales of urban horror produced by an increasingly cruel individualism and an increasingly brutal state ("Wars going on across the sea/Street soldiers killing the elderly/Whatever happened to unity?") with depictions of the inevitably angry and despondent, but nevertheless free and responsible, subjects it produces ("You should have gone to school, you could've learned a trade/But you laid in the bed where the bums have laid") through a hook that changed the reconciliation of "The Breaks" into a form of begrudging, tragi-comic acceptance: "It's like that, and that's the way it is". Other tracks, like Melle Mel and Duke Bootee's follow-up to "The Message", "New York, New York", increased the horror of the situations depicted and decreased the options open to the individuals therein. As these new, harsher sounds and lyrics began to spread through records and radio, MCs outside of New York carried this trend to its logical conclusion by transforming despondency into its own kind of responsibility, embracing the rage and violence that permeated the contained inner city as a source of individual power and freedom.

In 1985, Philadelphia's Schoolly D. independently released an album of amoral braggadocio, highlighted—again in a stark inversion of Hip Hop's founding ethos—by a tribute to the gang of which he was a member (the Park Side Killers), called "P.S.K.: What Does It Mean?". This initiated the "gangsta" rap genre that would be refined into its still-dominant form by pioneering West Coast MC Ice-T, who—having released a pair of "hard" singles that went further than "The Message" in calling for free responsibility despite the brutal confinement he brilliantly depicted—in 1986 released gangsta's defining song, "6 'N the Morning", the story of a "self-made monster of the city streets", that asserted that its "shit was for real, it was no La Di Da Di", and backed the claim with vivid and compelling details.[23] From "The Breaks" and "The Message" to the gangsta rap of MCs like Ice-T, Too $hort and their descendants, what we find in "reality" rap poetry is a precise and often revelatory description of the manner in which the inflexible constraints of finitude affected individuals in specific locales, with an emphasis on *subjective frustration* that alternates between comic forms of begrudging or reconciling acceptance and tragic forms of destructive and empowering rage.

Thus, in approximately the time it took for Hip Hop to emerge from the abandoned fires of the South Bronx to the clubs and record labels of Manhattan, rap poetry separated itself from the spiritual content of the original culture, in process shifting from a sanitized version of the party experience to the most diverse, compelling, controversial, and consumed form of poetry on the planet. This change, perhaps, reflects the difference between an *abandoned* populace, forced by their isolation from state institutions to refound communal values and rediscover their essential freedom through the collective act of aesthetic creation, and a *contained* population targeted, surveilled, and controlled by the social order, and which thus finds its consciously grasped spirit continually thwarted by unjust contingency, but which nevertheless has hope of inclusion and success through satisfying the varied interests of the popular audiences who—for extremely diverse reasons—expect such poetry from them. The nature of this shift is perfectly expressed by Bronx MC Dr. Jeckyll:

Back in the day, in 1976, when I started rapping [...] even though things were rugged and things were tough, we felt like there was an opportunity for us to be successful, so people would make raps that were different from today [...] Like I made a rap record [in 1983] called 'Gettin' Money', 'everything's funny when you're getting' money', 'cause I felt there was an opportunity to get money. Now rappers are making smash hits like [Method Man's 1994 single] 'Bring the Pain' because people feel like they're growing up in a time where there's no system for them to figure out how to get money. [...] Now, you've got *Reaganomics rap groups*, and Reaganomics took away after school programs, took away summer jobs, took away student loans, so you got a whole generation of rappers [...] who *grow up with no hope*, and all they see is pain.[24]

While it may seem counter-intuitive to suggest that the burning tenements of the Bronx in the 1970s contained more hope than the heavily policed inner cities of the 1980s and 1990s,[25] the stark contrast between the idealized presentations of subjectivity that dominated the pre-recording years of Hip Hop and the despondent truths of early "reality rap" signify precisely this shift. It is just because the aesthetic culture was explicitly and collectively *self-determining*, created without external influence or goal, that it felt liberating, spiritual, and true; but as it spread beyond its original borders, so did *both* the increasingly brutal repression of the containing police state *and* the possibility of economic and social gain for those who made art appropriate to it. As rap became more "real", more and more individuals, across the nation and globe, could either identify with or, from the safe confines of their own privilege, thrill themselves through rap's dramatic depictions of this imposed pain.[26] Because the forms of state constraint have only increased throughout the Clinton, Bush, and Obama years (and who knows how much worse they'll be after Trump), reality rap's inversion of Hip Hop's original cultural basis has never receded, and in the years after "6 'N the Morning", its tales would only get more aggressive, hopeless, and "real". As it developed,

> Gangsta rap took the 'keeping it real' mantra [...] to the extreme [and a]t the height of the genre's appeal record labels [...] even resorted to marketing the criminal backgrounds of rappers as a way to ensure 'street cred'. Eventually the line between performing gansta and living gansta became blurred.[27]

The more mainstream its music became, the further its popular forms seemed to remove rap from the collective and emancipatory values of its original culture, and the closer it adhered to the contingent and selfish desires of the modern romantic world that continued to force an increasingly large segment of the populace into an unjustly limited range of social options.

It is realities like this, perhaps, that help explain why Hegel, ultimately, was ambivalent about the "end of art". Art only arises in its "highest vocation" from situations devoid of right, because there a community "must work from its own resources [*aus sich selbst arbeiten*] and bring before the spiritual intuition [*geistige Anschauung*] a completely different, richer content" than that which results from the mere "rules" of "practical utility" that inform the kind of rote existence many enjoy in the modern state (26/I, 44, trans. modified). It is the very lack of higher spheres of spirit that forces the community to create a living culture which proceeds from, and sensibly presents, that essence. However, if an artistic culture is potent and sustained, the very self-determination towards which it strives ultimately helps to bring its community to the point at which they can embrace and actualize the radically individual values of modern romanticism, which even under the politics of containment dominate popular rap expression. This is perhaps why Hegel controversially claims that he cannot decide "which of these situations [...]—the civilized and developed life of a state, or an heroic [artistic] age—is the better" (185/I, 243); the latter simultaneously reflects the increasing self-consciousness of our universal essence among a self-determining and meritocratic community as well as the fundamental injustice of the determining situation within which they were forced to develop their aesthetic culture, while the former can more concretely actualize the political and economic fruits of the community's hard-won gains, but also fragments the unified culture into self-interested individuals making due as best they can in their situation, as it stands.

The specific trajectory of Hip Hop's re-construction of the classical Ideal, however, also clarifies Hegel's account of the essential limitations of not only romantic art, but art as a whole for actualizing the truth of spirit. Romantic art sensibly presents our free essence in terms of its links to the finitude of corporeal and situated human existence; that is, it "presents [...] the divine as interiority [but only as it is found] in the externality from which it always distinguishes itself".[28] While this emphasis on contingent particularity is most obvious in romantic, and especially dramatic, "poetry [which] takes pleasure in lingering over what is individual", this tendency is nevertheless "grounded in the fact that *art in general* loves to tarry with the particular" (981/III, 250–1, emphasis added), just because it is necessarily linked to our *sensible* finitude. While the contingently particular is the focus—and chief defect—of romantic art, Hegel claims *art as a whole* "is defective" precisely because it seeks "to bring the idea of *essence* to consciousness, [but does so] through intuition and imagination", and thus remains inevitably inflected by human finitude; that is, even in the ritual culture of classical art, we find "a religion still bound to sensuous externality".[29] If the heroic efforts of the symbolic and classical artists began "the purification of spirit from its unfreedom [*die Reinigung des Geistes von der Unfreiheit*]" in lawless "nature", the increasingly "real" presentations of individuals in romantic art reveal that a clear and complete expression of that freedom "is lacking not only in the sensuous beauty of artworks, but even more in that external, unbeautiful sensuousness" which eventually becomes art's focus.[30] Because of its necessary and essential connection to the sensuously particular, and thus to the *un*spiritual, it is inevitable that—as skill, tradition, and above all acceptance in the broader economic and political sphere, develop—art will focus more and more on finite individuality and sensible *form*, rendering less and less clear its relation to the universal free spirit that is art's, and our, essential *content*. That is, as the dialectic of aesthetic creation internally develops, it gradually *de-spiritualizes* the content it presents, forsaking the universal nature and import of its ground, just because the medium through which it conveys its message is finite sensuousness itself. As Will Dudley argues:

> When the universal truth is shown in individual form, the immanent connection between the universal and its necessary particulars remains unknown, and at the same time we learn more than we need to know about the contingent particulars of the individual in question.[31]

If spirit is *only* or *primarily* presented through artistic means, it is inevitable that freedom finds itself channelled into arbitrary individuality, which seeks, accepts, reinforces, or even creates the very fragmentation that thwarts the true actualization of our essence. But if spirit can be stably actualized in a form that retains its collective and emancipatory core, then even "beautiful art is only a *stage of emancipation* [*die schöne Kunst ist nur eine Befreiungstufe*]", for—*qua* sensuous—it remains too tied to the merely given conditions from which spirit must work to liberate itself in order to adequately and broadly convey our free essence.[32]

FROM RAP (BACK) TO HIP HOP

Consequently, as art deepens its ties to the world of constraining finitude, the spiritual community's emancipatory progress can only continue if it finds another, less sensuous, and thus more universal form through which to preach and preserve its essential content. If the tension within all art, made explicit by the development and increasingly contingent presentations of the romantic, is between the infinite and universal essence of our free spirit and the finite and particular nature of our sensing embodiment, then this new form can only be found if "the constrained content of the idea passes in and for itself into the universality identical with the infinite form [*Der beschränkte Gehalt der Idee geht an und für sich in die mit der unendlichen Form identische Allgemeinheit*]".[33] Because "the content of the idea has for its principle the determination of free intelligence" itself,[34] and because it is art's emphasis on situated finitude that renders it defective for this task, the new form of spiritual expression can only be found "in the element of *thought*; the sole medium in which pure spirit is for spirit, and emancipation is accompanied by reverence [*im Elemente des Denkens [...] dem Elemente, in welchem allein der reine Geist für den Geist, die Befreiung zugleich mit der Ehrfucht ist*]" for it.[35] In other words, when art becomes all too realistically, mundanely, and brutally romantic in its sensuous imagery, the spirit must pass into a more *direct* form of discourse, one which manifestly *proclaims*—rather than merely *embodies*—the divine freedom of human essence.

For Hegel, there are two—conceptually successive, but not competing—forms of discourse that render the spiritual content of art clear as it separates itself from its sensuous presentation. Firstly, "the beautiful art" of a classical culture "has its future in the true *religion*", which, for Hegel, effectively means a universalist brand of Christianity.[36] Like art, revealed religion has for its content the essential human freedom that grounds the ethical and creative forms of human action; unlike art, it "explicitly distinguish[es] universals from the individuals in which they are realized".[37] That is, by creating representational concepts (e.g. "God", "Incarnation of God in Christ", etc.) that convey human essence to an audience in the form of a non-sensuous "*idea [Vorstellung]*", religion supersedes the "immediacy and sensuousness of form and knowing" that both defines and limits art.[38]

However, while the history of religion marks the search for the representational ideas most adequate to the dissemination of spirit's truth, just because it still invokes metaphorical or symbolic representations of the content drawn from the life experiences of its community ("The Father", "The Son", etc.), even "true religion" "distorts the truth, in Hegel's view, since it falsely represents it as something we cannot know" without the mediation of representational form.[39] Religion's goal is to raise us to clear knowledge of our essential freedom, but it can still only do so by representing spirit as being outside of us, as in a distant God, or an inexplicable incarnation. Thus, while its images allow us not merely to sense, but more intimately to *feel* the spirit dwelling within, because religion seeks to "tell the truth that humans are free by means of a symbolic mythology that necessarily represents us as being dependent on an external authority",[40] much like art, the tension between the content it expresses and the form in which it is expressed is ultimately too great to clearly and broadly preach spirit to a community. Thus, what must be found is a discourse that "bring[s] the determinations of thought to language [...] without allowing the language it uses to violate the necessary self-determination of thought", that is, without placing between the hearer and the truth a potentially distorting intermediary.[41] Developing this discourse is precisely the task and goal of *philosophy*.

In sum: the romantic fragmentation of the polytheistic religion of art reflects the "splintering of [spiritual] content into many independent [sensible] shapes"; revealed religion reflects our striving to *merge* these shapes into one coherent system, but under representational, and thus still indirect and potentially distorting, ideas; and philosophy (ideally) "*unifies* [all of them] them into the simple, spiritual vision which then is raised into self-conscious thought" that can be directly presented to the people as the discourse of their own essence, precisely as that which is reflected in their artistic creations and religious traditions.[42] Philosophy's job, that is, is not to *critique* art (i.e. to demonstrate and catalogue the varied failures of its sensible forms to adequately convey the spiritual content), no more than it is to *eradicate* religion (e.g. by revealing the secular human source, and/or necessary limitations, of its representational ideas, thus rendering it superfluous); rather, philosophy must *complete* and *supplement* their work by bringing into the clearest language possible both the self-emancipating essence of humanity as expressed in them, as well as clarifying its relation to the forms of sensible art and religion that remain meaningful to most of its community.

Thus, while the infamously abstruse nature of his own system may seem to belie the point, for Hegel philosophy is not intended as an abstract, academic discourse, concerned with the most refined products of civilization, and available only to the few and the rare; rather, "Hegel wants philosophy to speak to ordinary people" within a community, in language they can understand and which reflects their own unique experiences, histories, and creations, as well as the universal spirit they share with all humanity.[43] Thus, much like art, any philosophy worthy of the name finds its essential purpose and goal in teaching self-emancipation to a specific community, in a language that speaks directly to them, just so that they can make concrete use of it in constructing, preserving, and improving their social and political situation, thus building upon and joining with the emancipatory struggles of others across history.

As we have seen above, the forms of constraining finitude imposed upon them ensured that the smooth transition from art to religion and philosophy was unavailable to the Hip Hop community; however, it is not even clear that the transition has *ever* been made as clearly and sequentially as Hegel seems to suggest. Given that even his own systematic texts are not only peppered with poetic flourishes, idiosyncratic obsessions, and semi-cryptic wordplay—to say nothing of the presence therein of racial, cultural, and personal biases from which Hegel implies philosophy can free us—we can hardly expect rigid distinctions between the three expressions of absolute spirit to be maintained by those with far fewer advantages and facing an almost incomprehensibly harsher set of challenges. As Hegel's accounts of art, religion, and philosophy seek to demonstrate, humanity is not just universally free, but also situationally determined, and thus *no* human discourse can completely free itself from the essential tension of our condition; in fact, the patently non-universal influences that find voice in his work essentially testify to the difficulty—perhaps even impossibility—of ineluctably finite human beings developing what he would consider a *purely* philosophical discourse, untainted by the influences of feeling, habit, and prejudice.

What we do find in the immediate wake of the original Hip Hop community's fragmentation, however, is the increasing recognition, among some of the culture's pioneers and most devoted disciples, of the need for a *non-aesthetic* discourse in which to articulate and thus preserve the culture's hard-won spiritual lessons against rap's increasing emphasis on contingent finitude. This new discourse would need to draw on Hip Hop's roots in the Bronx to determine the precise truth towards which its art was aiming, and which demanded more explicit, yet culturally relevant, expression if it was not to be lost; and it is only fitting that this task was first taken up by the man broadly credited with giving the culture its name: the original Master of Records.[44]

INFINITE KNOWLEDGE FOR PLANET ROCK: HIP HOP'S FIFTH ELEMENT

As noted above, the pioneering crews of Hip Hop did not immediately embrace recording. The more primal style of Herc and his MCs was not what was being sought by record producers in the wake of the Sugarhill Gang, and his crew never actually made it to wax. In fact, he even largely avoided the downtown clubs, claiming the largely spectacle-based scene in Manhattan "was bourgeois to me. My shit was elementary", and that he preferred to stay in the Bronx.[45] Flash was similarly sceptical and only recorded in response to what he took to be the insult to the culture's founders represented by "Rapper's Delight".[46] Of the early crews most actively sought by downtown labels, the "one who stood away longer" than any other was Afrika Bambaataa, who was also the most vocally critical of the transition to wax.[47] While among the first to transport the scene to downtown clubs, and certainly the one who most forcefully opened its horizon by encouraging the white punk and new wave kids who saw him in clubs to brave the Bronx to hear him on his home turf, Bambaataa was nevertheless worried the shift to records "would kill the scene in a way"; not just because it would cut MCing off from its spiritual home in the block party, but more pertinently because it would eliminate the need for distinct DJ crews with idiosyncratic sound systems and record collections as well as spaces of gathering for breakers and cyphers for the musical aspects of Hip Hop to be experienced. This reticence is unsurprising, for no-one had done more during the years of Hip Hop's classical period to identify, organize, and codify the culture into a self-standing religion of art, or to consider the threatening consequences of—and the potentially liberating possibilities opened up by—its popular reception.

Messianic from a young age, Bambaataa "always had visions, and always felt [he] was sent to do a job or something [f]or the creator". Born into a family of activists, he spent much of his teens hanging around the local Black Panther Party office and absorbing the speeches, books, and music of the civil rights and Black Power struggles and, as early as his mid-teens, he began to put his education into action. During the height of the gang wars, when he was a high-ranking member of the Black Spades, "Bambaataa made his rep by being unafraid to cross turfs to forge relationships with other gangs".[48] Thus, it was unsurprising that, as the gang era subsided in the Bronx in the first half of the 1970s (a process in which he played no small role), he began to recruit former members into a community service group that began under the moniker "The Organization" (or the "Bronx River Organization"), which, sometime between 1973 and 1976, was supplemented by the "Zulu Kings and Queens", which began as a breaking group that dominated Bronx battles, who were soon joined by a DJ/MC crew operating under his direction.[49] They took their name from the film *Zulu*[50] which Bambaataa saw as a child, and which struck him as an inspiring example of Blacks collectively and heroically fighting for self-determination against the seemingly insurmountable forces of racial oppression. A trip to Africa he won in a high school essay contest in 1975 deepened his interest in both the global possibilities for communal self-determination as well as the various Black liberation thinkers whose rhetoric and teachings he continued to absorb.[51] During this period, Bambaataa recalls:

> I started getting into the teachings of the most Honorable Elijah Muhammad, Minister Farrakhan, Malcom X, Black Panthers [and then] started incorporating a lot of that and then checking out stuff that I learned from when I was a Christian, and all these other grooves, and then hanging with all these black, white and Catholic schools, then just start[ed] incorporating that into the Zulu Nation, speaking to people from all walks of life.

As the new forms of art and community emerged in the Bronx, he quickly made the connection between these diverse discourses of liberation and the unique elements of aesthetic expression that anchored and sustained the developing culture around him.

Eventually, Bambaataa sought to use the Zulus as a vehicle for giving formal structure and direction to Hip Hop's spiritual content or, as Sha-Rock puts it, to explicitly "represent the positive and peaceful side of the beginning of the Hip Hop culture".[52] His account of this period is worth quoting at length:

> I grew up in the Southeast Bronx. It was an area where back in the late '60s, early '70s there was "broken glass everywhere," like Melle Mel said in 'The Message.' But it was also an area where there was *a lot of unity and a lot of social awareness going on*, at a time when people of color was *coming into*

their own, knowing that they were Black people [...] Seeing all the violence that was going on with the Vietnam War and all the people in Attica and Kent State, and being aware of what was going on in the late '60s, with Woodstock and the Flower Power generation, the Love Power Movement ... just being a young person and seeing all this happening around me put *a lot of consciousness in my mind to get up and do something.* [...] What I did is I took all these elements from all these great leaders and teachers that we had at the time and said I will start a group called the Zulu Nation. [...] So what I did, with myself and a couple of other comrades, is get out in the street, start talking to a lot of the brothers and sisters, trying to tell them how they're killing each other, that they *should be warriors for their community.* And when we started this music called hip-hop, which didn't have a name at the time, it brought a lot of these different elements together. We still had little spots of violence here and there, you know, at parties and stuff, but a lot of the time you had people who was coming together to kick the drug dealers out of the area—we used violence against a lot of the dope pushers and all that. We went from a negative thing to a positive thing.[53]

Bambaataa's drive to "bring different elements together" into one emancipatory vision extended to every aspect of his Hip Hop mission. First and perhaps foremost, it was the DJ and occasional MC who tagged BAM 117 that first explicitly sought "to bring the culture, the hip-hop culture, together from the break-dancers to graffiti artists to the DJs to the MCs, to all come together as one unit".[54] All of these aesthetic elements, for Bambaataa, sensibly expressed the growing awareness of emancipatory, communal spirit that he saw in the transition out of the negative going on around him, and he realized that articulating them as one unified force would allow the Hip Hop community to avoid replicating the divisions of gang culture into new schisms that threatened the new positivity (e.g. between the earlier writers and the breakers and DJs who followed them; between the DJ and breaking crews forming out of former gangs, whose aggression could go too far in battle, leading to further violence; between the gang members who attended the increasingly large and unwieldy jams and could act on old beefs, etc.). Thus, for Bambaataa, the unification of the elements into a complete culture was simply—but explicitly and directly—an extension of the "peace mission" that began with the tenuous gang truce that preceded the dawn of Hip Hop graffiti,[55] and in "coining the phrase 'hip-hop'" as defining the culture, he gave its emancipatory religion of art an explicit name, identity, and task.[56]

This drive for unity over division extended, secondly, to the still-prevalent racial tensions that existed in the Bronx, which both derived from, and reinforced, the lingering gang beefs in the area. As BOM5 recalls,

> He wanted to squash all this beef with the gangs. 'It's going to be a party. Everybody's welcome. Leave your gang colors at home. It's all about Peace, Love, Unity. Come learn about your brothers.' [...] My cousin came with me and we just went in. Once you see some Spanish people in there, you know there must be some peace going on! I met Bambaataa. They shook your hand! It was funny. My cousin says, 'See. Looks like things are changing!' [...] Thank God for Bambaataa realizing there was too much violence going on.[57]

Much of this change, of course, was achieved by channelling the negative violence of his former gang into what might be called the threat of "positive violence" through which "the Zulu nation [...] made sure that there was no trouble anywhere"; but freedom from fruitless violence was, assuredly, "what a lot of groups wanted—people to feel safe and come in and just listen to the music and everything", and transforming the menace of street gangs into informal community policing was well within the tradition of the Black Panthers who originally inspired him.[58]

However, as Hip Hop's influence spread outside the Bronx, where racial tensions operated differently, Bambaataa had to find *aesthetic* means to promote unity between distinct and increasingly distant groups (e.g. the Hip Hop heads of the Bronx who followed the culture to the downtown clubs, and the increasingly alienated—but still relatively privileged—punk and new wave crowd that already inhabited the clubs of downtown Manhattan, and started following the culture back to the Bronx; the club owners and attendees seeking the next wave of subcultural thrills in NYC, etc.).[59] This was achieved (third), through the unique and eclectic mix of records, breaks, and other sounds that the Zulu crew would play. While Herc, for example, was guided by the breakers to play the records that his audience wanted to hear, Bambaataa sought to use the interaction of breaks from distinct records to *challenge* the narrow musical preferences of his audience. Having the most diverse collection of records of any crew in the early years, the Zulus developed a reputation for playing "obscure things" alongside party classics and funky breaks, specifically and consciously to force people out of their comfort zones and to see the value in other (musical) cultures.[60] Bambaataa's selections manifestly demonstrated that anything from sitcom themes to field recordings to proto-metal to doo-wop classics could find a home in Hip Hop, compelling his partygoers to *open their minds to other ways of being and doing and thus to the universal spirit that unifies them all*, providing a sonic equivalent to what had been the culture's ethos from the earliest graffiti. Creating a genuinely polyglot musical environment helped shatter the barriers between seemingly distinct musical genres, thereby giving aesthetic form to the creolization of cultures and subcultures necessary to bring the increasingly diverse audiences that attended Zulu parties into creative and potent unity. Thus, "Bam's sound became a rhythmic analogue to his peace-making philosophy [as] his setlists had the same kind of inclusiveness and broad-mindedness he was aspiring to build" in all of his work, aesthetic and otherwise.[61]

And this wasn't the only way the Zulus played "records that makes [people] think"; they were also (fourth) perhaps the first crew to explicitly "add messages" to their jams, with Bambaataa "telling the MCs to say more than just throw your hands in the air, how many people smoke the reefer [but to r]aise money for sickle cell anemia, raise money for our community centre",[62] or to warn against hard drug use (as in their anti-PCP campaign, "Stop Smoking That Dust"). While this linked Hip Hop culture to the enduring remnants of the emancipatory politics of the 1960s, the Zulus would also heavily emphasize the music of that period, hosting tribute nights to James Brown or Sly Stone, during which they would incorporate speech fragments from Malcolm X, Martin Luther King, Fred Hampton, and other progressive icons into their rich sonic stew. For audience members like former Savage Skulls gang member and eventual Zulu Nation disciple Lucky Strike, the combination of records, speeches, and a safe environment conducive to both educational conversation and competitive fun drove home the point that the Zulus "were teaching me things about my own culture that I never knew and things that I never learned in school".[63]

Thus, in their broad, unifying, and explicitly political playlists, their linking of partying and community dialogue, as well as their creation of the safest and most welcoming zone for fun and interchange in the borough, the "Zulu Nation was returning the Bronx to an era of style, celebration and optimism".[64] Creating a potent mix of the political, the spiritual, and the aesthetic—which brought together the humanistic cry for Black authenticity in 60s funk and Kraftwerk's future-oriented, virtually disembodied "robot pop", the slogans and lessons of the largely college-based anti-war movement and the concrete and largely "street"-centric Black Panther community service programmes, and "the hippie-infused flower power movement, and the Muslim teachings of the Nation of Islam and the Nation of Gods and Earths"—"Bambaataa redesigned the hip-hop party scene as 'edutainment,' a mix of fun and socially conscious music and discourse"; a mix, moreover, that demonstrated that an uncompromising vision of "Afrocentric empowerment" derived from his studies of Black history and specific to the racially repressed populations of the urban America was not only not opposed to, but was in fact essentially linked with, a kind of "all-inclusive universalism [that] is inherently anti-race [as much as it is] anti-racist, as it focuses on the commonality of humanity".[65] It was this practical mix of the particular and the universal, or of the historically determined and the eternally valid, that gave the Zulu Nation their spiritual mission, reflecting Bambaataa's drive "to move hip-hop from [aesthetically presented] street consciousness to [a form of consciously embraced] Afrocentric empowerment" as "part of an emancipatory politic" destined to include the entire globe.[66]

Thus, it is perhaps predictable that (fifth) Bambaataa played a lead role in "taking the music and culture of the Black and brown Bronx into the white art-crowd and punk-rock clubs of lower Manhattan".[67] Seeing, embracing, and actively promoting the inevitable spread of Hip Hop to the broader sphere, Bambaataa forged connections with other counterculture movements, and the success of his work in Manhattan with the white punks in particular fostered in him a strong "ambition to take [Hip Hop] worldwide".[68] Zulu chapters began to dot the city, eventually becoming almost as diverse as his setlists, and consequently—to reflect both its increasingly varied and distant chapters, and its increasingly broad appeal and influence—the Zulu Kings and Queens were renamed the *Universal* Zulu Nation, becoming "the first hip-hop institution", formally linking its distinct geographical and cultural groups into a cohesive, and potentially global, "people", united by their practice of and/or love for Hip Hop's aesthetic culture and its emancipatory spirit.[69]

As we have seen, however, the very spread of Hip Hop that Bambaataa helped usher in, precisely because it both grew and diversified its audience, coincided with the *separation* of its aesthetic elements—particularly those of rap music as its poetry passed into the dramatic—from the ethical and spiritual codes that gave the culture its unity.[70] Watching rap poetry develop in increasing isolation from its founders, and thus from the values they helped usher into being, Bambaataa quickly came to see that, in many ways, "hip hop lost its way" in the move to the clubs and especially recordings, and thus that aesthetic means were *insufficient on their own* for continuing its peace mission.[71] Hip Hop art—whether it was the new dramatic poetry achieving critical and popular acclaim, the graffiti that was once again conquering galleries selling the vicarious thrills of "street art" to elites, or the breaking that would soon feature in everything from Hollywood films to presidential campaigns—was no longer carrying Hip Hop's spiritual message to the world. Consequently, in order to ensure the correct spiritual foundation for his envisioned Hip Hop institution, the man who first articulated the interconnection between the four aesthetic elements "added a fifth element—'*knowledge*'", which named the clear and distinct explication of the spiritual ground upon which the others rest, and from which they draw their validity and strength.[72]

   True to his DJ style, Bambaataa combed through the various philosophies, speeches, and conversations that he imbibed over the entirety of his life and began the—as it would turn out ever-evolving, precisely because increasingly universalizing—process of collating the "fundamental code of conduct [that] gave broad directive to the Zulu 'way of life'" into what he called the "Infinity Lessons".[73] Predictably, they did not embrace any doctrinaire creed, as Bambaataa had always been a seeker rather than a dogmatist, and Hip Hop had always been about rising above the merely received, rather than merely carrying the past forward; rather, the manner in which Bambaataa approached religious and cultural traditions was essentially identical to "the way he did political ideologies and his own records. He pulled out what was precious and tossed the rest [and thereby] *created new mythologies*".[74] As the original Lesson #4 succinctly states, "The religion of the Zulu Nation is truth wherever it is", rather than any given (and thus merely inherited) doctrine.[75] Primarily, however (and in a resonance with Hegel's account of Lutheranism), the infinity lessons hold that "any real change must come not from mere uncovering of the systems of power and oppression but from *recognizing the god within oneself*" that can resist and reform them.[76] The lessons, beliefs, and rules of the Zulu Nation were thus all directed towards inducing in all of the world's people—but especially the oppressed—a firm and clear knowledge of the drive towards collective self-emancipation which is essential to humanity in general, yet locally manifested in an infinite variety of distinct ways. Correspondingly, the Zulus sought through all of the religions and philosophies of the world for the language, concepts, and images most appropriate to preach the gospel of universal, self-determining freedom to as broad a collection as possible;

this essential mission is laid out in Zulu Belief 14, "We believe in Power, Education in truth, Freedom, Justice, Equality, Work for the people and the upliftment of the people".

Thus, while the lessons never really cohere into a distinctly recogniz-able creed, they do quite explicitly move beyond Hip Hop *as art*, towards something between a *religion* (which "remixes" previous doctrines into a discourse, often related through myths and parables, that preaches and celebrates the "divinity" in all) and a *philosophy* (which seeks to determine and systematically express the trans-historical truth of humanity's essence, differentially reflected not only in Hip Hop but in all religious, aesthetic, and political traditions), by articulating a series of "quasi-theological" principles, rules, and meditations that would allow one to "'overstand,' that is, comprehend and confront the injustice of the world by manifesting one's power" as intrinsically free.[77] Through the quasi-mythical parables of the Infinity Lessons, Bambaataa gave Hip Hop's universal essence an expression that could be conveyed more directly than through its aesthetic products alone.

However, as Watkins notes, while Hip Hop is "made up of various expressive elements, [nevertheless] rap music stands out as the face of the movement. Thus, the state of rap music has become a key indicator of the state of hip hop", essentially from the release of "Rapper's Delight" for-ward.[78] While the Infinity Lessons worked to reveal the essential core of Bronx Hip Hop to the world through religious and philosophical lan-guage, and the Zulu nation sought to politically actualize its spirit through varied local chapters dedicated to community service, by 1981 Bambaataa understood that the culture he had helped shape would soon have global reach, if only through the spread of a rap music that was increasingly becoming distant from the fifth element; this meant, of course, that while most people would soon be touched by it, their first encounter Hip Hop would most likely be in distorted form. However, if the culture could not help but be co-opted by external forces, then Bambaataa realized it was also possible for the record labels, radio stations, and other culture vultures seeking to profit off Hip Hop's products to be used as a vehicle for dis-seminating the movement's spiritual content. If rap carried Hip Hop away from its spiritual community, then conversely records could also allow him to spread at least some version of his gospel of pro-Black universalism, open-minded quest for knowledge, and progressive struggle for collective self-determination to anyone and everyone, all across the world. If rap music was going to be Hip Hop's public face, then Bambaataa "could use

[his] albums to send messages [while] the record companies played their role of sending these messages to all these places", uniting the explicit lessons of the Zulu religious philosophy with the sensuously appealing power of art, in order to rapidly and globally spread the emancipatory gospel of Hip Hop, in a form of what would come to be called "conscious" rap.[79]

Gathering up a predictably eclectic mix of samples—dominated by a riff from Kraftwerk and elements of the Latin-tinged b-boy classic "The Mexican" by the British band Babe Ruth—Bambaataa "unleashed a grand statement for what he was now calling the hip-hop movement. It was called 'Planet Rock'".[80] The global theme reflected more than the diversity of sampled material; the Zulus were quite consciously "trying to reach the Black, Latino, and the punk rock white[…]" communities to whom Bambaataa had already been playing with a new and more explicit message, in a process extending his reach across the globe, precisely by constructing communal sonic turf on which all could equally find footing.[81] Lyrically, "Planet Rock" was a celebration of Hip Hop jams as sites of unpretentious, joyous, universal community that sought only to reveal that, qua human, "our world is free". Sonically quite distinct from the hard funk of the Bronx, but still built from classic breakbeats, the track appealed not only to its home base but to the forms of street dance developing in Los Angeles (with its own local, evolving traditions of popping and locking), creating a point of contact between the different dance cultures in what were quickly becoming rap music's two primary geographical home bases. Capturing his polyglot sound in a single, coherent track made "Planet Rock" unlike anything that preceded it and, with lyrics that celebrated global connectedness to the point of even dropping coherent words in favour of merely joyous vocalizations that could include literally *anyone* in the sing-along,[82] it was a record that was consciously crafted for maximal travel, audience, and impact. Its hook even identified the global spread of emancipatory consciousness with early slang for Herc's breaks: "Planet Rock—it's the sure shot". As Sujatha Fernandes puts it, with

> its mix of European technorock, [60-era] funk, and [Hip Hop-era] rapping, 'Planet Rock' was a model of fusion that imagined unity across cultures the same way Bambaataa had created unity across gang lines. […] 'Planet Rock' preached universal brotherhood and transcendence [just as] Bambaataa envisioned universal consciousness.[83]

Rapturously received on a global tour, the single helped Bambaataa to eventually form Zulu chapters on every continent. Thus, having first articulated it independently of its aesthetic expression, the Zulus used rap music to give Hip Hop culture's message of collective consciousness and universal emancipation—effectively the inversion, or perhaps the "negation of the negation", of romantic rap music and the industry that produced and promoted it—as strong an aesthetic presentation as it could possibly receive, under the direction of the very man who first saw fit to clarify and name it. As the song's producer Tom Silverman argues, "Planet Rock" was thus "the record that initiated that [Hip Hop] wasn't just an urban thing, [and proved] it was inclusive. [...] That's when hip-hop became global".[84]

Hip Hop Between Art, Religion and Philosophy

In 1982—less than a decade after Herc's first party, and a mere 12 years after TAKI 183 first lit up the walls—the heroic culture of the Bronx achieved global acceptance and reach, carried by the humanistic optimism of "Planet Rock"; a few weeks later, it was eclipsed on the global stage by the alienated and isolating rage of "The Message". In a sense, these pioneering singles aesthetically present the tensions that continue to reverberate between Hip Hop as an emancipatory culture and rap music as its public face. While Bambaataa's single brought the original culture's universal consciousness and gospel of collective self-determination into cohesive and compelling aesthetic expression, the record credited to Flash's crew reflected the subsequent tendency towards increased emphasis on contingent individuality and the brutal refusal of the surrounding state, and world, to accept its most marginalized members as full citizens. While there can be no question, here, of doing anything resembling justice to the trajectories of either Hip Hop culture or rap music since 1982, in closing this chapter, we can make a few schematic remarks regarding both that follow from the preceding history.

It is, of course, the "reality rap" that followed in the wake of "The Message" which has come to dominate not only the public and academic understanding of Hip Hop, but to some degree the grasp of the culture internal to its ever-expanding global community. However, while its stark, brutal, and often hopeless vision reflects the inversion of the original culture, even the most seemingly spiritless forms of "gangsta" rap are not simply the products of external appropriation or romantic fragmentation.

If rap music has always appealed to the racial prejudices and thrill-seeking drive of the comfortable and privileged, and reflected the self-seeking individualism of the late capitalist state whose cruel fragmentation Hip Hop initially arose to resist, reality rap nevertheless also flourishes because the marginalized communities that still form Hop Hop's communal base continue to be unjustly denied genuine inclusion in the social and political institutions that would make the culture's emancipatory spirit a living reality. That is, despite the fact that, arguably starting with "The Message", "the gangsta style was a meticulous pose, a shrewd, market-driven performance that craftily exploited America's fear of poor, ghetto youths" as the basis for compelling, yet ultimately socially unthreatening drama, it is nevertheless equally true that "as the gangsta style evolved [...] it became, for some, the unfiltered voice of a generation of angry and alienated black men who inhabited America's ghettos" and expressed the perfectly understandable rage felt by the increasingly large surplus and stultified populations around the world.[85] We might say that "reality rap" reflects *both* Hegel's prediction of the inevitable end of art's internal development in individualistic romanticism (through its increasingly spiritless and spectacular presentations of the ugliness of finitude and desire, arguably peaking in the late 1990s output of labels like Death Row Records and Bad Boy Entertainment) and the repressive denial of free spirit's more direct and emancipatory actualization due to precisely the kinds of enduringly unjust social exclusion that Hegel steadfastly refuses to acknowledge (as we see in reality rap's "conscious" variants, or what used to be called "knowledge rap", from the militantly confrontational Black Nationalism of Public Enemy to the more explicitly Zulu-inspired work of the Native Tongues collective).[86] While the former provides spectacular thrills for the comfortable in the surrounding state, as well as channelling the potentially emancipatory energy of the oppressed into individually empowering, but collectively destructive, acts of creative expression, the latter carries forward Bambaataa's push to use the popularity of rap music and the full range of its aesthetic tools to preach Hip Hop's culture's core message to the contained communities that form its base, as well as to the broader, containing social sphere. The distinction between the two, of course, is marked by the very term now commonly used to mark the second; while its "harder" variants remain determined by corporeal and situational finitude, and thus by lyrical and dramatic depictions of alienated individuality, "conscious" or "knowledge" rap is always explicitly directed by the universal and emancipatory *thought* of our emancipatory essence which the art was initially created to express. All of Hip Hop's descendants, however, have remained politically potent and necessary even if, as Greg Tate argues, "for no other reason than [their] rendering people of African descent anything but invisible, forgettable, and dismissible" under the politics of containment, whose cruel, lived effects many would like to keep hidden.[87]

As we have seen, however, the problem is that art remains too tied to finitude, too focused on the particular, and ultimately too oblique in its presentation of spiritual truth for even its best "conscious" variants to remain prominent in the field of art. While the late 1980s is often referred to as rap's "Golden Age" precisely because its most innovative, commercially viable, and critically successful music fell somewhere on the "conscious" side of the spectrum, by the mid-1990s (in particular, after the 1992 release of Dr. Dre's landmark celebration of nihilistic hedonism, *The Chronic*), "gangsta" romanticism, along with the capitalist dreams of "bling" rap, came to almost exclusively dominate not only the mainstream expression of rap's dramatic poetry, but the image of Hip Hop culture in the broader popular imagination. As "rap as marketable product" became ever more divorced from the values of the culture that gave it birth, those who still embraced some variant of the original Bronx/Zulu values would seek not only to preserve Hip Hop's "conscious" poetry, but to find even more explicit ways to articulate its emancipatory spirit in non-aesthetic terms; and the most influential figure in this effort "un-rap" the culture from the "capitalist take-over of Hip Hop" is undoubtedly KRS-One.[88]

While his debut album, *Criminal Minded* (1987), is often cited as a source for some of the "gangsta" tropes mentioned above, as he saw the spiritless variants of reality rap begin to dominate the popular understanding of Hip Hop, like Bambaataa before him, KRS-One presciently grasped the deleterious effect they were going to have on both the original culture and the communities that shaped and preserved its evolving art forms. In response, and following the tragic murder of his partner in Boogie Down Productions, DJ Scott La Rock, he founded the Stop the Violence movement. While it is best known for the brilliant "posse" single it produced ("Self-Destruction" (1991), sometimes referred to as "Hip Hop's 'We Are The World'"), featuring a panoply of pioneering East Coast artists preaching the Zulu message of "Peace, Love, Unity, and Having Fun" against the spectacular celebration of fruitless violence and appetite that soon dominated the airwaves, the organization was also responsible for "many summits and conferences [which sought] to establish an authentic Hip Hop common spirit and began to give meaning and purpose to Hip Hop globally".[89] As mainstream interest in "conscious" rap subsided around 1994,[90] and "gangsta"/"bling" reality firmly took hold of the popular music, KRS-One and his organizations

> realized that rap was something that was *done*, while Hip Hop was something that was *lived*. We realized that Hip Hop was far more than just a music genre, that it was a *collective urban consciousness* that produced not only the expression of rapping, but also breakin, Deejayin, graffiti writing. [sic, emphasis added]

That is, he took up Bambaataa's fundamental insight regarding Hip Hop's universal knowledge, now explicitly grasped as something distinct from any aesthetic products Hip Hop might produce, and yet common to any creations that should pass under the culture's name, as their unifying and determining ground. To save Hip Hop culture, a new discourse was needed—more explicit not only from the discourse of rap music, but from the quasi-mystical Infinity Lessons, and which nevertheless spoke directly to those who were coming under the sway of rap—that could explicitly "guide a new generation of Hiphoppas spiritually and establish the groundwork for a new Hip Hop nation", and thereby lay the ground to *politically* actualize the essential freedom that birthed the artistic culture.

"This led", on the one hand, "to the 'I am Hip Hop' *philosophy* in 1994 [emphasis added]", which eventually produced *Ruminations*, his book of "Urban Inspirational Metaphysics [which] uses the experiences, logic, and reasoning of the urban environment to explain spirituality as it pertains to the essence of one's being while living in the inner city" environment where Hip Hop culture was born and, even as it globalizes itself, still largely finds its spiritual home;[91] and, on the other hand, to "the establishment of the Temple of Hip Hop in 1996", which sought to lead fragmented individuals into "the beginning of Hip Hop spiritual life. Not a lot of bells and whistles, not a lot of claims to divinity, just simply living a life that shows appreciation for the force that rescued" the founding community from abandonment, and could potentially liberate the globe from containment, thus putting the guiding philosophy of Hip Hop in *religious* form, replete with a founding sacred text (*The Gospel of Hip Hop: First Instrument*), attendant rituals, sacraments, and prayers.[92] These texts have significantly informed the analysis in this book because they reflect "remixes" of a large variety of surveys and conversations within the Hip Hop community itself, written to serve "as an actual balancing force within Hip Hop's cultural image in world history" against its appropriation by forces antithetical to its essence, in part through the philosophical articulation of the emancipatory truth of humanity's essence, and in part through the religious organization of communal life around "a covenant that provides peace and prosperity to all who claim Hip Hop as their culture". As Public Enemy's "media assassin" Harry Allen argues, such a covenant was necessary in order to force those attracted to the aesthetic products of the culture to pick a side between its spiritual foundation and its commercial exploitation:

> If you're gonna give in a tape and say 'I'm into Rap,' you have to *define yourself*. Are you going to be a Rap artist or a Hip Hop artist? Because if you say you're gonna be a Hip Hop artist, this little book[93] here put together by the minds of people in Hip Hop is what you should know. This will also weed out who's not down and who really is. In addition to that, we won't have the problems that Hip Hop is having because of rap artists.[94]

Along with Bambaataa and the Zulu Nation, KRS-One and the Temple of Hip Hop have perhaps been the most vital force in Hip Hop culture working to preserve, codify, and politically actualize what we might call the *spiritual philosophy* that unifies it, along the way inspiring rappers as diverse as the "revolutionary but gangsta" militants in *dead prez*[95]; the satirical art-rapper, journalist, and activist Kool A.D.[96]; and the reformed-dealers-seeking-mystical-redemption of the Wu-Tang Clan.[97]

In line with Harry Allen's words above, however, the future of this work is as yet uncertain. While conscious rap may in fact be both more prevalent and more popular than ever, and Hip Hop's other elements have attracted millions of devotees worldwide, as KRS-One's Temple literature notes, it is nevertheless also true that their "approach to Hip Hop is indeed unique" in the broader field; in fact, when compared with the varied forms of romantic rap that pass under Hip Hop's name in the broader sphere, it is arguably of limited influence. It is certainly true that the Zulu and Temple organizations and their varied comrades (e.g. the original Rock Steady Crew, which preserves and teaches the b-boy practice and ethic worldwide) have not only preserved Hip Hop's connection to its founding pioneers and principles in the public imagination, but helped further its political ambitions—most notably in the Hip Hop

Declaration of Peace, accepted by the United Nations in 2001, in part formally to recognize "Hip-Hop as an international culture of peace and prosperity".[98] It is, however, telling that the document was also conceived "to show Hip-Hop as a positive phenomenon which has nothing in common with the negative image of Hip Hop as something that corrupts young people and encourages them to break the law", or to combat the spectacular ugliness and romantic fragmentation that shape the most broadly popular forms of rap music, and thus the general public's understanding of the core culture.

This tension between Hip Hop's spiritual core and its marketed image is even found in "two of the most visible attempts [at] institutionalizing hip-hop politics", the Hip-Hop Summit Action Network (HSAN, founded 2001) and the National Hip Hop Political Convention (NHHPC, founded in 2003).[99] Conceived initially by rap music's first true mogul, Russell Simmons' HSAN quickly leveraged its roster of prominent rappers, producers, and entrepreneurs to gain a seat at the table during state-level political negotiations; for example, helping to push for modifications to the notorious Rockefeller drug laws in New York. However, it has also faced sharp criticism for its top-down approach to voicing Hip Hop's position, which is often perceived as relying "too heavily on the appearances of hip-hop celebrities [...] and catchy slogans", rather than grassroots organizing and community consultation.[100] For many, the fact that HSAN *appears* more political than it truly *is* proceeds from the fact that its primary organization "contains no nonrap artists, ignores three elements of hip-hop [...] and has no youth component", and thus is cut off from the broader and expanding culture.[101] While certainly influential in popular media, HSAN has largely remained distant from the community which made it possible, as reflected in the (quite limited, easily reversible) gains it made. Conversely, the more broad-based NHHPC, convened largely as a response to the perceived flaws in Simmons' group, "sought to gain its political prestige and influence from below" in order to ensure that "hip hop's political future would not be left in the hands of the very corporate interests that blunted its political edge".[102] However, despite the well-attended and broad-based conventions which re-affirmed and helped clarify the fact that Hip Hop was a distinct and emancipatory culture whose political potential was grounded in the grassroots community that kept alive its aesthetic elements and spiritual knowledge, it as yet has failed to produce significant gains in, or arguably even concrete and actualizable programmes for, institutional transformation.

Thus, while Simmons could parlay his credibility in rap music into tangible, if tenuous reform, this came in a form all too familiar to those who had long been spoken for, as opposed to being heard; conversely, while all relevant voices contribute to the unifying vision of NHHPC, they as yet lack the social or institutional power necessary to force transformative action. Both groups have so far failed "to develop what could be called a unique 'hip-hop' mode of politics" that would translate the culture's emancipatory promise into concrete social progress[103]; simultaneously, however, they also demonstrate the essential need for that promise to be kept, as well as the tensions that must be negotiated in order to do so.

CONCLUSION

All of this, of course, simply reinforces the fact that the tension—aesthetically expressed through "Planet Rock" and "The Message"—between Hip Hop as the expression of emancipatory consciousness (first in art, then in a "spiritual philosophy", and ultimately as a nascent, if unfulfilled and still emerging, politics that actualizes its previous discourses in state institutions) and rap music as the culture's most marketable and perhaps most "aesthetic" product (sometimes connected to its foundation, but easily and predominantly separable from it) is, in some ways, the enduring legacy of the original culture of the Bronx. As Chicago MC Super LP Raven puts it in the classic underground polemic *Bomb the Suburbs* (and in most Hegelian terms), "Hip-hop is a process that is *supposed to eliminate itself*. For hip-hop to achieve its goals it would have to *disappear*", precisely because it finds its goal, not in art, but in discourses and social practices that more directly express, and social institutions that more stably and concretely actualize, the emancipatory spirit that animated its original community; however, because of the adamant refusal of the American state to truly confront and correct the corrosive impact of its racial hierarchies and the inability, as yet, of its artists, organic intellectuals, and activists to find the discourses and courses of action that will sufficiently educate and unify its increasingly broad and diverse constituency to mobilize them into political action of lasting consequence, "hip-hop *keeps coming back*, 'cause the problems are still here".[104] Hip Hop unjustly, but heroically, endures not only as sensible evidence of the frustrations and distortions of human essence under late capitalism (typified by "reality" rap, and in the more "establishment" politics and economic opportunities it tends to produce), but as the spiritual promise of a future liberation to come (found

in the Hip Hop community as grassroots aesthetic, religious, philosophical, and political struggle for self-determination and the more "underground" politics and economies it inspires).

The "conscious" lyricism that defined reality rap's "Golden Age", and
typifies much of the "underground" music which followed it (on labels like
Rawkus Records, Definitive Jux, Rhymesayers, etc.), unites these two sides
in an uneasy but potent synthesis that infuses reality rap's broad appeal
with what we might call Hip Hop philosophy's essential message; however,
in inevitably seeking to appeal to the finite interests of its audience, even
the best conscious rap can always be confused with, or can internally fall
prey to the temptations of, the merely romantic presentation of reality and
subjectivity. The breakers, DJs, and graffiti artists who carry forward Hip
Hop's other elements may, of course, similarly give into the romantic
temptations of mere virtuosity and personal empowerment; but the lower
market value of these aesthetic products, and their intrinsic link to an adjudicating community and thus to collectively determined and meritocratic
values, may make them (along, perhaps, with the long-standing underground tradition of "battle rapping") the primary *aesthetic* representation
of Hip Hop's spiritual vision at present. But, as Super Ravven indicates,
these primarily serve, not as ends in themselves, but as means of keeping
the vision of an anti-racist, pro-Black, progressively self-determining, and
increasingly universal community alive and united until it rightfully receives
or forces genuine inclusion in academic, cultural, and political structures,
allowing art's central role to recede, as it should, to the past.

The question of how to do so, of course, is precisely the one posed by
Brother D., and—in what one might call the cunning of reason—the
spread and influence of the very rap music that he condemned will assuredly play a leading role in formulating and implementing its solution.
While, as Paul Gilroy argues, the "[m]arket-driven black popular culture"
presented in much rap music "is *making politics* aesthetic [but] usually as
a precondition for marketing hollow defiance",[105] Hip Hop endures everywhere *the aesthetic is made political* by using its unique elements, ethical
principles, and collective modes of being to educate, agitate, and organize
the globe's most marginalized to force emancipatory social and institutional change. The Zulu Nation and following it the Temple of Hip Hop
have arguably reflected the most significant efforts to move the culture's
truth beyond art, within the conditions that still seek to stifle its communities; however, during the time of this writing, allegations against Afrika
Bambaataa and the initial reaction to them by KRS-One rocked rap music

and Hip Hop culture.[106] Whether these figures and their organizations will continue to play leading roles in the ongoing development of Hip Hop culture, or whether new voices and collectives will rise remains to be seen.[107]

What is clear, however, is that Bambaataa was right that rap music can serve as a powerfully compelling *vehicle* for promoting, and even popularizing, the struggle for emancipation; but this, as KRS-One has long held, means that the essential destiny of Hip Hop—seemingly unique among the contemporary arts, popular or otherwise—demands that its increasingly global community "turn [their] Hip Hop view of the world (our *sight*) toward the subjects of *philosophy, history, religion and politics*", precisely in order to distinguish the emancipatory and universal spirit evinced by the culture from the romantic, appropriating forces that continually seek to seize control over its discourse by way of its most popular aesthetic products.[108]

NOTES

1. All of the quotes in the prologue are either from the lyrics to the song in question or to Hager, *Hip Hop*, Ch. 6.
2. In *"There Ain't No Black in the Union Jack": The Cultural Politics of Race and Nation* (Chicago: University of Chicago Press, 1985), Paul Gilroy links the record to the general trend towards militant politics in soul music, with which he considers early "message" rap continuous. While remaining one of the best resources for studying the movement of rap music across both the "Back Atlantic" and racial boundaries, as well as the manner in which rap exemplifies "the chronic conflict between black musics and the forms in which the leisure industries have sought to commodify and sell them" (214), he downplays, in my view, the degree to which Brother D. "denounced" rap, and even Hip Hop culture, rather than merely the surrounding culture's "discos" (183), and thus the tension it raises between aesthetic struggles and more directly political ones. Of course, the guiding thread of this entire book has been that the emancipatory potential of rap music/Hip Hop culture is grounded in the fact that, as Gilroy puts it, the "arts, which [...] blacks were allowed instead of freedom, have become a means to make their formal freedom tangible" (215); however, the failure of Brother D. to make an impact in the culture, or to attract true descendants arguably until Public Enemy's second album nearly a decade later, should, I think, make us re-evaluate the role that art can play in securing political freedoms, at least when not directly tied to local communities. On the import of the local for the future of rap music, see Perry.

3. As he puts it elsewhere, "the real beginning of dramatic poetry must be sought [...] where the principle of free individuality makes the completion [*Vollendung*] of the classical form of art possible for the first time" (1206/III, 535, trans. modified).

4. Purely lyrical poetry, of course, continues to feature strongly in the music, as we see in the imaginative genius of MCs like MF DOOM and GZA, or the tradition of hookless, stream of consciousness raps exemplified by tracks like "Mural" by Lupe Fiasco, "Hot Tub Rhyme Machine" by Kool A.D. (which features the couplet "Sippin'" on Faygo/Flippin' through Hegel") and the now-legendary Flex freestyle by Black Thought. The introduction of the "hype man"—arguably originating with Public Enemy's Flavor Flav in the mid-1980s—kept alive the epic celebration of the performers and crowd at a live show. But the genre has come to embrace themes, styles and topics as broad as any other form of literature, and has produced everything from experimental poets (e.g. Aesop Rock, Kool Keith, and Beans) whose linguistic abstractions rival those of the high modernists, to satirists (e.g. Lil B, El-P, and Tyler, the Creator) who recall everything from William S. Burroughs to Paul Krassner to the Church of the Subgenius.

5. The phrase is broadly credited to Chuck D. from Public Enemy.

6. Charnas, 48. A large number of early rap records, in fact, were in the "novelty" category, often created to cash in on pop culture trends (Bobby Robinson from Enjoy Records, e.g. produced "I'm the Packman" in 1982, which was quickly followed by Shawn Brown's John Wayne parody, "Rappin' Duke" ("duh-ha, duh-ha"), and Mel Brooks' film promotion parody "To Be Or Not To Be", more popularly known as "The Hitler Rap"), but which occasionally formed an avenue for some of the new rap crews to break mainstream, as when Brooklyn's Disco 3 changed their name and image for their debut, self-titled record *The Fat Boys*. Moore and Ford would go on to produce more novelty records, like the Rodney Dangerfield-sung parody, "Rappin' Rodney".

7. Although it was re-released every Christmas for a decade thereafter and eventually went gold.

8. *Philosophy of Mind/Werke* 10, §562. All translations from this text are my own.

9. Rutter, 49. While offering one of the most cogent accounts in the literature of Hegel's assertion that, in comedy, "it is the protagonist's stubborn subjectivity which is fixed, or necessary, while the objective realm goes free" (223), and correctly noting that, for Hegel, the "comedic protagonist is drawn from the lower classes, and it is the playwright whose generous imagination sets him free" (227), it is somewhat disconcerting that Rutter fails to address the class or racial implications of this claim. I dis-

cuss the tendency among Hegel scholars to remain within Hegel's blind spots in the conclusion.

10. Cornel West, *Democracy Matters: Winning the Fight Against Imperialism* (New York: Penguin, 2004), 179. While offering one of the most compelling defences of the relationship between Hip Hop's aesthetic elements and the religious-philosophical-political dimensions of the culture that we will discuss below, West nevertheless follows many in conflating the early and "golden" ages of rap music of the 1980s and early 1990s with the pre-recording pioneers of the Bronx party culture, in order to link Hip Hop's origins to rap music's political protest tradition: "The first stages of hip-hop were hot. Coming from the margins of society, the lyrics and rhythms of Grandmaster Flash and the Furious Five, Kool Herc, Rakim, Paris, the Poor Righteous Teachers, Afrikaa [sic] Bambaataa, and, above all, KRS-ONE and Public Enemy (Led by Chuck D) unleased incredible democratic energies" (180); compare, e.g. with Perry and Tayannah Lee McQuillar, *When Rap Music Had A Conscience: The Artists, Organizations, and Historic Events that Inspired and Influenced the 'Golden Age' of Hip-Hop From 1987–1996* (New York: Thunder's Mouth Press, 2007). The vexed story of "The Message", in my view, deserves far more scholarly investigation and debate.

11. Chang, *Can't Stop*, 178. Compare *The Adventures of Grandmaster Flash*, 157: "nobody in the group liked it […] the shit was way too dark, way too edgy, and way too much of a downer. It was the furthest thing from a party rap anyone could imagine".

12. While this story is becoming better known, you can still find examples of the song being credited to the singular genius of the foundational Bronx crew. For example, McQuillar credits the song's fame to "Flash's unrivaled cutting and scratching skills combined with Melle Mel's scorching and fear-filled stories" (14), despite the fact the latter had to be coerced into largely reciting a professional songwriter's lines, and the song lacks any audible DJing technique whatsoever. This is likely typical of both the public confusion made inevitable by the questionable practices of Sugar Hill and other labels and of the drive to anachronistically push "conscious rap" back to the earliest manifestations of the culture. I hope to show that such a link can be made, but through a different pioneering single and arguably "conscious" rap tradition.

13. *The Adventures of Grandmaster Flash*, 159. As he movingly details in this memoir, he did eventually successfully sue the company over his contract, but tellingly asked for no damages; he only asked for the rights to his *name*.

14. Etter, 65.

15. Rutter, 223.

16. Chang, *Can't Stop*, 178–9. After "The Message" became a smash, Flash was haunted by being told—by not only his record label, but even some of his crew—that he was "just a DJ" (Cf., *The Adventures of Grandmaster Flash*, 166–74).

17. Anticipating some of my arguments in the conclusion, I would also note that this is an inversion of the history of Hip Hop culture presented by Bailey: "Hip-hop may have begun as something violently abrasive to the generic Western interests that helped create the climates of poverty in urban communities, but, since its birth, it has grown into the expression of unity, peace, and collective struggle" (66). This reveals the extent to which Bailey, like many scholars, while briefly detailing (in an occasionally questionable narrative) Hip Hop's Bronx origin, effectively begins with rap music's so-called Golden Age of post-"Message" conscious rap poetry, as though both originating in and defining of the broader culture. One sees this in his terse claim that "In 1982, Grandmaster Flash came out with 'The Message,' which highlighted this inner-city struggle", without any comment on the track's sordid history or its distinction from previous rap and Hip Hop lyrics and music (35). For the record, at the time the song dominated the airwaves, Flash recalls thinking "every time I hear it, I get the same sinking feeling in my gut....*I'm losing something here*" (*The Adventures of Grandmaster Flash*, 156), echoing his later realization that "[s]omewhere along the way, the heart and soul of what I had helped create had disappeared" (201) because "The Bronx was my home. The Bronx was where I did my thing. But somehow, the Bronx had been left behind" in rap's triumph (200). This claim is true both literally, in figures like Caz and Herc who effectively got robbed of their innovations, and figuratively in that the collective spirit of the crew, cypher, and party suddenly became "a story about getting paid" as the primary chance to escape despair (201).

18. This would reach its peak with the hysteria over Ice-T's manifestly non-rap song "Cop Killer", recorded by his heavy metal side project Body Count, and Bill Clinton's craven attack on Public Enemy affiliate Sister Souljah for some decontextualized words. For discussion, see Chang, *Can't Stop*, 392–405.

19. Fernandes, ix.

20. Ibid., 4.

21. Ibid., 3.

22. Toop, 124. The story, here, is predictably somewhat complicated, and space considerations obviously don't allow a complete airing of the tale of its national, then global, spread. While the early records certainly brought it to broad public attention, Hip Hop culture arguably received its first truly national and international exposure through the appearance of the

Rock Steady Crew in the movie *Flashdance* (1983; directed by A. Lyne), kicking off a (very brief) popular obsession with breaking. However, none of the elements beyond rap music were readily monetized, which inevitably limited their appeal to the economic forces that allowed for popular exposure. Thus, in the wake of the success of records like "Rapper's Delight" and "The Breaks", those seeking either to profit from the elements of culture or to make a living in and through it quickly gravitated to MCing, and "The Message" in many ways set the template for an MC's "authenticity".

23. While the tale is obviously fantasy, Ice-T could, of course, write from his experience in the city's criminal underworld. The aesthetic appeal of blending the authentic and the fantastical in "gangsta" rap is, in many ways, Ice-T's central and underappreciated contribution to rap poetry.

24. Speaking in *The Show*, emphasis mine.

25. Flash also claims that "throughout 1986, I could see what Reaganomics was doing in the Bronx [...] If anything, the Bronx was getting worse. Worse than it had been in the days of the gangs. Worse than it had been in the summer of '77. Worse than ever" (*The Adventures of Grandmaster Flash*, 214).

26. Fernandes offers an excellent account of the global spread and appeal of the former tendency; for a particular unsavoury—and, due to the later literary achievements of one of its authors, unfortunately broadly read and praised—example of the latter, see David Foster Wallace and Mark Costello, *Signifying Rappers* (New York: Back Bay Books, 1990). The concern arising from "realistic" portrayals of Black American life in art that, in Gilroy's terms, a "mass white [audience] might discover deep pleasures in the image of blacks as victims of racism" (*Black Atlantic*, 153) or that, as Christopher J. Lebron, drawing on the work of Zora Neale Hurston, puts it, "those consuming that testimony are not doing so to genuinely learn anything new about Black Americans. Rather, they already have concluded that their condition is wretched and merely seek confirmation" (*The Making of Black Lives Matter: A Brief History of an Idea* (New York: Oxford University Press, 2017), 58) should, in my view, be raised far more frequently in the Hip Hop Studies literature, for reasons I will discuss more fully in the conclusion.

27. Watkins, 103. Some of the causes and effects of this trend, particularly as they affect issues of gender and sexuality in rap music, are treated well in *Hip-Hop: Beyond Beats and Rhymes* (2006; directed by Byron Hurt).

28. *Philosophy of Mind/Werke* 10, §562.

29. Ibid.

30. Ibid.

31. "Telling the Truth: Systematic Philosophy and the *Aufhebung* of Poetic and Religious Language," in Jere O'Neill Surber, ed. *Hegel and Language* (Albany: SUNY Press, 2006), 127–141 (133).

32. *Philosophy of Mind/Werke* 10, §562, emphasis added.

33. Ibid., §563.

34. Ibid.

35. Ibid., §562, emphasis added.

36. Ibid., §562. I try to clarify the logic of Hegel's preference for religions of free self-knowledge, as reflected for him primarily in the Lutheranism of his day, but perhaps now best exemplified by other religions, in "Liberation Theology: Hegel on Why Philosophy Takes Sides in Religious Conflict", *Symposium: Canadian Journal of Continental Philosophy* 17:2 (Fall 2013), 141–157.

37. Dudley, 133–4.

38. *Philosophy of Mind/ Werke* 10, §565.

39. Dudley, 135.

40. Ibid., 136.

41. Ibid., 137.

42. *Philosophy of Mind*, §572, emphasis added.

43. Dudley, 137. Cf., Hegel's infamous 1805 draft letter to Voss: "Luther made the Bible speak German, and you have done the same for Homer—the greatest gift that can be made to a people. For a people remains barbarian and does not view what is excellent within the range of its acquaintance as its own true property so long as it does not come to know it in its own language. If you will kindly forget these two illustrations, I may say of my endeavor that I wish to try to teach philosophy to speak German" (*Hegel: The Letters*, trans. Clark Butler and Christiane Seiler, with commentary by Clark Butler (Bloomington, IN: Indiana University Press, 1984), 107).

44. Bambaataa's role, I should note, is not *unanimously* accepted among the players in early Hip Hop's unification. For example, Martha Cooper, who played a pioneering role in gaining mainstream exposure for the elements, argues that "graffiti and break-dancing would not necessarily have been connected if we, the media people, had not wanted to lump them together. [...] Hip-hop was packaged and in a sense we packaged it" (quoted in I. Miller, 152). While there is some controversy regarding the exact timing and origin of the unification of its elements under the moniker Hip Hop, on balance I think the evidence indicates that it was an internal, rather than an external, development and that Bambaataa both popularized the name and initially forwarded its explicit spiritual vision.

45. Brewster and Broughton, *The Record Players*, 175.

46. Cf., Watkins: "His response to an initial offer to record the music he was helping to create was incredibly naïve: 'Let's keep it underground. Nobody outside the Bronx would like this stuff anyway.' And then he heard the Sugarhill Gang on the radio. [...] The success of the record haunted him; he realized that he had missed out on an opportunity to be the first to record the music" (29).

47. Bambaataa in Brewster and Broughton, *The Record Players*, 198. Unless otherwise marked, all quotes in this paragraph and the next are from this text, 192–3. As with much in Hip Hop's first decade, there are conflicting accounts of his relation to recording. Hager, for example, suggests that he actively sought a deal early, but was rebuked; I stick with the most commonly told story, here, which primarily echoes Bambaataa's claim that "When we started seeing the recordings, a lot of us in the Zulu Nation stayed away from that at first because people thought once it got into vinyl we thought it was going to kill the culture" (Fricke and Ahearn, 196). The first attempts he made at recording further soured him on the attempt to shrink the culture down to a 12-inch record.

48. Chang, *Can't Stop*, 95.

49. Again, dates as to its founding differ, as do those of when he began the Organization, and in most cases evidence of Bambaataa suggesting a given date at one time or another can be found. Hager claims that even while he was in the Black Spades, he used the group to organize voting registration drives and to raise money for various Black-focused charities (e.g. for sickle-cell anaemia testing). Chang dates "The Organization" roughly from the beginning of the decline of the gangs in 1971, and suggests it became The Zulu Nation between 1974 and 1976, or around the time most commonly suggested for when he formally began DJing; this roughly matches the story told in *Beat This*, which is a kind of cross between a documentary on Bambaataa's influence on Hip Hop culture, and a stylized explication of the Zulu spiritual philosophy. But recent research suggests the Organization moniker remained as late as—or perhaps even did not arise until—1975, and one commonly cited date for Bambaataa's first party is November 12, 1976, with the Zulu name arising subsequent to it. The 1973 date comes from the timeline on the Zulu Nation website at the time of writing, although it isn't clear if that is meant to reflect the dance-based Zulu Kings and Queens, or the more educational and political institution of the Organization. *From Mambo to Hip Hop* gives a good sense of how absolutely foundational the Zulu Kings and Queens were in the history of breaking. And my thanks once again to Serouj Aprahamian, whose ongoing work will assuredly help clarify this vital timeline, for sharing his research.

50. 1964; directed by Cy Endfield.

51. "I went to Africa [...] I was in Ivory Coast, Nigeria, and Guinea Bissau [...] That was a big inspiration, seeing black people controlling their own destiny, seeing them get up and go to their own work. Seeing their own farmers and agricultures, it was very interesting, when you were seeing all the negativity that you were seeing as a young cat, and all the stuff just coming out of the '60s with the civil rights and human rights, so it was very inspirational seeing this" (Brewster and Broughton, *The Record Players*, 193).

52. Sha-Rock, with Iesha Brown, *Luminary Icon: The Story of the Beginning and End of Hip-Hop's First Female MC* (Sudbury, MA: eBookit.com, 2015); audiobook version.

53. Fricke and Ahearn, 44, emphasis added.

54. "Son of Bambaataa", Afrika Islam, speaking in Fricke and Ahearn, 55.

55. Ibid.

56. Travis L. Gosa, "The fifth element: knowledge," in Justin A. Williams, ed. *The Cambridge Companion to Hip-Hop* (Cambridge: Cambridge University Press, 2015), 56–70 (58).

57. Fricke and Ahearn, 52. As the early tagger DOZE recalls, "I got down with Zulu Nation primarily because of its inclusiveness. [...] the Zulu Nation was like, 'You are poor, you are black, you are brown. We all have something in common with hip-hop. Let's try to unite, let's get it together.' Thank God for the Nation; there were gangs before that and all kinds of crap going on" (quoted in I. Miller, 113).

58. Ibid., 50. The often shifting accounts Bambaataa himself gives have often led the Zulus to be misunderstood, with some claiming it was really just "a collective of rap artists devoted to promoting social and political awareness in their listeners" (Hess, 73). McQuillar captures some of the more robust nature of Nation as Bambaataa's "movement to preserve hip-hop in its truest artistic form and [thereby to] create-self-awareness" in their audience (43).

59. As he recalls, "Once we started playing downtown, once it started getting towards the late '70s early 80s you start seeing the white punk rockers started coming to the black and Latino areas to hear the music. They would come to the Bronx. People were scared at first, you know you had the media said 'Oh there's gonna be race violence,' which we showed them was a bunch of shit" (Brewster and Broughton, *DJ Revolutionaries*, 198).

60. "I play stuff where people talk about 'I don't like Latin,', so I play a Latin artist, and get them movin'. I'm a play a rock artist, say 'I ain't into heavy metal,' so I play something like Led Zeppelin, or Foghat or something, then move into that" (Ibid., 201); compare Ewodzie, 118. Hager reports that this is the reason Bambaataa was "the only DJ [that Kool Herc]

respect[ed] because [Bambaataa] always plays music [Herc] never heard before" ("Pied Piper"); this also would have made his sets more popular with the early graffiti artists, who, coming from an earlier time and a more multi-racial constituency, were often heavily into classic rock and Latin music.

61. Chang, *Can't Stop*, 97. Recently asked to look back on what he was most proud of, Bambaataa succinctly and predictably replied, "Bringing people together. Settling their differences and spreading the hip hop culture all around the globe" (Brewster and Broughton, *DJ Revolutionaries*, 201), which quickly makes the connection between his days as truce-broker among gangs to, as we shall see, his becoming Hip Hop's first global ambassador.

62. Brewster and Broughton, *DJ Revolutionaries*, 200.

63. Fricke and Ahearn, 52.

64. Chang, *Can't Stop*, 101.

65. Gosa, 64; 58; 65.

66. Ibid., 58.

67. Chang, *Can't Stop*, 92.

68. Brewster and Broughton, *DJ Revolutionaries*, 197; as he puts it here, "I just had a vision. I said we just have to make this move."

69. Chang, *Can't Stop*, 90.

70. As Sha-Rock puts it in *Luminary Icon*, "Hip Hop began to take on a new form [because t]he world was now seeing the rap side of the culture" on its own, rather than as essentially linked with the other elements and the community which developed them.

71. Ibid.

72. Ibid, emphasis added.

73. Ibid. The most recent Infinity Lessons, along with some of the original documents, are available at http://new.zulunation.com/infinity-lessons/ (accessed May 2017). All citations from the Infinity Lessons and Core Beliefs can be found from their main page.

74. Chang, *Can't Stop*, 94, emphasis added.

75. Quoted in Ibid., 106.

76. Aine McGlynn, "The Infinity Lessons of the Zulu Nation," in Mickey Hess, ed., *Icons of Hip-Hop: An Encyclopedia of the Movement, Music, and Culture*, vol. 1 (Santa Barbara: ABC-CLO, 2007), 269–70 (269, emphasis added). As she writes of the "infinity" and "universality" of the lessons, "One of the most beautiful and appealing aspects of the lessons is that they are never complete. They can, at any time, by any member, be added to. […] There is, however, a set of fundamental ideas around which they shift and develop. Among them is the focus on coming to know the self" as spiritually "divine" (ibid.).

77. Chang, *Can't Stop*, 106.

78. *Hip Hop Matters: Politics, Pop Culture, and the Struggle for the Soul of a Movement* (Boston: Beacon Press, 2005), 52.

79. Chang, *Can't Stop*, 172.

80. Ibid., 170.

81. Fricke and Ahearn, 315. Even the new MCs enlisted for the project, like Pow Wow and G.L.O.B.E., named themselves in honour of this collectivist mission.

82. This was, evidently, a contingency: a nervous Pow Wow dropped his lyric sheet and spontaneously improvised a verse built solely around the sound "zoom", which would become the song's most beloved moment.

83. *Close to the Edge*, 2–3.

84. Chang, *Can't Stop*, 173.

85. Watkins, 45.

86. It is worth noting that, despite his critiques of "The Message" for its inversion of the original, as "reality rap" spread around the globe, Flash became increasingly troubled "that young brothers were using drugs and guns to get by rather than turntables and microphones. [It b]othered me that nobody was talking about it on wax […] it bothered me that nobody was talking about black life in rap music. Now I don't judge anyone for how they choose to get over […] but it didn't seem right to me that the place where it came from didn't have a voice. Right about then, it needed one bad" (*The Adventures of Grandmaster Flash*, 213–14). And it was precisely the arrival of Public Enemy and KRS-One's Boogie Down Productions, along with the revolutionary, multisyllabic, and internally dense lyrical rhymes of Rakim, that filled this need—aesthetically and educationally—and thus signalled for Hip Hop's most important and influential DJ that the spirit of Hip Hop could and indeed would live on in rap music (cf. 215–217).

87. Greg Tate, "Hiphop Turns 30", *Village Voice*, Dec. 28, 2004, which also captures the tension between the "conscious" and "reality" variants in Hip Hop's popular legacy: "Nothing less […] than the marriage of heaven and hell, of New World African ingenuity and that trick of the devil known as global hypercapitalism".

88. M. Miller, 60.

89. https://thetempleofhiphop.wordpress.com/ (accessed, May 2017). Unless otherwise noted, all citation quotations in this section are from this webpage, which succinctly charts the history of KRS-One's activities outside of rap music, including his underappreciated Human Education Against Lies (H.E.A.L.) organization.

90. Listen to "Ferocious Soul", the "hidden" track that opens Public Enemy's *Muse Sick-n-Our Mess Age* (1994) for a remarkable prediction of the criti-

cal and popular eclipse of "conscious" rap in favour of the most conform-
ist "gangsta" variants.

91. KRS-One, *Ruminations*, 37.

92. KRS-One, *Gospel*, 14.

93. He is referring to a then-projected compendium of Hip Hop knowledge
to be derived from meetings of the major minds in the culture, but which
went on to serve as the foundation for the *Gospel* and *Ruminations*.

94. Quoted in *Gospel*, 508, italics and underscoring used to mark off different
aspects of the oral conversation recorded in the book removed for
clarity.

95. "KRS-One made a huge impact on my life/from the foods that I choose,
every rhyme that I write", "The Movement".

96. "Bump KRS for philosophy", "Special Forces".

97. Cf., RZA speaking in *Something from Nothing: The Art of Rap* (2012;
directed by Ice-T and Andy Baybutt).

98. https://thetempleofhiphop.wordpress.com/hip-hop-declaration-of-
peace/ (accessed May 2017). Among its primary authors were KRS-One,
Rock Steady Crew Vice-President and breaking historian Pop Master
Fabel, Afrika Bambaataa, and Harry Allen.

99. Lester K. Spence, *Stare Into The Darkness: The Limits of Hip-Hop and
Black Politics* (Minneapolis: University of Minnesota, 2011), 97. While
we will just barely touch on the issue, here, this is an excellent introduc-
tion to/analysis of the major efforts to articulate and institutionalize a
Hip Hop politics. For further discussion of the possibility of actualizing
the spirit of the aesthetic culture in more concrete political forms, see
Watkins, Kitwana, and William "Upski" Wimsatt, *Please Don't Bomb The
Suburbs: A Midterm Report on My Generation and the Future of Our
Super Movement* (New York: Atlantic, 2010); for a sceptical view, see John
McWhorter, *All About The Beat: Why Hip-Hop Can't Save Black America*
(New York: Penguin, 2008).

100. Watkins, 155.

101. Spence, 114.

102. Watkins, 158–9. Among other things, attendees had to demonstrate
community support by garnering signatures endorsing their attendance
from within their local scenes.

103. Spence, 128.

104. 105, emphasis added.

105. *Against Race*, 206, emphasis added; more on this in the conclusion.

106. It would be unjust to complete a book that focuses so much on their
contributions to Hip Hop culture without mentioning the disturbing and
compelling charges against Bambaataa, as well as the controversies surrounding the responses by both KRS-One and the Zulu Nation; however,

both because the allegations have been denied by Bambaataa and because the responses of his followers have been subject to substantial change and occasional misrepresentation, this troubling episode in the ongoing history of Hip Hop culture will have to remain on the periphery of our analysis. While I would insist that future scholarship should still give both of these pivotal figures and their organizations *an even greater voice* than they have hitherto received in the literature, for all the reasons outlined above, the unfolding fallout of these events *should also form a core aspect* of ongoing discussion about the culture's direction. The same, as I will suggest in the conclusion, is true of the need to *both* revive what is vital and enduring in Hegel's thought, *and* to explicitly confront his deep and serious personal and philosophical flaws.

107. Crazy Legs, Grandmaster Caz, Sha-Rock, and Kool Herc remain among the most dedicated guardians of the first decade's techniques, principles, and legacy, and many important leaders have emerged from the "conscious" side of rap music. Chuck D., like KRS-One, has worked in his books, lectures, and activism to forge an essentially Black, but vocally universalist, liberation movement out of his revolutionary MCing, and with his group Public Enemy has tirelessly and successfully worked to force lasting change within the music industry (among other things, they were the first group to record an East/West posse cut; the first group to found their own record label, to launch their own internet radio station and to distribute music via mp3 downloads; the first to defend torrents and downloading in Congress; and the group who finally put Kool Herc on wax). On their fascinating history, see Russell Myrie, *Don't Rhyme for The Sake of Riddlin': The Authorized Story of Public Enemy* (New York: Canongate, 2009). In recent years, the university lecture circuit has included rappers like Talib Kweli and Heems, both of whom have also been extremely active in journalism, music criticism, and municipal politics. But perhaps the most successful efforts to further Hip Hop goals in recent years have found their rap spokesperson in Killer Mike, whose campaign #BankBlack led thousands of people to draw their money out of conglomerate banks, and invest in local, Black-owned credit unions, and who was instrumental in swinging the extremely close 2017 Atlanta mayoral election to a progressive Democrat. While there is no-one more cognizant of the distinction between the original Hip Hop culture and subsequent rap music, or who more vociferously defends even what would appear to be the latter's most spiritless commercial offerings, when one considers his internal critiques of rap music on tracks like "Rap is Dead", arena-filling (and, I know from experience, life-changing) work with El-P in Run The Jewels, continuous and highly influential municipal activism in Atlanta, surrogacy for Bernie Sanders'

landmark presidential campaign, inspired journalism on issues related to rap music, censorship and police brutality, and lucidly educational rapping on tracks like "Reagan", Killer Mike may be the most potent figure bridging the principles of Hip Hop culture with the global reach of rap music active today.

108. Gospel, 100, emphasis added.

CHAPTER 7

Conclusion

In this book, I have sought to philosophically comprehend the emergence, development, and enduring tensions of Hip Hop through the Hegelian thesis that collectively self-determining artistic cultures emerge as a people's self-liberation from extreme situations of external determination; both reveal that collectively forging a social order, in and through creative contribution to a unified aesthetic culture and its attendant ethical values, allows communities that are radically deprived of functioning and inclusive political institutions to *sensuously demonstrate their essential freedom.* On the one hand, this implies that art—as Hegel suggests, but then quickly and conveniently forgets—is not merely a stage humanity has long since passed through on the way spirit's complete actualization in the modern state, but remains a *predictable and vital response* to forms of social abandonment or severe alienation that arises from, and palpably demonstrates, the striving for self-determination essential to humanity. On the other hand, if there has long been a feeling among scholars and artists alike that "hip hop was at its best and most vital when it was contained in the New York City neighborhoods where it began",[1] this is because its founding artists, creations, and values best exemplify the mission of Hip Hop as an *emancipatory culture,* whose spirit continues to act, as it were, as the conscience of rap music. What I have tried to show in this book is both that reading his *Lectures on Aesthetics* through the lens of Hip Hop reveals some ways we should change the way we think and write about Hegel, and

© The Author(s) 2018

J. Vernon, *Hip Hop, Hegel, and the Art of Emancipation,*
https://doi.org/10.1007/978-3-319-91304-9_7

conversely that examining the culture's history through the framework of Hegel's aesthetic theory should push us to change some of the ways we think and write about Hip Hop.

Given the preceding, I hope it will be clear that by "we", I primarily mean *scholars*, rather than those struggling to sustain Hip Hop as a unified and emancipatory culture, either by preserving and developing its aesthetic elements or by pushing its community and spirit towards actualization in the realms of religion, philosophy, and politics. I also hope the above demonstrates not only that Hip Hop's history charts a trajectory remarkably similar to that which Hegel charts for freely creative humanity in general, but that its organic intellectuals explicitly proclaim a remarkably similar self-understanding of the nature and import of their cultural creations, demonstrating the enduring power of a distinctive and largely derided thesis about the much-vaunted link between art and emancipation. While the consequences of the above analysis for future scholarship are multiple and varied, by way of conclusion, I'd like to briefly sketch one substantial critique that the preceding analysis contains for each field, starting with Hegel studies, and the very question of the academic "we".

While much recent work on the *Lectures on Aesthetics* has highlighted the fact that art's "business is to realize and to bring to consciousness who and what we are as creatures engaged in attaining our freedom",[2] the field also broadly and often uncritically adopts Hegel's view that "the essence of what *we moderns* are is no longer best rendered comprehensible in art".[3] As Bungay notes, Hegel's "'We' means the sophisticated, intellectual public of early-nineteenth-century Germany"—or, by extension, the "modern public" in contemporary Western states—who, safely ensconced within stable institutions of right, can reflectively produce, consume, and debate the diverse forms of "romantic" art that are typically the focus of philosophical aesthetics, Hegelian or otherwise.[4] It is these audiences that scholars typically have in mind when they agree with Hegel that "art, on its highest side, is *for us* a thing of the past".[5] However, if art's emancipatory power and role "waxes as the expressive possibilities of sensuous configuration are more and more realized",[6] this is not only because higher forms of spirit's self-actualization—as manifested in revealed religion, public philosophy, and the institutions of a free state—have arisen to carry on art's work, but more pertinently because such audiences generally (if imperfectly) enjoy representation and protection within them.

Of course, the generalized social inclusion of this "we" by no means precludes the expression, aesthetic or otherwise, of dissatisfaction with the nature of modern civic life; no one would seriously claim that all are equally recognized or actualized in modern society, and such expressions are obviously often quite justified. However, it is telling that, for Hegel scholars such as Rutter, the often critical nature of contemporary, romantic art and subjectivity reflects the fact that what "people ordinarily feel, *modern people at any rate*, is the *profoundly middling* nature of the human character and human affairs".[7] Critiques of the Hegelian "we" have been made in the literature sympathetic to his *Aesthetics*, perhaps most forcefully by Pippin, who claims that Hegel's "greatest failure [in his *Lectures*, is that he] never seemed very concerned about [the] potential instability in the modern world, [or] about citizens of the same ethical commonwealth potentially losing so much common ground and common confidence that a general irresolvability of any of these possible conflicts becomes ever more apparent".[8] Nevertheless, in locating the aesthetic consequences of such a failure in modernist painting—Manet's revolution in particular—Pippin's reading largely remains within the purview of the generally included, yet personally dissatisfied citizen, for whom gallery art expresses and calls attention to our discontent. While recent scholarship has compellingly revealed the enduring import of Hegel's theory of art for understanding the largely romantic artistic developments in the twentieth century and beyond, its focus has remained on the art most amenable to the spiritual needs of the privileged "we" within which most scholars generally find themselves, and whose rote, if often stultifying, social inclusion implies that "art can still be one mode of truth or one need of the Spirit, just *not the highest mode* or the supreme need".[9]

As someone who has defended the core of Hegel's thought for most of his career, the most important and difficult lesson I have learned from writing this book is that Hip Hop does not merely represent a particularly powerful proof for his emancipatory theory of art; it amounts to visceral and undeniable evidence that what can only be called the *whiteness* of the "we" that dominates Hegel's historical narratives still largely affects the scholarship that surrounds them.[10] While there are assuredly many who find the rote existence of modern life "middling", or have lost the sense of common purpose that once gave "us" faith in its institutional structures, the varied forms of abandonment and containment that have been brought to bear on specifically targeted communities throughout the modern West compel a radically different, much more vital, and concretely liberating relationship to aesthetic creation[11]; and the unique and continuous repression of Black life in the United States is particularly and remarkably absent—

even as he enjoys a revival as a resource for grasping contemporary historical and political developments therein—from literature on a figure who was not only one of the chief apologists for colonial racism, but may be the source of some of "our" most pernicious anti-Black myths.[12]

As "we" work to revive Hegel's *Aesthetics* in order to comprehend the responses of contemporary art to the failings in modern society, as well as for defending the essential relationship between artistic expression and human emancipation, it is precisely to aesthetic subcultures such as Hip Hop that we must turn,[13] not only in order to grasp the timeless lessons contained in Hegel's thought, but also to expose its inherent and repressive flaws and to determine the degree to which they continue to endure (even if only by omission) in our own work. If Hegel remains one of our most vital thinkers of humanity's emancipatory destiny and its links with artistic practice, those of us working to articulate, defend, and further the contributions of his work must confront and correct the often (to say the very least) myopic lens through which he articulates his essential theory of freedom; and this is best done by engaging with the social movements and organic intellectuals—in art, and otherwise—that have emerged from those communities, largely of colour, that have risen to struggle against the brutal conditions of abandonment and containment that "our" inclusion, in part, imposes upon them. The consonances between Hegel's aesthetic theory and cultures like Hip Hop—to say nothing of the more direct influence his account of human freedom and historical progress appears to have had on philosophers of liberation from Frederick Douglass to W.E.B. Du Bois to Martin Luther King[14]—offer rich resources not only for determining and defending the spiritual core of Hegel's philosophy, but for using it as a guide to confront its bigoted trappings and combat their legacy; severed from such engagements, however, we risk not only losing sight of the living power of his thought but minimizing, excusing, or implicitly sustaining its many dead ends.

While the study of Hip Hop reveals the dangers of presuming a generic and unified "we" within Hegel studies (as well as in aesthetic and political theory more broadly), reading the culture's history through the Hegelian framework allows us to more clearly articulate and emphasize its—and, through it, humanity's—essential drive to produce an increasingly inclusive, emancipatory collective against the various forces that seek to contain communities through differentiation and fragmentation. As Ewoodzie notes, in the academic literature on Hip Hop, there is a tendency to "begin with what is currently known and then trace it back to its origins"; and the global dominance of the subsequently developed, consumable products of commercial rap music has led most scholars to "look at what has become the most important component of hip-hop and [then] trace it back to its beginnings".[15] This has, of course, ensured that rap is rarely totally detached from its Bronx origins or the broader culture, thus drawing necessary academic attention both to its founding community and to the enduring social ills that instigated it; however, it has also often reduced early Hip Hop to the mere condition for the emergence of the subsequently developed musical poetry which forms the central focus of scholarly work. Tricia Rose, for example, while affirming that the "primary context for [rap music's] development is hip hop culture", and thus that rap "cannot be fully severed from the sociohistorical moment" from which it emerged, nevertheless turns to that culture in order to ensure that "the specificity of rap music is [...] fully understood",[16] or to ask "what are the sociohistorical conditions that help to explain the specificity of rap's development?".[17] Similarly, while Reiland Rabaka notes that "what truly distinguishes the Hip Hop Movement [is primarily] the unique historical moment in which it emerged and rapidly evolved", he primarily understands it as "a kind of continuation of African American social commentary and political critique", and thus largely through the resistant lyrics of post-"Message" rap music.[18]

One strength of Hegel's account of art in its "highest vocation" is that it allows us to grasp Hip Hop's intrinsically political nature through its original, ritually collective, ethically grounded and grounding, and passionately yet thoughtfully lived religion of art. Subsuming Hip Hop under the more divergent and contested discourses of rap music, as the preceding argument suggests, can obscure the emancipatory and universalist spirit that received aesthetic expression—or, perhaps more accurately, aesthetic *demonstration*—in the Bronx, and towards which its enduring artists, organic intellectuals, and activists have continually sought to (re)direct the rap music that emerged from it. Thus, much as Hegel studies needs to attend more closely to vital work of the populations outside of its presumed "we", I would argue that Hip Hop scholars should work to include and/or amplify the voices of the original culture's pioneers and organic intellectuals whose work has, in my view, often been underrepresented in the literature. While it is assuredly not the only theoretical framework that can do so, Hegel's account of communal, progressively developing aesthetic cultures can provide balance to the rap-centric approach to Hip Hop, precisely because—despite the many flaws noted above—its focus on the essential link between the human need for art and our drive for communal self-emancipation allows us to systematically explicate and justify not only its specific and multiple aesthetic elements and their development, but moreover the expressed self-understanding of the enduring culture's founders and leaders, which often contrast sharply with the more dominant voices and trends in commercial rap music.

Of course, it is precisely its defence of the seemingly outmoded link between art and human freedom that puts this book at a far remove from the vast majority of Continental philosophy and cultural studies in the years since 1970, as well as from the significant strain of rap-centric Hip Hop scholarship which embraces the anti-Hegelian—and thus anti-universalist, anti-progress, as well as largely anti-freedom—domain of what can loosely be called a "postmodern" approach to political aesthetics.[19] While we cannot, here, do anything like full justice to either postmodern aesthetics in general or to the varied trends in rap scholarship beyond it, in closing I'd like to contrast the preceding analysis to one of the founding texts of "postmodern Hip Hop studies", Russell Potter's *Spectacular Vernaculars*.[20]

Potter—who, as we saw in the Introduction, writes precisely to challenge the "ubiquitous academic 'we'" that ignores or distorts the indigenous theories of the oppressed—claims that "hip-hop culture" exemplifies "a central trait or trope of the postmodern: its refusal of [...] progressive models of time".[21] That is, in stark contrast to the "universalizing, humanistic framework" of thinkers like Hegel, who seek to identify the heroic struggles, progressive unification, and actualized or envisioned victories of an emancipatory community, Potter holds that Hip Hop's aesthetic achievements "are not monuments to some romanticized 'human spirit'", but "*aim for* a world made *hole*, aporic, fracturing the fragmented", refusing all teleology and striving towards no goal beyond leaving intriguing "scratches on the decaying surfaces of post-industrial urban America".[22] Hip Hop has no real foundation,[23] and no discernible arc, precisely because it is grounded in no universal trait or essence; rather if "there is communality in hip-hop [...] it is the communality of the recognition that 'it's like that, and that's the way it is'—that the time for naïve idealism is past, that the world's in a non-stop state of emergency that no amount of rose-coloured rhetoric can amend".[24]

Nevertheless, Potter insists that Hip Hop's "radical postmodernism" retains "liberatory potential", but this tellingly consists of "*push*[ing] *the boundaries of the political*, [and] in the process *redefining the very struc-*

tures of resistance".[25] Predictably, given his rap-centric approach, he holds that if "there is a field in which hip-hop's revolution will be fought, it will be *first and foremost that of language*".[26] While his understanding of language is broad enough to include the musical discourse created by producers and DJs, Potter limits the contributions of both to their creative application of Hip Hop's "fundamental practice [...] *citation*, [or] the relentless sampling of sonic and verbal archives".[27] On the one hand, given his emphasis on the appropriation of material from original contexts into new and subversive ones, for Potter this implies—precisely as Hegel predicts, with regard to the inevitable conclusion of romantic art—that Hip Hop's linguistic resistance is "a theorized practice which is fundamentally *ironic*, [because] fundamentally *postmodern*"[28]; but on the other hand, this ironic subversion of communal unity and teleological purpose—again, just as Hegel suggests of late or post-romantic art—entails that "hip-hop is about a *fundamental oppositional stance*", rather than the struggle towards a constructive, actualizable vision of the near or distant future.[29] Believing in nothing beyond its own opposition to *all* forms of community, as well as all ethical and aesthetic values, Hip Hop is defined, above all, by its *essentially negative and subjective attitude*. Thus, for Potter, it is not battling, skill development, cypher participation, or even the consciousness-raising of the Golden Age "rap nationalists" that best express the culture's spirit; rather, it is the "gansta rapper Bo$$ [who] puts this attitude succinctly: 'I don't give a fuck, not a single fuck, not a single solitary fuck, motherfucka!'—that is hip-hop attitude in a nutshell".[30]

It would, of course, be hard to deny the prevalence of this attitude in much, particularly post-1990 rap music, and thus this theoretical approach is certainly justified in many cases; the diverse forms of romantic genius that have been produced in rap's music and poetry since 1979 assuredly warrant academic discourses appropriate to them, and thus varied forms of musical and literary criticism will be required to make sense of the increasingly broad field. What I want to contest, however, is the identification of *Hip Hop* with the merely subjective and subversive values that dominate the commercial products that have always existed in uneasy tension with it. As we have seen, even if a significant number of rap artists and/or their promoters have routinely voiced it, there could arguably be *nothing further* from the self-expressed, unifying, and fundamentally emancipatory values of the original Bronx culture than the merely reactive and ironic undermining of the lived ethics of unique individual contribution to a community's progressive self-determination. I have thus tried, in this book, to demonstrate *both* that the "Hegelian perspective on aesthetics demands a *critique* of the assumptions of [...] postmodernism" precisely by emphasizing the "*ethical content* that art" manifests—and arguably should retain—under particular social conditions,[31] *and* that Hip Hop is a palpable proof that such a "modern" vision remains powerfully active in the age of postmodern fragmentation, precisely because it demonstrates that art can be used to collectively determine, as KRS-One puts it, "what it means for us to be and remain free, to take responsibility for ourselves, [and] to be able to chart our own path" into the future.[32]

Potter, admirably, calls upon scholars not to theorize Hip Hop from the outside, as though its aesthetic "practices are somehow naïve, somehow lacking their own indigenous theories" and theorists, even calling out the scholarly treatment of the "'organic intellectual', [who is often] raised as a hopeful sign, [but then] is dropped all too quickly when he or she refuses to walk in step with the announced theoretical vanguard"[33]; however, as I hope to have shown above, these practices and theories, as well as the organic intellectuals that articulate them, are essentially reflective of the universalist, progressive, "humanist turn" to which Potter's work, like so much "vanguard" academic theory in the age of neo-liberalism, is adamantly opposed.[34] As Gilroy notes, much postmodern "[t]extuality [has] become[...] a means to evacuate the problem of human agency [or] a means to specify the death (by fragmentation) of the subject", and it is precisely the late-capitalist forms of atomization that Hip Hop fought valiantly to overcome, and the essentially human capacity for collective emancipation that it worked to celebrate, preserve, and strengthen. To elide the voices of the culture's pioneers, internal theorists, and institutional leadership in favour of the most "subversive" voices in commercial rap thus risks "collud[ing] in the belief that black vernacular [art] is nothing other than a playful, parodic cavalcade of Rabelaisian subversion [which] decisively weakens the positions of the artist, the critical commentator, and the community as a whole".[35] We would do well to compare Potter's view of Hip Hop with that of the culture's founding father, Kool DJ Herc:

> 'Keeping it real' has become just another fad word. It sounds cute. But it has been pimped and perverted. It ain't about keeping it real. It's got to be about keeping it right. [...] Hip-hop has always been about having fun, but it's also about taking responsibility. And now we have a platform to speak our minds. Millions of people are watching us. Let's hear something powerful. Tell the people what they need to hear. How will we help the commu-

nity? What do we stand for? What would happen if we got the hip-hop generation to vote, or to form organizations to change things? That would be powerful. [...] We're surviving now, but we're not yet rising up. [...] That's what I hope the hip-hop generation can do, to take us all to the next level.[36]

It is just as revealing to contrast Potter's account of Hip Hop communality with that of culture's leading organic intellectual, KRS-One:

In the back of our collective hip-hop minds we actually believe that it is hopeless, that corruption is the norm and 'things ain't never gonna change,' [...] This is the attitude that fuels so much of the rebellion of the culture. [...] But now that we've started and have established ourselves in the minds of urban people everywhere, we need a new course of action. [...] We must become better, yes, better than those who sought to exploit us and our resources. We must became an authority over them through righteousness and discipline.[37]

If there is one thing the Hegelian framework can help make clear, it is that Hip Hop did not simply, or even primarily, liberate *the forms of sensation or self-expression* from previously given restrictions, enabling a merely semiotic, subversive, or oblique form of resistance; it demonstrably emancipated *a community* from the worst form of race-based social exclusion in America in the post-civil rights era by sensibly demonstrating the possibility and value of the collective struggle to determine and progressively strive towards both individual and institutional actualizations of our creative, rational, and free essence. And it is precisely this link between aesthetic creativity and the universal drive for progressively self-determining human emancipation that remains undertheorized—and, in fact, generally stands as theoretically *condemned*—in our "postmodern age". Despite the obvious and contemptible flaws in his work, I hope to have shown that the arch-nemesis of most postmoderns offers powerful and still viable tools for shifting our priorities and understanding, so long as we recognize what "Hegel could not imagine[:] that America's greatest contribution to the future may spring from her African past".[38] However, even if (for, of course, in many ways good reason) we remain sceptical of the value of Hegel's thought either in general or specifically for analysing Hip Hop, if the ongoing history of the culture is to be philosophically grasped in a manner true to its origins, then we must link its emergence to a compelling account of *our universal, progressively actualized, and above all self-determining capacity to will emancipatory change in both ourselves and our social world*; an account, moreover, which can explain not only the role that a specifically aesthetic culture plays in manifesting that will under particular conditions, but the diverse ways in which art, as that culture develops, furthers, preserves, or even subverts the will's progress. This, of course, requires both doing justice to what makes the culture *irreducibly unique*, and exposing its *essential continuities with free human creation in general.*

Doing so, of course, would also help clarify Hip Hop's crucial connection to the progressive, world-historical struggles waged by Black activists in America during the decades which preceded it. These movements not only forcefully and irrevocably exposed the foundational lies of racial repression that still define so much of the country's civic life, but moreover made strident institutional and cultural progress against them. If their very existence killed Hegel's Whiggish narrative of humanity's unified historical progress, their dialectical navigation of the irreducible particularity of an unjustly repressed community and the essential universality of its emancipatory ground and social import nevertheless revealed what was living in his account of historically actualized free will, and offered genuine hope that America's promise may yet be fulfilled. However, the still-unsolved assassination of Martin Luther King, followed by the state murders of Mark Clark and Fred Hampton,[39] signalled a rollback of these victories so severe that it is readily understandable why so many have retreated—whether begrudgingly, selfishly, or as a form of merely subjective revolt—into "not giving a fuck"; this was, after all, the clear aim of its architects, and a good deal of subsequent academic theory has served not only to articulate, but to *justify* this "postrevolutionary despair".[40]

As I have tried to show, however, Hip Hop reflects a markedly and vitally different course. Against the most brutal forms of late-capitalist atomization, it found a way to *aesthetically preserve* the historical struggle for objectively actualized freedom, and thus "represents an iconic, godly embodiment of a universal struggle for justice, peace, and human rights, [and] a prefiguration of more positive forms of global interconnection" to come,[41] which carried on the previous decades of struggle in the most viable form available in that place and time. Born at the precise moment when all neo-Hegelian predictions of continual ethical evolution in the world's leading industrial democracy appeared to crumble, what is perhaps most striking about the culture is its manifest *refusal to forsake the possibility of progress* towards a just, humane, and free world. Above all, Hip Hop viscerally demonstrates that *humanity intrinsically refuses to be defined by the contingent determinations of situational finitude, precisely because we are all essentially and unstoppably driven towards individual and communal self-determination.* It not only reveals the emancipatory role that can be played by art, but the genuinely universal nature and essentially progressive trajectory of humanity, thereby not only actualizing the most enduring truth that emerges from Hegel's thought, but palpably refuting the many falsehoods in his text that conceal it.

Multiracial in origin and expanse, but pro-Black and anti-white supremacy at its core; founded in an aesthetic meritocracy of uniquely individual contribution to one's community through study, practice, and innovation, but directed towards the increasingly collective and institutionalized liberation of humanity as a whole, "hip-hop is the symbol for people internationally for how you need to organize based on the reality that we've done it" in the realm of art, and can work to carry forward that struggle through more explicit and direct means.[42] One last time, KRS-One:

> The question, then, for us today is, are we prepared to heed the call in our generation? Can we create and govern ourselves? This would be the true origin of Hip Hop, a civilization established first as art in the minds of enlightened African Americans but then manifested as a raceless civilization of self-expressed human beings. [...] It is now time for us (Hip Hop) to become 'orderly', meaning purposeful, methodically arranged, obedient to our own principles [...] Let us be the nation America attempted to be, and receive the tranquility America attempted to secure.[43]

Ultimately, whether it is waged aesthetically, religiously, philosophically, or politically, it may be that Hip Hop should now primarily serve as the proper name for the increasingly global, interconnected, disciplined, and youth-led movement fighting not only *against* the politics of abandonment and containment that have eroded our institutions of right since the end of the 1960s, but more importantly *towards* progressively collective and inclusive structures of self-government. If this is true, it is because, at its best, the rap music that proceeded from the original culture has become the most powerful vehicle for spreading *both* vital information about the nature, extent, and above all the subjective and communal impact of repressive inclusion, *and* the spiritual knowledge developed first within the original culture, and then among the most-effected communities, necessary to properly guide what must become a broad-based, multifaceted, and increasingly collective struggle against it.

And, to my mind, there is no better example of rap's political potential than "Hip Hop", the enduring anthem from the *dead prez* album from which this book draws its subtitle. I thus give the final word to the final line of its final verse: "This is *real* Hip Hop, and it don't stop, 'til we get to po-po off the block".

NOTES

1. Hess, 2.
2. William Maker, "Introduction", in William Maker, ed. *Hegel and Aesthetics* (Albany: State University of New York Press, 2000), vii–xxvi (vii).
3. Ibid., xv, emphasis added.
4. *Beauty and Truth*, 23; 79.
5. Willian Desmond, "Art and the Absolute Revisited", in Maker, ed. *Hegel and Aesthetics*, 1–12 (2, emphasis added).
6. Carl Rapp, "Hegel's Concept of the Dissolution of Art, in Maker, ed. *Hegel and Aesthetics*, 13–30 (14).
7. *Hegel on the Modern Arts*, 261, emphasis added.
8. *After the Beautiful*, 60.
9. Rapp, 14, emphasis added.
10. On the social construction of whiteness, and its particular function in Western and academic philosophy, see Charles W. Mills, *The Racial Contract* (Ithaca: Cornell University Press, 1999). I certainly don't exempt myself from this critique; chief among my regrets about past publications is the deflection of the charge of Eurocentrism in my first venture into defending Hegel's grasp of history as the collective struggle for progressive self-determination, "Hegel, Edward Sanders and Emancipatory History", *Clio: A Journal of Literature, History and the Philosophy of History*, 42:1 (2013), 27–52.
11. By no means a Hegelian, Paul Gilroy speaks of this relationship in very similar terms, arguing that for the "descendants of slaves [...] [a]rtistic expression [...] becomes the means towards both individual self-fashioning and communal liberation" and thus under specific "conditions, artistic practice retains its 'cultic functions'" (*The Black Atlantic: Modernity and Double Consciousness* (Cambridge: Harvard University Press, 1993), 40; 57).
12. Bernasconi, "Hegel's Racism" is required reading on these issues.
13. While there are obvious differences between them and Hip Hop, I think comparable histories could be written of other aesthetic cultures—for example, hardcore in L.A. and Washington and footwork in Illinois and Indiana—produced by the marginalized communities of collapsing empire. There is, in fact, considerable continuity between Hip Hop and a recent

dance-based culture to emerge in New York: Litefeet. It retains not only the sculptural depiction of human divinity (achieved through a potent form of slow motion movement, combined with prop tricks and gymnastic feats, rather than through floor work or power moves consummating in a freeze), but graffiti's focus on the subway system (many early practitioners performed inside the cars themselves for spare change, and the space became a central part of the dance, leading, with sad predictability, to a heavy-handed legal crackdown) and a novel form of beat-centric music (which often emphasizes the physical sounds of clapping and snapping alongside the sampled, almost chanting vocals of producers and participants, but rarely features anything resembling lyrical MCing); despite the marked de-emphasis on rapping, some of its participants have gone so far as to call it "the second coming of Hip Hop". Hat tip, once again, to Serouj Aprahamian.

14. On the vexed and varied relationships that Douglass and Du Bois may have with Hegel, see Gilroy, *The Black Atlantic*; I follow one route directly linking Hegel to King in "'A Passion For Justice': Martin Luther King, Jr. and G.W.F. Hegel on 'World-Historical Individuals'", *Philosophy and Social Criticism* 43:2, 187–207.

15. *Break Beats in the Bronx*, 5.

16. *Black Noise*, 26; xiv, emphasis added.

17. Ibid., xiv.

18. *Hip Hop's Amnesia: From Blues and the Black Women's Club Movement to Rap and the Hip Hop Movement* (Plymouth: Lexington, 2012). 247; 246.

19. Having begun my career in deconstruction, I'm well aware of how unsatisfactory this term is, and how strenuously pivotal thinkers like Jacques Derrida worked to distance their work from the label as loosely used within the academy and beyond. Concepts from Gilles Deleuze, for example, are often invoked in Hip Hop studies in ways that seem distinct from his commitments (see, e.g. James Braxton Peterson, *The Hip-Hop Underground and African American Culture: Beneath the Surface* (New York: Palgrave Macmillan, 2014), or Awad Ibrahim, *The Rhizome of Blackness: A Critical Ethnography of Hip-Hop Culture, Language, Identity, and the Politics of Becoming* (New York: Peter Lang, 2014)); however, the discussion which follows builds upon my critique of Deleuze's aesthetic theory, "Deleuze on the Musical Work of Art", in *Intensities and Lines of Flight: Deleuze and Guattari and the Arts*, eds. Antonio Calcagno, Jim Vernon and Steve Lofts (Rowman and Littlefield, 2014), 55–65, and I believe similar cases could be mounted against many recent figures and movements in Continental philosophy-inspired cultural theory. As regards postmodernism's impact on Hip Hop scholarship, see Gilroy, *Against Race*, for an investigation into why "it seems no longer appropriate or even plausible to speculate about

the freedom of the subject of black politics in the overdeveloped countries" (184–5).

20. While I read this case as exemplary, it obviously is not indicative of every "postmodern" reading of Hip Hop's aesthetic politics; however, written early in the field's development, and enjoying a citation count well above 500, it is safe to say it is not only substantially influential within the specialist literature, but is often read as representative of the field by those outside of it. For a generally similar account, see Bailey; other influential texts that read rap as a distinctly postmodern practice include Andre Craddock Willis, "Rap Music and the Black Musical Tradition: A Critical Assessment", *Radical America* 23:4 (1991), 29–38, and Richard Shusterman, "The Fine Art of Rap," *New Literary History*, 22: 3 (1991), 613–632. While Rose is compellingly critical of some postmodern accounts, in part because they focus on rap to the exclusion of the wider culture, claims such as "Hip Hop artists used the tools of obsolete industrial technology to traverse contemporary crossroads of lack and desire" (35), or that Hip Hop's "style can be used as a gesture of refusal or as a form of oblique challenge to structures of domination" (36) seem quite close to broader themes in the postmodern aesthetics of resistance as found in Potter and Bailey; the same is true of Fred Moten's recent claim that "hip-hop is [...] a non-coercive rearrangement of desire that moves—that somehow obliterates the distinctions between being made to move and wanting to move and wanting to be made to move—in that gap, that break, which is a field of feel in dance, in which the representation itself is negated by an overwhelming affirmation" (*Black and Blur* (Durham and London: Duke University Press, 2017), 273). Although we have a different understanding of what its history reveals, I agree with Adam Krims, *Rap Music and the Poetics of Identity* (New York: Cambridge University Press, 2000) that, even if it "seems, at times, that rap music would have to have been invented by postmodern theory, had it not been there, poised to exact its tribute", nevertheless a "strong case could be made that the history of hip-hop culture demonstrates precisely how [such] cultural practices can be deployed to reinforce, at least as much as to challenge, dominant discourses" (8).

21. Potter, 3. It is, indeed, in the understanding of time and history that we find postmodernism's most serious challenge to the conception of both art and politics defended in this book; however, the arguments for, and consequences of, non-chronological/progressive theories of temporality are, in my view, underdeveloped by Potter. For one of the most compelling and nuanced attempts to reveal the import of postmodern theorists of time like Derrida and Deleuze for aesthetic and political practice, see Jay Lampert, *Simultaneity and Delay: A Dialectical Theory of Staggered Time* (London: Bloomsbury, 2012), especially chapters 7–9.

22. Ibid., 61; 8, emphasis added to "aim for". Compare Bailey, for whom Hip Hop "departs from modernity's *sensus communis* [and thus reflects] a manifestation of the postmodern or the post-historical" (1), or Shusterman, for whom rap essentially refutes the "dogma that good art should [...] focus[...] only on universal themes" (619).

23. Which explains Potter's perplexing claim that "hip-hop culture arose in *places like* the South Bronx" (142, emphasis added).

24. Ibid., 8. In citing Run DMC, note how late in the culture's development he finds its core message.

25. Ibid., 8; 15, emphasis added.

26. Ibid., 64, emphasis added.

27. Ibid., 53.

28. Ibid., 18, emphasis added to "ironic".

29. Ibid., 153. For Hegel, "this negativity of irony is [...] the *vanity* of everything factual, ethical, and substantial, the nullity of everything objective and valid in and for itself [...] the ironical [...] lies in the self-destruction of the noble, great, and excellent; and so the objective art forms too will have to present only the principle of absolute subjectivity, by showing what has value and dignity for humanity as void in its self-destruction" (66/I, 96–7, trans. modified). See Judith Norman, "Hegel and German Romanticism", in Stephen Houlgate, ed. *Hegel and the Arts*, 310–336, for a detailed discussion of Hegel's vexed relationship with the German Romantics, who exemplify this "irony [which] is undiscriminating in its negative intents, running roughshod over the good and noble" (313). Correctly, she critiques Hegel's limited understanding of the Romantic movement, emphasizing its potential productive side, which she also locates in Derrida's deconstruction, *pace* the nihilism, mere subversiveness or meaningless "free play" often attributed to it. In postmodern appreciations of Hip Hop, we see this, for example, in Henry Louis Gates, Jr., *The Signifying Monkey: A Theory of African American Literary Criticism, 25th-Anniversary Edition* (New York: Oxford University Press, 2014), which argues that "hip-hop sampling" or citation (xxxii), like the appropriation of pop songs in "jazz performances [or] the play of black language games" in verbal sparring matches (57) reflects the uniquely African American practice of Signifyin(g), "a game of language, independent of reaction to white racism or even to collective black wish-fulfillment" (77), which emphasizes "the figurative difference between the literal and the metaphorical, between surface and latent meaning" (89). While the literary theory Gates derives from the traditions of Signifyin(g) is remarkably close to certain aspects of Derrida's thought, like Derrida he emphasizes the potentially constructive contributions of this play, finding sampling's citation to be "more admiring than mocking [...] ironic or critical" of its

source materials, which thus marks a transformative extension of the various traditions from which it springs, reflecting a "remarkably self-conscious art form" that seeks to build upon, rather than undermine, its past (xxxii). Thus, while thinkers like Derrida and Gates should make us question Hegel's somewhat crude caricature of romantic irony, and by extension postmodern philosophy, a text like Potter's may indicate how presciently Hegel intimated where such thought—precisely because of its emphasis on subversive appropriation—might inevitably be taken up by others.

30. Ibid., 71. Again, compare Bailey, for whom Hip Hop "is much more of an '*attitude*'" than anything else; an "attitude, which is, in essence, a *reaction contra* the rigidly limiting aesthetic of modernism", which "*rejects* conventional moral wisdom" precisely because "its creators share with most postmodernists the tendency to *revere subversives*" (7, emphasis added).

31. Etter, 207, emphasis added.

32. *Gospel*, 28.

33. Potter, 10; 6.

34. Ibid., 132.

35. *Black Atlantic*, 77; 84.

36. Chang, *Can't Stop*, xii–xiii.

37. *Gospel*, 576–7. In fact Potter admits, seemingly against his own "postmodern politics", the need for Hip Hop to move to non-aesthetic means of resistance, claiming, "If hip-hop wants to make a serious challenge to commodification, it needs to do more than simply make lyrical resistance" (113), just as Bailey claims that Hip Hop holds out a promise for "individuals who seek an alternative to atomization" (*Philosophy and Hip-Hop*, 16–7). However, as KRS-One argues, this would imply, as it were, a *change in attitude*, and one *towards* the "outmoded" values of humanism, universalism, ethical duty to one's community through earnest social contribution, and emancipatory progress that we associate with figures like Hegel.

38. Verharen, 457. Verharen uses Cheikh Anta Diop's critique of Hegel and his account of Egyptian philosophy, as well as the work of Alain Locke and W.E.B. Du Bois, to envision a "human unity" that "can be reached only through evolutionary processes grounded in self-knowledge" (482), but which requires us to "preserve a cultural identity directly linked to Africa" (489), against Hegel's removal of it from progressive history. While this, I would argue, manifests a different vision of progress than that forwarded by Bambaataa and KRS-One, there are assuredly resources in this suggestion for writing alternative histories of Hip Hop's development, lesson and direction, as well as for countering the increasingly dominant voices of the postmodern in its scholarship.

39. The state actors in the murders of Hampton and Clark are exposed with exacting detail in Jeffrey Haas, *The Assassination of Fred Hampton: How the*

FBI and the Chicago Police Murdered a Black Panther (Chicago: Lawrence Hill Books, 2010). While few now doubt there was some level of state complicity in King's assassination, the precise agents and contributions remain unclear. The case for the FBI's active role is best laid out by the man who successfully prosecuted the case regarding it in civil court, William Pepper, *An Act of State: The Execution of Martin Luther King* (New York: Verso, 2008), but a compelling argument for the role of more diffuse and local networks, involving local law enforcement, but which the FBI may have actually sought to subvert, is made in Stuart Wexler and Larry Hancock, *The Awful Grace of God: Religious Terrorism, White Supremacy and The Unsolved Murder of Martin Luther King, Jr.* (Berkeley, CA: Counterpoint, 2012).

40. Peter Hallward, "The Politics of Prescription", *South Atlantic Quarterly* 104:4 (Fall 2005), 769–789 (769). While he is often sharply critical of Hegel, my case, here, is indebted to Hallward's pioneering work on trends in academic political and aesthetic theory since the 1970s.

41. Paul Gilroy, *Darker than Blue: On the Moral Economies of Black Atlantic Culture* (Cambridge, MA: Belknap Press of Harvard University Press, 2011), 88. He is speaking, here, of Bob Marley who he presents—along with Curtis Mayfield and Jimi Hendrix—as a kind of cultural antipode to the crass materialism and cultural narcissism reflected in much recent rap music. As the preceding should make clear, however, Hip Hop intellectuals like Bambaataa and KRS-One share Gilroy's push for an aesthetic pairing of "Black power on the one side and, on the other, the hope of a future in which race has been drained of meaning" (100). I hope that this book's analysis offers evidence of Gilroy's claim that cultural forms like Hip Hop reflect a "political relationship" forged across racial and ethnic communities through aesthetic cultures, which "reconstruct[s] and rework[s] tradition as they pursue their particular utopia. A vision of the world in which 'race' will no longer be a meaningful device for the categorization of human beings, where work will no longer be servitude and law will be dissociated from domination" (*There Ain't No Black in the Union Jack*, 218). However, while Hip Hop assuredly proves that "people can act socially and cohesively without the structures provided by formal organizations" (247), the Zulu Nation, the Temple of Hip Hop, and other, more directly political institutions grounded in the philosophical and religious spirit that emerged from the culture suggest an intrinsic limit to *merely* aesthetic struggle. Thus, while we assuredly need to stress and defend the enduring role art plays in struggles for historical emancipation, the tensions explored in the previous chapter may mean that Gilroy's suggestion that such "expressive cultural forms and the intercultural conversations to which they contribute are a dynamic refutation of the Hegelian suggestion that thought and

reflection have outstripped art and that art is opposed to philosophy as the lowest, merely sensuous form" of emancipation is challenged, rather than confirmed, by Hip Hop's ongoing history (*Black Atlantic*, 73).

42. Hip Hop scholar Marcyliena Morgan, interviewed in Kitwana, 152.
43. *Gospel*, 817; 574–5.

BIBLIOGRAPHY

Aprahamian, Serouj. Debunking the Historical Hype: A Look into the True Origins of Wall Writing. Bombingscience.com. https://www.bombingscience.com/debunking-the-historical-hype-a-look-into-the-true-origins-of-wall-writing/. Accessed Sept 2017.

Asante, M.K., Jr. 2008. *It's Bigger Than Hip Hop: The Rise of the Post-Hip-Hop Generation*. New York: St. Martin's.

Banes, Sally. 2004. Physical Graffiti: Breaking Is Hard to Do. In *And It Don't Stop: The Best American Hip-Hop Journalism of the Last 25 Years*, ed. Raquel Cepeda, 7–11. New York: Faber & Faber.

Bernasconi, Robert. 1998. Hegel at the Court of Ashanti. In *Hegel After Derrida*, ed. Stuart Barnett, 41–63. New York: Routledge.

———. 2003. Hegel's Racism: A Reply to McCarney. *Radical Philosophy* 119: 35–37.

Bloom, Joshua, and Wald E. Martin Jr. 2013. *Black Against Empire: The History and Politics of the Black Panther Party*. Berkeley: University of California Press.

Brewster, Bill, and Frank Broughton. 2010. *The Record Players: DJ Revolutionaries*. New York: Black Cat.

———. 2014. *Last Night a DJ Saved My Life*. New York: Grove.

Bubner, Rüdiger. 2007. The 'Religion of Art'. In *Hegel and the Arts*, ed. Stephen Houlgate, 296–309. Evanston: Northwestern University Press.

Bungay, Stephen. 1984. *Beauty and Truth: A Study of Hegel's Aesthetics*. Oxford: Oxford University Press.

Butler, Paul. 2009. *Let's Get Free: A Hip-Hop Theory of Justice*. New York: The New Press.

Butler, Clark, and Christiane Seiler, trans. 1984. *Hegel: The Letters*. Bloomington: Indiana University Press.

© The Author(s) 2018   245
J. Vernon, *Hip Hop, Hegel, and the Art of Emancipation*,
https://doi.org/10.1007/978-3-319-91304-9

Castleman, Craig. 1997. *Getting Up: Subway Graffiti in New York*. Cambridge, MA: MIT.

Chalfant, Henry, and Martha Cooper. 1984. *Subway Art*. New York: Thames and Hudson.

Chang, Jeff. 2005. *Can't Stop, Won't Stop: A History of the Hip-Hop Generation*. New York: Picador.

———. 2006. Introduction: Hip-Hop Arts: Our Expanding Universe. In *Total Chaos: The Art and Aesthetics of Hip-Hop*, ed. Jeff Chang, ix–xv. New York: Perseus.

Chang, O'Brian Kevin, and Wayne Chen. 1998. *Reggae Roots: The Story of Jamaican Music*. Philadelphia: Temple University Press.

Charnas, Dan. 2010. *The Big Payback: The History of the Business of Hip-Hop*. New York: New American Library.

Cheney, Charise. 2005. *Brothers Gonna Work It Out: Sexual Politics in the Golden Age of Rap Nationalism*. New York: New York University Press.

Chuck, D., with Yusef Jah. 1997. *Fight the Power: Rap, Race, and Reality*. New York: Delta.

Churchill, Ward, and Jim Vander Wall. 2002. *Agents of Repression: The FBI's Secret Wars Against the Black Panther Party and the American Indian Movement*. Cambridge, MA: South End Press.

Coates, Ta-Nehisi. 2017. *We Were Eight Years in Power*. New York: One World.

Cunningham, David. 2004. *There's Something Happening Here: The New Left, the Klan and FBI Counterintelligence*. Berkeley: University of California Press.

Desmond, William. 1986. *Art and the Absolute: A Study of Hegel's Aesthetics*. Albany: SUNY Press.

———. 2000. Art and the Absolute Revisited. In *Hegel and Aesthetics*, ed. William Maker, 1–12. Albany: SUNY Press.

Donogho, Martin. 2007. Art and History: Hegel on the End, the Beginning, and the Future of Art. In *Hegel and the Arts*, ed. Stephen Houlgate, 179–215. Evanston: Northwestern University Press.

Dudley, Will. 2006. Telling the Truth: Systematic Philosophy and the Aufhebung of Poetic and Religious Language. In *Hegel and Language*, ed. Jere O'Neill Surber, 127–141. Albany: SUNY Press.

Dyson, Michael Eric. 2007. *Know What I Mean?: Reflections on Hip Hop*. Philadelphia: Basic Civitas Books.

Edwards, Paul. 2015. *The Concise Guide to Hip-Hop Music: A Fresh Look at the Art of Hip-Hop from Old-School Beats to Freestyle Rap*. New York: St. Martin's Griffin.

Etter, Brian K. 2006. *Between Transcendence and Historicism: The Ethical Nature of the Arts in Hegelian Aesthetics*. Albany: SUNY Press.

Ewoodzie, Joseph C., Jr. 2017. *Break Beats in the Bronx: Rediscovering Hip-Hop's Early Years*. Chapel Hill: University of North Carolina Press.

Fernandes, Sujatha. 2011. *Close to the Edge: In Search of the Global Hip Hop Generation*. London: Verso.

Flores, Juan. 1996. Puerto Rocks: New York Ricans Stake Their Claims. In *Droppin' Science: Critical Essays on Rap Music and Hip Hop Culture*, ed. William Eric Perkins, 85–105. Philadelphia: Temple University Press.

Fricke, Jim, and Charlie Ahearn. 2002. *Yes Yes Y'all: The Experience Music Project Oral History of Hip-Hop's First Decade*. Cambridge: Da Capo.

Gates, Henry Louis, Jr. 2014. *The Signifying Monkey: A Theory of African American Literary Criticism*. 25th-Anniversary ed. New York: Oxford University Press.

George, Nelson. 1998. *Hip Hop America*. New York: Viking.

———. 2012. Hip-Hop's Founding Fathers Speak the Truth. In *That's the Joint: The Hip Hop Studies Reader*, ed. Murray Forman and Mark Anthony Neal, 2nd ed., 44–54. New York: Routledge.

Gilman, Sander. 1982. *On Blackness Without Blacks: Essays on the Image of the Black in Germany*. Boston: G.K. Hall and Co.

Gilroy, Paul. 1987. *"There Ain't No Black in the Union Jack": The Cultural Politics or Race and Nation*. Chicago: University of Chicago.

———. 1993. *The Black Atlantic: Modernity and Double Consciousness*. Cambridge, MA: Harvard University Press.

———. 2000. *Against Race: Imagining Political Culture Beyond the Color Line*. Cambridge: Belknap Press of Harvard.

———. 2010. *Darker Than Blue: On the Moral Economies of Black Atlantic Culture*. Cambridge: Belknap Press of Harvard.

Glazer, Nathan. 1979. On Subway Graffiti in New York. *The Public Interest* 54: 3–11.

Gordon, Jane Anna. 2014. *Creolizing Political Theory: Reading Rousseau Through Fanon*. New York: Fordham University Press.

Gosa, Travis L. 2015. The Fifth Element: Knowledge. In *The Cambridge Companion to Hip-Hop*, ed. Justin A. Williams, 56–70. Cambridge: Cambridge University Press.

Grandmaster Caz. 2012. *Written: The Lyrics of Grandmaster Caz*. Godalming: The Lyric Book Company.

Grandmaster Flash, with David Rita. 2008. *The Adventures of Grandmaster Flash: My Life, My Beats*. New York: Broadway Books.

Guevera, Nancy. "Women Writin' Rappin' Breakin'". In Droppin' Science: Critical Essays on Rap Music and Hip Hop Culture, William Eric Perkins, 49–62. Philadelphia: Temple University Press, 1996.

Guzman-Sanchez, Thomas. 2012. *Underground Dance Masters: Final History of a Forgotten Era*. Santa-Barbara: Praeger.

Haas, Jeffrey. 2010. *The Assassination of Fred Hampton: How the FBI and the Chicago Police Murdered a Black Panther*. Chicago: Lawrence Hill Books.

Hager, Steven. 1984. *Hip Hop: The Illustrated History of Break Dancing, Rap Music, and Graffiti*. New York: St. Martin's.

———. *Hip Hop*. Self-published.

Hallward, Peter. 2005. The Politics of Prescription. *South Atlantic Quarterly* 104 (4): 769–789.

Hazzard-Donald, Katrina. 1996. Dance in Hip Hop Culture. In *Droppin' Science: Critical Essays on Rap Music and Hip Hop*, ed. William Eric Perkins, 220–235. Philadelphia: Temple University Press.

Hegel, G.W.F. 1956. *Lectures on the Philosophy of History*. Trans. J. Sibree. New York: Dover.

———. 1970. *Werke* (Various Volumes). Frankfurt am Main: Suhrkamp.

———. 1975. *Aesthetics: Lectures on Fine Art*, vols. I & II. Trans. T.M. Knox. New York: Oxford University Press.

———. 1977. *Phenomenology of Spirit*. Trans. A.V. Miller. New York: Oxford University Press.

Henrich, Dieter. 1985. The Contemporary Relevance of Hegel's Aesthetics. In *Hegel*, ed. Michael J. Inwood, 199–207. Oxford: Oxford University Press.

Hess, Mickey. 2007. *Is Hip Hop Dead?: The Past, Present, and Future of America's Most Wanted Music*. Westport: Praeger.

Houlgate, Stephen. 1997. The "End" of Art. *Owl of Minerva* 29: 1–21.

———. 2005. *An Introduction to Hegel: Freedom, Truth and History*. Oxford: Blackwell.

———, ed. 2007a. *Hegel and the Arts*. Evanston: Northwestern University Press.

———. 2007b. Introduction: An Overview of Hegel's Aesthetics. In *Hegel and the Arts*, ed. Stephen Houlgate, xi–xxviii. Evanston: Northwestern University Press.

Ibrahim, Awad. 2014. *The Rhizome of Blackness: A Critical Ethnography of Hip-Hop Culture, Language, Identity, and the Politics of Becoming*. New York: Peter Lang.

James, David. 2009. *Art, Myth and Society in Hegel's Aesthetics*. London: Continuum.

Jenkins, Sacha. 2004. The Writing on the Wall: Graffiti Culture Crumbles into the Violence It Once Escaped. In *And It Don't Stop: The Best American Hip-Hop Journalism of the Last 25 Years*, ed. Raquel Cepeda, 288–299. New York: Faber and Faber.

Johnson, Imani Kai. 2015. Hip-Hop Dance. In *The Cambridge Companion to Hip-Hop*, ed. Justin A. Williams, 22–31. Cambridge: Cambridge University Press.

Jonnes, Jill. 2002. *South Bronx Rising: The Rise, Fall, and Resurrection of an American City*. New York: Fordham University Press.

Kajikawa, Loren. 2015. *Sounding Race in Rap Songs*. Oakland: University of California Press.

Kaminsky, Jack. 1962. *Hegel on Art: An Interpretation of Hegel's Aesthetics.* New York: SUNY Press.

Katz, Mark. 2012. *Groove Music: The Art and Culture of the Hip-Hop DJ.* New York: Oxford University Press.

Keyes, Cheryl. 2004. *Rap Music and Street Consciousness.* Champaign: University of Illinois Press.

Kitwana, Bakari. 2005. *Why White Kids Love Hip-Hop: Wankstas, Wiggers, Wannabes, and the New Reality of Race in America.* New York: Basic Civitas.

Kohl, Herbert, with photos by James Hinton. 1969. Names, Graffiti, and Culture. *Urban Review* 3: 24–37.

Kolb, David. 2000. The Spirit of Gravity: Architecture and Externality. In *Hegel and Aesthetics*, ed. William Maker, 83–95. Albany: State University of New York Press.

Krims, Adam. 2000. *Rap Music and the Poetics of Identity.* New York: Cambridge University Press.

KRS-One. 2003. *Ruminations.* New York: Welcome Rain.

———. 2009. *The Gospel of Hip Hop: First Instrument.* New York: Powerhouse Books.

Kurlansky Mervyn, and Jon Naar, eds. with text by Norman Mailer. 1974. *The Faith of Graffiti.* New York: Praeger.

Lampert, Jay. 1995. Hegel and Ancient Egypt: History and Becoming. *International Philosophical Quarterly* 35: 43–58.

———. 2012. *Simultaneity and Delay: A Dialectical Theory of Staggered Time.* London: Bloomsbury.

Lebron, Christopher J. 2017. *The Making of Black Lives Matter: A Brief History of an Idea.* New York: Oxford University Press.

Macdonald, Nancy. 2001. *The Graffiti Subculture: Youth, Masculinity and Identity in New York and London.* New York: Palgrave.

Maker, William. 2000. Introduction. In *Hegel and Aesthetics*, ed. William Maker, vii–xxvi. Albany: State University of New York Press.

McGlynn, Aine. 2007. The Infinity Lessons of the Zulu Nation. In *Icons of Hip-Hop: An Encyclopedia of the Movement, Music, and Culture*, ed. Mickey Hess, vol. 1, 269–270. Santa Barbara: ABC-CLO.

McQuillar, Tayannah Lee. 2007. *When Rap Music Had a Conscience: The Artists, Organizations, and Historic Events That Inspired and Influenced the 'Golden Age' of Hip-Hop from 1987–1996.* New York: Thunder's Mouth Press.

McWhorter, John. 2008. *All About the Beat: Why Hip-Hop Can't Save Black America.* New York: Penguin.

Miller, Ivor R. 2002. *Aerosol Kingdom: Subway Painters of New York City.* Jackson: University of Mississippi.

Miller, Monica R. 2013. *Religion and Hip Hop.* New York: Routledge.

Mills, Charles W. 1999. *The Racial Contract.* Ithaca: Cornell University Press.

Moten, Fred. 2017. *Black and Blur*. Durham/London: Duke University Press.

Myrie, Russell. 2009. *Don't Rhyme for the Sake of Riddlin': The Authorized Story of Public Enemy*. New York: Canongate.

Naar, Jon. 2007. *The Birth of Graffiti*. New York: Prestel.

Newton, Huey P. 1996. *War Against the Panthers: A Study of Repression in America*. New York/London: Harlem River Press.

Norman, Judith. 2007. Hegel and German Romanticism. In *Hegel and the Arts*, ed. Stephen Houlgate, 310–336. Evanston: Northwestern University Press.

Ogbar, Jeffrey O.G. 2007. *Hip-Hop Revolution: The Culture and Politics of Rap*. Lawrence: University of Kansas Press.

Orejuela, Fernando. 2014. *Rap and Hip Hop Culture*. Oxford: Oxford University Press.

Pabon, Jorge 'Popmaster Fabel'. 2012. Physical Graffiti: The History of Hip-Hop Dance. In *That's the Joint: The Hip Hop Studies Reader*, ed. Murray Forman and Mark Anthony Neal, 2nd ed., 57–61. New York: Routledge.

Paul 107. 2003. *All City: The Book About Taking Space*. Toronto: ECW Press.

Pepper, William F. 2008. *An Act of State: The Execution of Martin Luther King*. New York: Verso.

Perkins, William Eric, ed. 1996. *Droppin' Science: Critical Essays on Rap Music and Hip Hop Culture*. Philadelphia: Temple University Press.

Perry, Imani. 2004. *Prophets of the Hood: Politics and Poetics in Hip Hop*. Durham: Duke University Press.

Peterson, James Braxton. 2014. *The Hip-Hop Underground and African American Culture: Beneath the Surface*. New York: Palgrave Macmillan.

Pippin, Robert. 2014. *After the Beautiful: Hegel and the Philosophy of Pictorial Modernism*. Chicago: University of Chicago Press.

Piskor, ed. 2013. *Hip Hop Family Tree, Vol. 1*. Seattle: Fantagraphics.

Pittman, John P. 2005. 'Y'all Niggaz Better Recognize': Hip Hop's Dialectical Struggle for Recognition. In *Hip Hop & Philosophy: Rhyme 2 Reason*, ed. Derrick Darby and Tommie Shelby, 41–53. Chicago/La Salle: Open Court.

Potter, Russell A. 1995. *Spectacular Vernaculars: Hip-Hop and the Politics of Postmodernism*. Albany: SUNY Press.

Pough, Gwendolyn D., Elaine Richardson, Aisha Durham, and Rachel Raimist, eds. 2007. *Home Girls Make Some Noise: Hip Hop Feminism Anthology*. Mira Loma: Parker Publishing.

Powers, Stephen. 1999. *The Art of Getting Over: Graffiti at the Millennium*. New York: St. Martin's Press.

Price-Styles, Alice. 2015. MC Origins: Rap and Spoken Word Poetry. In *The Cambridge Companion to Hip-Hop*, ed. Justin A. Williams, 11–21. Cambridge: Cambridge University Press.

Rapp, Carl. 2000. Hegel's Concept of the Dissolution of Art. In *Hegel and Aesthetics*, ed. William Maker, 13–30. Albany: SUNY Press.

Reeves, Marcus. 2008. *Somebody Scream: Rap Music's Rise to Prominence in the Aftershock of Black Power*. New York: Faber and Faber.

Robinson, Cedric. 2000. *Black Marxism: The Making of the Black Radical Tradition*. Chapel Hill: University of North Carolina Press.

Romero, Elena. 2012. *Free Stylin': How Hip Hop Changed the Fashion Industry*. Santa Barbara: Praeger.

Rose, Tricia. 1994. *Black Noise: Rap Music and Black Culture in Contemporary America*. Middletown: Wesleyan University Press.

Rutter, Benjamin. 2010. *Hegel on the Modern Arts*. Cambridge: Cambridge University Press.

Schloss, Joseph. 2004. *Making Beats: The Art of Sample-Based Hip-Hop*. Middletown: Wesleyan University Press.

———. 2009. *Foundation: B-boys, B-girls, and Hip-Hop Culture in New York*. New York: Oxford University Press.

Shabazz, Jamel. 2001. *Back in the Days*. New York: powerHouse Books.

Sha-Rock, with Iesha Brown. 2015. *Luminary Icon: The Story of the Beginning and End of Hip-Hop's First Female MC*. Sudbury: eBookit.com; Audiobook Version.

Shusterman, Richard. 1991. The Fine Art of Rap. *New Literary History* 22 (3): 613–632.

Spence, Lester K. 2011. *Stare into the Darkness: The Limits of Hip-Hop and Black Politics*. Minneapolis: University of Minnesota.

Stewart, Jack. 2009. *Graffiti Kings: New York Mass Transit Art of the 1970s*. New York: Melcher Media.

Stone, Alison. 2016. *The Value of Popular Music: An Approach from Post-Kantian Aesthetics*. Cham: Palgrave Macmillan.

Taibbi, Matt. 2017. *I Can't Breathe: A Killing on Bay Street*. New York: Spiegel & Grau.

Tate, Greg. 2004. Hiphop Turns 30. *Village Voice*, December 28.

Taylor, Charles. 1979. *Hegel and Modern Society*. New York: Cambridge University Press.

Thompson, Robert Farris. 1996. Hip Hop 101. In *Droppin' Science: Critical Essays on Rap Music and Hip Hop Culture*, ed. William Eric Perkins, 211–219. Philadelphia: Temple University Press.

Toop, David. 1991. *Rap Attack 2*. New York: Serpent's Tail.

Usher, Carlton A. 2006. *A Rhyme Is a Terrible Thing to Waste: Hip Hop and the Creation of a Political Philosophy*. Trenton: Africa Wold Press.

Verharen, Charles C. 1997. 'The New World and the Dreams to Which It May Give Rise': An African and American Response to Hegel's Challenge. *Journal of Black Studies* 27 (4): 456–493.

Vernon, Jim. 2007. *Hegel's Philosophy of Language*. London: Continuum.

———. 2011. Siding with Freedom: Towards a Prescriptive Hegelianism. *Critical Horizons* 12 (1): 49–69.

———. 2013a. Hegel, Edward Sanders and Emancipatory History. *Clio: A Journal of Literature, History and the Philosophy of History* 42 (1): 27–52.

———. 2013b. Liberation Theology: Hegel on Why Philosophy Takes Sides in Religious Conflict. *Symposium: Canadian Journal of Continental Philosophy* 17 (2): 141–157.

———. 2013c. Why We Fight: Hegel's Struggle for Recognition Revisited. *Cosmos and History: The Journal of Natural and Social Philosophy* 9 (2): 178–197.

———. 2014a. I Am We: Dialectics of Political Will in Huey P. Newton and the Black Panther Party. *Theory and Event* 17: 4.

———. 2014b. Deleuze on the Musical Work of Art. In *Intensities and Lines of Flight: Deleuze and Guattari and the Arts*, ed. Antonio Calcagno, Jim Vernon, and Steve Lofts, 55–65. Lanham: Rowman and Littlefield.

———. 2017. 'A Passion for Justice': Martin Luther King, Jr. and G.W.F. Hegel on 'World-Historical Individuals'. *Philosophy and Social Criticism* 43 (2): 187–207.

Voloj, Julian, and Claudia Ahlering. 2015. *Ghetto Brother: Warrior to Peacemaker*. New York: NBM Publishing.

Waclawaek, Anna. 2011. *Graffiti and Street Art*. London: Thames & Hudson.

Walker, Klive. 2005. *Dubwise: Reasoning from the Reggae Underground*. Toronto: Insomniac Press.

Wallace, David Foster, and Mark Costello. 1990. *Signifying Rappers*. New York: Back Bay Books.

Watkins, S. Craig. 2005. *Hip Hop Matters: Politics, Pop Culture, and the Struggle for the Soul of a Movement*. Boston: Beacon Press.

West, Cornel. 2004. *Democracy Matters: Winning the Fight Against Imperialism*. New York: Penguin.

Westbrook, Alonzo. 2002. *Hip Hoptionary: The Dictionary of Hip Hop Terminology*. New York: Harlem Moon.

Wexler, Stuart, and Larry Hancock. 2012. *The Awful Grace of God: Religious Terrorism, White Supremacy and the Unsolved Murder of Martin Luther King, Jr.* Berkeley: Counterpoint.

Willis, Andre Craddock. 1991. Rap Music and the Black Musical Tradition: A Critical Assessment. *Radical America* 23 (4): 29–38.

Wimsatt, William 'Upski'. 1994. *Bomb the Suburbs*, Revised 2nd ed. Chicago: The Subway and Elevated Press Company.

———. 2010. *Please Don't Bomb the Suburbs: A Midterm Report on My Generation and the Future of Our Super Movement*. New York: Atlantic.

Winfield, Richard Dien. 2000. The Challenge of Architecture to Hegel's Aesthetics. In *Hegel and Aesthetics*, ed. William Maker, 97–111. Albany: SUNY Press.

Filmography

And You Don't Stop: 30 Years of Hip-Hop. Directed by Dana Heinz Perry and Richard Lowe. Perry Films, 2004.

Bboy: A History of Breaking. Directed by Marc-Aurèle Vecchione. Arte France, 2016.

Beat Street. Directed by Stan Lathan. MGM, 1984.

Beat This: A Hip-Hop History. Directed by Dick Fontaine. BBC, 1984.

Flashdance. Directed by Adrian Lyne. Paramount, 1983.

Flyin' Cut Sleeves. Directed by Henry Chalfant. Sleeping Dog Films, 1993.

Founding Fathers. Directed by Ron Lawrence and Hassan Pore. Highlife Entertainment, 2009.

Fresh Dressed. Directed by Sasha Jenkins. Mass Appeal, 2015.

From Mambo to Hip-Hop: A South Bronx Tale. Directed by Henry Chalfant. City Lore, 2006.

Graffiti Rock. Directed by Clark Santee, presented by Michael Holman. Skywise, 1984.

Hip-Hop: Beyond Beats and Rhymes. Directed by Byron Hurt. God Bless The Child, 2006.

Infamy. Directed by Doug Pray. QD3 Entertainment, 2005.

Just To Get A Rep. Directed by Peter Gerard. Accidental Media, 2004.

Rock Steady, Directed by Anthony Ralph. Twenty Twenty Films, 1982.

Rubble Kings. Directed by Shan Nicholson. Saboteur, 2015.

Scratch. Directed by Doug Pray. Palm Pictures, 2001.

Something from Nothing: The Art of Rap. Directed by Ice-T and Andy Baybutt. Jolly Good, 2012.

The Freshest Kids. Directed by Israel. QD3 Entertainment, 2002.

The Hip-Hop Years. Directed by David Upshal. Channel 4, 1999.

The Show. Directed by Brian Robbins. Rysher Entertainment, 1995.

Whatever Happened to Hip Hop?. Directed by Sonali Aggarwal. 358inc., 2009.

Zulu. Directed by Cy Endfield. Paramount, 1964.

Index[1]

[1] Note: Page numbers followed by 'n' refer to notes.

© The Author(s) 2018   255
J. Vernon, *Hip Hop, Hegel, and the Art of Emancipation*,
https://doi.org/10.1007/978-3-319-91304-9

Printed by Printforce, the Netherlands